WRESTLING
WITH THE DIVINE

WRESTLING WITH THE DIVINE

A JEWISH RESPONSE TO SUFFERING

Shmuel Boteach

JASON ARONSON INC.
Northvale, New Jersey
London

The author gratefully acknowledges permission to quote from the following source:
From WHEN BAD THINGS HAPPEN TO GOOD PEOPLE by Harold S. Kushner. Copyright © 1981 by Harold S. Kushner. Reprinted by permission of Schocken Books, published by Pantheon Books, a division of Random House, Inc.; and Macmillan General Books, a division of Macmillan Publishers Ltd.

This book was set in 11 pt. Garamond by Alpha Graphics of Pittsfield, New Hampshire, and printed by Haddon Craftsmen in Scranton, Pennsylvania.

Library of Congress Cataloging-in-Publication Data

Boteach, Shmuel.
 Wrestling with the divine : a Jewish response to suffering / Shmuel Boteach.
  p. cm.
 Includes bibliographical references and index.
 ISBN 1-56821-176-7
  1. Reward (Jewish theology) 2. Suffering–Religious aspects–
Judaism. 3. God (Judaism) 4. Judaism–Doctrines. I. Title.
BM645.R55B68 1995
296.3'11–dc20   94-1288

Manufactured in the United States of America. Jason Aronson Inc. offers books and cassettes. For information and catalog write to Jason Aronson Inc., 230 Livingston Street, Northvale, New Jersey 07647.

To my parents,
Yoav Boteach
and
Eleanor Paul,
who have demonstrated to me
that no pain or adversity
could ever quash the human spirit.
In the face of suffering
one must stand up
and fight back.
Never submit and never bear witness
to the pain of another in silence.

CONTENTS

II
The Problem of Suffering:
Reconciling the Benevolent God
with the Existence of Evil

Acknowledgments

I would like to offer special thanks to Rabbi Manis Friedman, dean of Beis Chana Women's Institute in St. Paul, Minnesota, who, through numerous conversations on the subject of suffering, helped crystallize many of the thoughts contained herein. Rabbi Friedman is celebrated throughout the world as one of the finest speakers and authors on Jewish themes and I delight in the clarity and depth that he brings to every subject he addresses. He has also been a trusted guide to me since I assumed my position at Oxford and has shown me warmth and friendship that has significantly enhanced my ability to navigate some of the stormier waters that my responsibilities present.

I also wish to thank the man who has served as my superior and friend for six years, Rabbi S. Faivish Vogel, director of the Lubavitch Foundation, United Kingdom. A man of profundity, professionalism, and eminence, he has offered me his wisdom and guidance through all my years at Oxford. It was he who, with the blessing of the Lubavitcher Rebbe, was responsible for my coming here and embarking upon the most enlightening experience of my life.

I would also like to thank the students and academics of the University of Oxford, who, as devoted friends and colleagues, challenge me constantly to provide new and insightful responses to the major problems confronting society and civilization within the framework of Jewish tradition and thought.

ix

It is their incessant questions and debates that have served as the principal stimulus for this book. I must also thank the many student volunteers of the Oxford University L'Chaim Society, now the university's second largest student organization and of which I am director, who, through their efforts to promote and publicize all of our activities, afford me some much-needed time to write. Without their dedication and assistance, my responsibilities as rabbi to the university would hardly ever allow me to put pen to paper. Likewise, I thank the many friends and financial supporters of the L'Chaim Society, too numerous to list but very significant all the same, without whom none of our activities, including my writings, would be possible. It is they who must take the principal credit for the plethora of activities and speakers that we are able to provide for the students and larger community at Oxford, and I remain eternally grateful.

In the same vein, I must thank my wonderful office staff: my research and administrative assistants, Kathy Brewis and Julie Markoff, for their dedication and patience in helping to edit my writings and essays, and Lucy Ireland for running around after me.

No life is without its share of pain and suffering, be it internal, external, or otherwise. What has made my life not only bearable, but special and glorious, is the constant companionship and devotion of my loving wife Devorah, whose unyielding support for me over the past six years has encouraged and comforted me at all times. I am truly thankful to the Creator of all life for providing me with such a supportive family. And although the world is still far from perfect, the joy of being surrounded by those who love you affords life a special shine and gloss that can make even ordinary things distinctive and beautiful.

I pay homage to my teacher, inspiration, and guiding light, the Lubavitcher Rebbe, Rabbi Menachem Mendel Schneerson. The Rebbe is a fighter without compare who has sparred with the heavens on so many occasions in defense of his people and humanity at large. It was in the course of watching the Rebbe thunder at the skies during numerous public orations that I attended, demanding to know from God how long it would be until the Messiah came, how long it would be before humankind ceased suffering, how many more Jewish soldiers would have to die in defense of their people, and what had happened to all the promises that He had made through His righteous prophets, that I understood that heartache has no place in our world and that the only human response is to defeat and eradicate every trace of agony and misery for all eternity. His defiant example continues to be the inspiration for millions of Jews around the world who cry out for an epoch of abundance and goodness, and I not least among them. May the Almighty grant him renewed strength and health to take up the staff of leadership for our people once again.

Finally, I thank the Master of the Universe for the unrelenting kindness He has shown me throughout life. I continue to marvel at His benevolence because I know myself to be undeserving. May He, in His infinite mercy, extend His magnificence to all created things and grant us all a good and happy life in the plain and simple meaning of the term.

I

THE BELIEF
IN REWARD
AND PUNISHMENT

Overview to Part I

IF JUDAISM IS TO LIVE AGAIN: THE PROBLEM OF SUFFERING

Every people possesses certain historical characteristics. Perhaps one of the saddest commentaries about the nation of Israel is that amid the various historical characteristics that may be said to be indigenous to the Jewish people, the adjective *suffering* will nearly always top the list. Simply stated, the Jewish people are known universally as a people who have experienced unspeakable horrors, hardship, and misery. Yet God promised our forefathers that it would never be like this. The statements he made to Abraham, Isaac, and Jacob seemed to ensure a good and bountiful life for their offspring. Thus, the travail of the children of Israel, and the repeated persecution that they have endured throughout history, are shrouded in mystery.

This book is an attempt to shed light both on the collective suffering of nations in general and on that of the solitary human being in particular. It is also an attempt to posit a response to suffering, to suggest what we should do both when enduring suffering on our own and when witnessing the suffering of others. I hope my position will not be misconstrued, as it is the nature of the issue to cause much contention and misunderstanding. My position will be supported in the book by arguments, anecdotes, and, above all, real-life examples, since there are no greater proofs than these.

That religion has survived the onslaught of ideas and events of the last 130 years is near miraculous. Prior to the 1860s, organized religion enjoyed a social and cultural supremacy that is totally unknown in our time and may not be known again. To be sure, even in the nineteenth century there were heretics, atheists, agnostics, and those who scoffed at religion and its claims. The difference, however, was that they were not in the majority, and it was therefore *they* who had to justify their rejection of religion. These early atheistic thinkers can almost all be described as "aggressive atheists" because they had to spend a considerable amount of time rationalizing their position of theistic denial. Because organized religion was the norm, they were automatically classed as radicals and outcasts of religious society and were obliged to draw upon their highest cognitive faculties if they were to lend credibility to their attitudes and dignify their opinions.

Today, the situation has come full circle. It is no longer those who reject religion who are on the defensive, but those who affirm the traditions, beliefs, and practices of their forebears. Since atheism, or at least agnosticism, is now commonplace, it is religious individuals who are forced to explain themselves to the world around them. As a rabbi in Oxford for the last six years, I have seen how religion has taken on more and more of a rational bent, in an effort to be more appealing in the prevailing intellectual social climate. Those who practice religion are constantly questioned, sometimes even attacked, for their beliefs, and must therefore find reasons to justify their positions.

Over the past millennia, there have been several attempts on the part of the giants of Jewish thought to codify the essential principles of the Jewish faith. Judaism is a religion of 613 commandments, along with thousands of tributary laws and commandments associated with the original 613. Nevertheless, Maimonides reduced these to thirteen cardinal articles. Rabbi Joseph Albo encapsulated the essence of Judaism further into three major principles. But notwithstanding how one codifies the cardinal tenets of the Jewish faith, the following principles will certainly be included, upon which there can be no compromise for traditional Judaism.

First, there exists an eternal God Who is the Creator of heaven and earth and everything contained therein, especially all forms and walks of life. These did not arise spontaneously, but rather were called into being by a special act of creation on the part of an all-powerful Being. Second, this all-powerful and eternal Creator communicated His will to humans through His Torah, which is of direct divine origin. Third, of those things revealed in the will of the Creator, it is the belief that man is the jewel of creation, endowed with special purpose and intelligence, which serves both as a privilege and as a grave responsibility. Fourth, man has the freedom of choice to be good or evil, to accommodate the wishes of the Supreme Being Who created him in His image, or to lead an immoral existence, thereby ignoring the will of his Creator, and without sensitivity to his fellowman. Fifth, because of the special responsibility carried by man, as well as the freedom to act in accordance with his own will, man will be held accountable for his actions and remunerated accordingly. He will be rewarded with a good life for his acts of kindness and generosity but will be punished with suffering and travail commensurate with his acts of evil and indifference. Finally, notwithstanding the gross evil that might pervade the world at present, and the apparent prosperity of the wicked in our world while the righteous suffer, this seemingly unjust state of affairs will be corrected in a future messianic era in which goodness will abound. Strife, jealousy, and contention will be removed from our world and will be replaced with love, truth, sincerity, and friendship. And all evil will be eradicated from this earth.

In the modern era, however, we have witnessed how all of these sacred principles have been subtly eroded. Charles Darwin in his theory of evolution argued that life may have arisen spontaneously and without the agency of a purposeful Creator. Thus, while Darwin never actually refuted the existence of God, his claims entailed that it was unnecessary to affirm a belief in Him. The complexity and diversity of the universe, along with the existence of all organic forms, might be explained through the mechanisms of genetic mutation and natural selection along with the earth's own indigenous processes. Thus God was no longer an integral part of the picture. Furthermore, Darwin challenged the belief that man is unique within creation. From an evolutionary viewpoint, man is an animal. He descends from primates and is anatomically almost identical to his cousins, the apes. The only real thing that separates man from the apes is the development of his intelligence. Man is therefore not in any way *qualitatively* superior to the animals. Rather, the only thing that separates them is the extent of their evolutionary development.

Freud took this a step further by asserting that man is far less a master in his own mental household than he had supposed. Whereas Judaism had always emphasized the absolute belief in man's freedom of choice, Freud argued for the existence of autonomous faculties of the mind, the *id*, for example, which could not be subjected to man's conscious control. Whether or not one likes it or agrees with it, the id would always remain primal, uncultured, and uncivilized, thriving on and serving as the impetus for man's most basic instincts. Nor was there a means for evading the dictates of the id. The more man sought to suppress it, the more it would manifest itself in the form of neurotic symptoms and even psychosis. By postulating a base and animalistic impulse at the very heart of man, Freud indirectly emphasized the kinship between man and the animals.

Modern-day psychology has taken this argument further by advancing theories that view man as the sum total of his upbringing, composed of his early childhood experiences, the love or neglect shown to him in his infancy, and so on. Essentially, then, man has no choice at all, but is instead conditioned from his earliest youth by the society and people around him as to what life and activities he will subsequently choose.

Furthermore, the assertions of biblical criticism and scholarship seemingly made a shambles of the claims of divine authorship of the Bible. By maintaining that the Bible is a complex set of books that should not all be treated identically, and by pointing to the discrepancies in style between the different books of the Bible as well as to the contradictions of biblical claims that are now coming to light as a result of archaeological investigation, the belief in collective divine revelation at the foot of Sinai was dealt a powerful blow. And although an acceptance of the claims of the JEDP hypothesis is not as widespread as, say, that of evolution or psychoanalysis, it has made strong inroads in all the academic communities, so that extreme doubt has been cast in the minds of the students and intellectuals. In fact, from my experiences in Oxford over the past six years, it is specifically the claims of biblical critics that pose the greatest challenge to belief for Oxford students who study the Bible.

But none of the aforementioned phenomena have undermined the case for religion in the twentieth century as greatly as the most pressing and urgent issue of all, that of oppression and human suffering. The wholesale slaughter that has occurred in this century, the utter inhumanity revealed in our midst, has led us to believe that we are alone in this universe. In this respect, it is the Holocaust, more than anything else, that serves as the primary challenge to the religious convictions of our generation. The fact that so many innocents died in so gruesome a way shakes belief to its very core. How could it have happened? And how can we continue to believe in a loving, caring Creator in its aftermath?

To be sure, the presence of suffering does nothing to refute the existence of God. In March 1992 the L'Chaim Society hosted Elie Wiesel in Oxford. At a lunch at my home he was asked by a student whether or not he still believed in God after the Holocaust. His response was: "Of course I believe in God after the Holocaust, and my belief in Him has not wavered a bit in its wake. But specifically because I believe in Him, I am very angry at Him. He does exist. There can be no question of that. But why then did He allow this to happen?"

The existence of suffering is the greatest challenge to faith, therefore, because it undermines the most central premise of our faith: that God not only exists, but that He cares and He listens. That every time a human being aches or grieves, he can entreat his Creator to take notice and expect Him to come to his aid, to provide comfort and love, and to embrace man as His child. A child whose father has run away from home, leaving the child to his own devices, could hardly care less if the parent still lives elsewhere on the planet. It is far more damaging to the belief of the faithful, and far more damning of God, if He does indeed exist, yet remains indifferent to the torment of man.

Man is intelligent enough to recognize his own limitations. He is overwhelmed by his own insignificance in this vast universe of infinite expanse and feels the need to attach himself to a supreme Being who will always cradle and never abandon him. Who among us is so arrogant as to believe that he is good enough on his own? Who among us is so brazen as to deny his own mortality? And who among us is so brave as to desire to walk through the labyrinth of life without the grace and love of a benevolent Creator?

But what if the vicissitudes of life indicate that there is no one holding our hand, but only an indifferent observer who watches man from his high perch in heaven, as though man were a mere laboratory rat? Man indeed may be insignificant and may indeed come to realize his own unworthiness. But the significance that man achieves is specifically by virtue of the fact that he is created and looked after by a Being of infinite significance. A child who goes to school and is bullied by classmates always dreams of his father or mother coming to his rescue in the role of protector. It is only this belief that sustains children through the most trying times because, having recognized their own vulnerability, they must have something upon which to rely, and that lends their being importance. Man cannot feel as if he is all alone in this universe. He requires, as a matter of necessity, a belief and conviction that there is a God Who not only created but controls the heavens and the earth, Who will answer his call in his hour of need, and Who will comfort him through tragedy, misery, and pain—a God Who is not only transcendent, as in the Cartesian model of the deity, but immanent and Who takes part, indeed supervises, the unfolding events of history.

Of what use is a God who creates man but subsequently leaves him to his own devices to get along? Of what use is the Creator of man, Who, having called him into existence, subsequently decides to abandon him to fate and the elements? In the words of Rabbi Abraham Joshua Heschel, "Dark is the world to me for all its cities and stars. If not for the certainty that God listens to our cry, who could stand so much misery, so much callousness? The mystery and the grandeur of the concern of the infinite God for the finite man is the basic insight of biblical tradition. This mystery is enhanced by the aspect of immediacy. God is *imme-*

diately concerned. He is not concerned through intermediate agents. He is personally concerned" (*The Insecurity of Freedom*, p. 254). After witnessing the ravages of the Holocaust, Judaism must postulate a response to the calamities that befall man while on this earth, if it is to live again.

1

WITHOUT ULTERIOR MOTIVES: THE PROBLEM WITH DIVINE REWARDS

A t the start of Moses' mission to Pharaoh to free the Jews from Egypt, we read how Moses, in his ongoing dialogue with God, offers a complaint. It is significant because it serves as the very first challenge recorded in the Bible claiming a divine miscarriage of justice. Moses has just been sent by the Almighty to demand the Jewish people's release from Pharaoh. What resulted from this first encounter was that not only did Pharaoh refuse to free them, but he also gave orders that the Jewish slaves should not be given straw to build bricks, amid the requirement to fill the same quota per day. This invites a sharp response from the future lawgiver. "And Moses returned unto the Lord and he said, 'Lord, why have You dealt ill with this people? Why is it that You have sent me? For since I came to Pharaoh to speak in Your name, he has dealt ill with this people; neither have You delivered at all Your people'" (Exodus 5:22-23).

Among the various difficult challenges posed to religion today and the religious believer, the most difficult, in my opinion, is that which is also the oldest—the problem of suffering. Darwinian evolution, biblical criticism, or archaeological excavation may pose a seeming contradiction to specific claims for the Bible and organized religion, which the devout believer will no doubt seek to reconcile. But human suffering poses a contradiction to the overall and most important claim in religion, namely that

11

there is a benevolent God who seeks a dialogue with every created being and listens to our call when we cry out, who cares and listens, who is attentive to our prayers, and is a personal God. When someone is afflicted with some incurable illness, or when war snuffs out the life of the young, then one of the fundamentals of religious belief must fall. Can we still accept that God is all-powerful and causes everything that happens in the world, and that God is just and fair, so that the good people are rewarded and only the wicked are punished, when good people suffer?

This work in its entirety is dedicated to resolving this ancient dilemma that has for many millennia served to separate man from God and cast doubt on what I feel to be the most important and central of all Jewish theological assertions, namely, that God is not merely transcendent, but immanent; that He is not merely a God who resides in the heavens, but is firmly entrenched on earth; that He seeks not so much a rapport with the angels but a dialogue with man. That we should undertake such a study is entirely consonant with Jewish tradition and history, although our findings may pose a challenge to God, whereas Christianity advocates faith and acceptance of the divine will above all else, and Islam actually translates as "submission," the word *Israel*, which means "he who wrestles with God." Jews have always struggled with cosmic "whys" and "wherefores" rather than blindly accept or submit to tragedy and fate.

In his celebrated *Shloshah-Asar Ikkarim* (Thirteen Principles of Jewish Faith), Maimonides lists Principle #11 as the belief in divine reward and punishment. He writes as follows:

> Principle #11 is that He, be He exalted, will reward an individual who will fulfill the commandments of the Torah, and will punish an individual who will violate its injunctions, and that the greatest reward is *Olam Haba*—the Hereafter, while the greatest punishment is *Karet*—to be "cut off" [from life in the Hereafter]. We already discussed this matter adequately. (See Maimonides, "Introduction" to *Perek Helek*).
>
> The following verse clarifies this principle. [When Israel sinned grievously with the transgression of the Golden Calf, Moshe said

to the Almighty], "Now, if you would, please forgive their sin. If not, then blot me out from the Book which you have written" (Exodus 32:32). Whereupon, the Almighty, be He blessed, answered him, "He who has sinned against Me, him will I blot out of My Book" (Exodus 32:33). This proves that He knows who serves Him and who transgresses against Him, to reward the one, and to punish the other. (Maimonides, "Introduction" to *Perek Helek*)

This principle of faith, along with the other twelve, constitutes part of the liturgy of many synagogue prayer books and is recited on a daily basis at the conclusion of the morning prayers in the following format: "I believe with a perfect faith that the Creator, blessed be His name, rewards with goodness those who keep his commandments, and punishes those who transgress his commandments."

These words seem simple enough and are easily digestible. From our earliest childhood we have all been raised by our parents, even those who were completely nonobservant, to believe that if we act good then good things will come our way, and conversely that "crime doesn't pay." We have even been taught to feel a certain indignance about those who lie, steal, and cheat, yet prosper doing it. We are bothered by those who are evil yet get away with it. Thus, when confronted with this particular principle of Jewish faith, our gut reaction is to accept it unquestioningly.

What makes this principle even more attractive and palatable to the human mind is that it confirms the notion that each of us is empowered with freedom of choice. Indeed Maimonides himself incorporates the belief in freedom of choice within this principle. This is proven conclusively by Rabbi Yosef Albo, in his *Sefer Haikkarim*, where he questions why it is that Maimonides did not include the concept of *bechirah*, or freedom of will, among his fundamental articles of Torah faith, particularly in view of the fact that in his *Mishneh Torah* (*Mishneh Torah, Hilkhot Teshuvah* 5:3) Maimonides himself refers to the concept of free will as "a great fundamental principle," and as "a pillar of the Torah and its commandments" (*Shloshah Asar Ikkarim* 1:3). He writes:

Freedom of choice is granted to each individual. If he desires to lead himself along the righteous path and to be a *tzaddik*, the choice is in his hands, and if he desires to lead himself along a path of wickedness and to be a wicked person, the choice is in his hands. This is as is written in the Torah (Genesis 3:22): "Behold, the man has become as one of us, to know good and evil." This means, "Behold, this species of man has become unique in the world, and there is no other species like him in this respect, that he by himself, with his own thought and intellect, shall know [to discern between] good and evil and he can do whatever he desires. Nor is there anyone to prevent him from doing either good or evil." And since this is so (Genesis 3:22), "Perhaps he will put forth his hand [to take also of the tree of life]." (*Mishneh Torah, Hilkhot Teshuvah* 5:1)

Without the principle of freedom of choice, Maimonides observes further, the entire structure of the Torah or divine commandments would be ludicrous and would disintegrate, while the principle of *s'har ve-onesh* (reward and punishment) would likewise be entirely incongruous.

Were the Almighty to decree upon the individual to become either righteous or wicked, or were there something that might draw an individual by his very nature toward a particular path, or toward a particular intellectual approach, or toward a particular philosophy, or to the performance of a particular deed, like the fabrications that the foolish astrologers contrive, how could He command us through the Prophets, "Do this," or, "Do not do that," "Improve your ways," or, "Do not pursue your wicked [impulses]," if it was already decreed upon the person from his very inception, or by his innate nature, to be drawn toward a certain type of behavior, from which it is impossible for him to deviate? And what basis would there be for the entire Torah? And according to what law and what justice could the evildoer be punished or the righteous rewarded? (Genesis 18:25): "Shall the judge of all the earth not do justice?" (*Mishneh Torah, Hilkhot Teshuvah* 5:4)

Rabbi Albo concludes, therefore, that because the concept of freedom of choice is so fundamental to the entire concept of reward and punishment, and because they are such inextricably interwoven and interdependent concepts, Maimonides did not find it necessary to list them as two separate principles. Instead, he included the concept of reward and punishment as one of the "Thirteen Principles," with the awareness that this concept of reward and retribution actually presupposes and is predicated upon the fundamental Torah concept of choice and free will.

But the comfort felt in regard to the concepts of freedom of choice and reward and punishment does little to explain the strongest question that stares us in the face immediately upon learning of this principle in the treatise of Maimonides: What is it about the belief in reward and punishment that makes it a foundation of the Jewish faith?

The simple meaning of a foundation or pillar is something that serves as a support to an entire edifice standing above it, or, in our case, a single tenet of the Jewish religion that, were it to be removed, the entire structure of the religion would crumble.

When we learn, for example, of the first of Maimonides' thirteen principles, the belief that there is a God, we can readily understand how if one were to reject this principal Judaism could not stand. Of what authenticity is a religion, creed, or faith, if God does not exist? The very idea of divine commandments, such as those found in Judaism, is absurd without the notion of a God who commands.

Similarly, if one were to reject a belief in the second of the thirteen principles, that the Torah originates in the Heavens, then, once again, Judaism as a religion is an absurdity. Even if there is a God, it is preposterous to speak in His name and make statements about what man should believe and what God requires of him, if God Himself never communicated those wishes to us. Revelation, therefore, is an absolute essential of the Jewish faith.

But what is it about the belief in reward and punishment that makes it a foundation for the fulfillment of all of the Torah's commandments? To make the promise of divine gifts a fundamental tenet of Judaism seems at best vain, and at worst counterproductive. For in its most basic, most pure form, is not religion a statement of the fact that God comes first, and that the individual should concern himself with God's needs and not (just) his own? Yet here we formulate, as one of the pillars upon which all of Jewish worship rests, the belief that it is worthwhile being good to God, not for its own sake, but because He will in turn be good to the believer.

It should be emphasized that the need to serve God for no ulterior motive is not just a logical premise, but is something that is emphasized many times in all sectors of Jewish scholarship.

In the well-known mishnaic treatise *Ethics of Our Fathers*, which deals with the moral and ethical values advocated by the Sages as the most precious, we read (1:3): "Do not be like servants who serve their master for the sake of receiving a reward, but rather be like servants who serve their master without the intent of receiving a reward; and let the fear of Heaven be upon you."

Likewise, Maimonides himself codifies in his magnus opus, *Mishneh Torah* (*Laws of Repentance* 10:1) as a *halakhah*, that

> one should not say: "I hereby am fulfilling the commandments of the Torah and studying its wisdom in order that I should receive all of the blessings which are enumerated with it; or in order that I shall merit life in the world to come. And I will distance myself from all sin which the Torah cautions me against, in order that I be saved from all curses enumerated in the Torah; or in order that I not be cut off from life in the world to come." It is not proper to serve God in this way for someone who serves God in this way serves Him out of fear [of punishment], and this was not the great path of the Prophets and neither that of the Sages. And the only people who serve God in this way are simpletons, women, and children, whom, due to lack of education, are taught to serve God out of fear until their intellect matures and they are able to serve Him out of love.

Thus, we see clear directives from the Torah's most important works that completely negate the notion that the pretext for fulfillment of the Torah's commandments should be a belief in reward and punishment. How then can we establish reward and punishment, not only as *a* belief among many in Judaism, but as one of *the* principal doctrines of the Jewish faith?

In the very next law following the one quoted earlier (*Laws of Repentance* 10:2), Maimonides goes on to explain that the best way to serve God is "to worship Him with disinterested love." This is a very great virtue indeed, yet, one that not everyone merits to attain. This was the attribute of our forefather Abraham whom God himself referred to as "Abraham my beloved." Thus Maimonides explains how of the two ways to serve God, love and fear, the former is by far the greater of the two, but not everyone merits to reach that high plateau. The majority are forced to content themselves with fulfilling the commandments because of the reward promised them, and are cautious not to transgress God's commandments because of the consequent punishment.

Accordingly, we might have been able to explain that the reason why the belief in reward and punishment has been established as a pillar of Judaism is simply due to the fact that in most cases this belief serves as *the* pretext for the individual to obey God's commandments. As such, it is a concession that nevertheless realistically reflects the actual state of the people.

Following this line of thought, the characterization of the belief in reward and punishment as a foundation of Judaism is one of sheer pragmatism. Since without being promised a reward a significant number of people would simply ignore God's will, it thus becomes important to establish clearly and fundamentally that indeed the Almighty rewards those who heed his edicts. Maimonides, therefore, might have advocated serving God in return for divine gifts for reasons of expediency alone.

Looking at this more closely, though, we must utterly reject this interpretation for the following two reasons. First, accepting this insight would force us to embrace the notion that for the unfortunate masses who are incapable of achieving a loving relationship with God, there are thirteen principles of Jewish faith. But for that tiny minority who are able to serve God through love, there are only *twelve* principles of Jewish faith. For those who serve God as a result of disinterested love do not need to base their service of God on reward and punishment. Can we then really accept the fact that the cardinal rules of Jewish faith do not apply to all people equally? Any intelligent person can understand how utterly arbitrary this becomes. Judaism is built on immutable divine articles and not expedient and ephemeral whim.

Second, the fact is that the purpose of these foundations of belief formulated by Maimonides is not merely to encourage man and afford him enthusiasm in worshiping God. Maimonides, in choosing these thirteen principles, was not looking for a method to help the individual overcome complacency in the face of God's will. Rather, and it is important to establish this fact as applicable to all of the thirteen principles, they were established as the thirteen principles of faith because they are indeed the principles that together form the very essence of Judaism. They are not rallying points for the observance of Judaism; rather, they are the core, verily the quintessence of the Jewish faith.

For example, the belief that the Torah is divine is not a means to increase one's excitement in fulfilling its laws. Rather, we take this to be an absolute and immutable truth. The Torah comes from Heaven and was not written by Moses. What is meant by a foundation is exactly what it implies, that without this belief or premise, the entire Torah falls.

It can be appreciated, therefore, that what is taken for granted by the masses, that a belief in reward and punishment is emphasized repeatedly in the Torah just to persuade the individual to be Jewishly observant, is ludicrous. Indeed it is a great shame that the topic of reward and punishment is looked upon so superficially by the average student of Judaism, and is treated the same way that it is treated in other world religions, although in truth the Jewish approach may be radically different.

Even taking a cursory glance at Judaism one may appreciate that its concept of God is radically different from the other widespread religions of the west. In Judaism God is never a means to an end. God is not described as the road to salvation. Rather, God is always the supreme goal and objective. And one is forewarned never to use God as a means to achieve one's personal goals, notwithstanding how lofty or sublime those goals might be.

We thus must deal with this question seriously. How is it that the Jewish religion, which prods man to serve God from love and from a desire to pursue truth, should seemingly degrade itself and ask man to fulfill God's law because he will benefit if he does, and to refrain from transgressing God's will because he will be diminished by doing so?

As we shall explain, this question itself stems from an improper and superficial understanding of the true nature of reward and punishment. What will be required if we are to properly understand this pivotal concept is to explore its internal dimension. Thus it is necessary for us to first preface our answer with an elucidation of the essence of reward and punishment, after which we shall understand why a firm conviction that God rewards the righteous serves as a pillar of Jewish religious endeavor.

2

THE REWARD FOR
A *MITZVAH* IS THE
MITZVAH ITSELF

W e must first emphasize that the very concept of reward and punishment is a halakhic one. That is to say
that God is obligated by Torah law to recompense
man for his divine worship. Proof to this effect can be brought
from the *Mishneh Torah* of Maimonides, which he himself describes, in his introduction, as a book of law only, not of agga-
dic or midrashic legend.

In the ninth chapter of his *Laws of Repentance*, Maimonides
codifies a series of laws that serve as the parameters for how
God rewards, and likewise, how He punishes, man. The fact
that Maimonides includes a discussion of reward and punishment in an halakhic compendium is ample proof that God's obligation to man is subject to the jurisdiction of Jewish law. One
should not be led to believe that the intention of Maimonides
in outlining these laws is to lecture or sermonize his readers
about the beauty and rewards of keeping the Torah, as if Maimonides were a polemicist intent on impressing his readers.
Rather, his intention is to teach Jewish law. As stated earlier,
reward and punishment are *laws* within Judaism, not rallying
points for higher levels of observance.

Another proof of the halakhic status of reward and punishment may be found in numerous talmudic statements in which
the receipt of reward for the fulfillment of the *mitzvot* is compared to the salary paid to an employee by his employer. Case

21

in point, in *Ethics of Our Fathers* (2:16) we find the proclamation of our Rabbis that "if you have studied much Torah, much reward will be given to you; and your employer is trustworthy to pay you your reward for your labor."

Similar references may be found in the written Torah and its commentaries. In Leviticus where God promises reward for the fulfillment of His commandments, He states, "If you follow my laws and are careful to keep my commandments, I will provide you with rain at the right time so that the land will bear its crops and the trees of the field will provide fruit" (26:3). Commenting on this passage, Rashi notes the exposition of the Sages that this promise by the Almighty "may be compared to a king who hired workers and promised to pay them, etc." The implication of the Sages is this: since according to Torah law an employer is obligated and may never refrain from paying the earned reward of his employee, we may rest assured that the Almighty, the formulator of this law, will honor his commitments and repay the just reward of those who obey His Will.

This fascinating concept of God committing Himself to comply with the very laws that He institutes is found in many places throughout rabbinic literature. For instance, commenting on Psalm 147, in which it is written, "He tells His words [in Torah] to Jacob, His statutes and ordinances to Israel," the Midrash (*Shemot Rabbah* 30) comments, "That which God commands Israel to observe, He Himself observes." Similarly, in a fantastic pronouncement the Talmud states in *Berakhot* (6aa) that God dons *tefillin* just as He commands man to put on *tefillin*. The Talmud even goes as far as asking, "The *tefillin* of the Master of the universe, what is written in them. . . ."

The above demonstrates clearly that reward and punishment enjoy halakhic status in Jewish thought, and thus God is *obligated*, by Torah law, to compensate man for doing His work.

Thus far, the argument seems simple. God comes to man and asks man to serve Him. Man complies and thus God is hiring man, as it were. God is thus obligated to pay or reward man for services rendered.

But there is a serious flaw in this argument. In Jewish law a worker is only paid a salary if he has chosen, of his own free accord, to work for his employer. But if for any reason he is in servitude or enslaved, he receives no compensation. For example, if a thief steals an object and then is caught, he is obligated to repay double the value of what he has taken. If he lacks the means to repay the amount, he becomes enslaved to the owner of the object and must work it off. In such circumstances a master pays no salary to his servant, aside from general obligations the master incurs such as to feed, clothe, and house the servant. But these obligations do not serve as a salary for the slave, but rather as obligations incumbent upon the master to treat his servants humanely, so much so that the Talmud comments, "Having a Jewish servant is really like obtaining a master for oneself." This means that one cannot treat a servant as one would treat an animal; there are certain human rights that cannot be violated, and the servant must be fed. But these should not be misconstrued as earnings.

If this is so, why is God obligated to compensate the Jewish people for fulfiling His *mitzvot*? Throughout the Torah the Jewish people are constantly referred to as God's servants, not employees, as in, "For unto Me [are] the children of Israel servants; they are My servants, whom I brought forth out of the land of Egypt" (Leviticus 25:55).

Furthermore, even a servant whose body belongs to his master still remains an independent individual. Only his productivity is in servitude to his master. But the Jewish people have no intrinsic self-identity other than the fact that they are chosen as God's people to serve Him and spread His teachings throughout the world. This statement needs no proof inasmuch as the entire history of the Jews is one of a people who, at times, would have liked to have been like everybody else but are eternally unable to cast off the burden of what they represent. The Jews cannot assimilate, for, in everybody's eyes, they are the Chosen people, chosen to serve as God's emissaries to bring the message of moral and ethical goodness and ethical monotheism to the entire world. As the *Mishnah* states (*Kiddushin*, chap. 8), "[A Jew should always state] I was created only in order to serve my Creator."

Why then should the Jewish people earn a reward? Had the order of events been that the world existed before God became its master, and up to that time human beings simply did whatever they pleased, but then God came along from a distant galaxy and told the Jews He had a specific task He wanted performed, He would then be obligated to reward them since they were "hired." But the situation is not like that at all. God created this world and called it forth from nothingness along with all of its inhabitants. He created the world so that He could be served. Thus, the world's inhabitants are not hired employees, but rather servants who were brought into existence to serve their master. Their very *raison d'etre* is for the purpose of executing the will of their Creator.

There are yet further questions on the concept of divine reward. Many important Jewish writings (see introduction to *Shnei Luchot Habrit*) note that the reward given for Torah and *mitzvot* is radically different from, say, the salary paid to a laborer. A laborer might work picking cotton, cutting corn, or weaving wool and in return receive money, gold, or silver. There exists no intrinsic relationship between the work performed by the laborer and the remuneration that he receives for his work. Rather, the reward is something that serves as an impetus for the laborer to do the bidding of his employer. Not so is the reward for Torah and *mitzvot*. The reward of a *mitzvah* is said to be the direct result, and intrinsically related, to the performance of the *mitzvah* itself. Likewise, the punishment for a sin is said to be a direct result from the sin and whose connection can be immediately identified. Rabbi Shneur Zalman of Liadi expresses this aptly in *Tanya* (chap. 37), "For that which causes the reward of a *mitzvah* is the *mitzvah* itself." In other words, one of the intrinsic dimensions of a *mitzvah* is that as a consequence of the performance of the *mitzvah* the reward automatically emerges. And one of the intrinsic consequences of the performance of sin is that something evil will result from it, which we refer to as punishment. With this our Sages explain the verse, "Your evil will punish you," to mean that one is not punished for doing a sin, but rather it is the sin itself that brings about pain and suffering.

To illustrate this point, let us use a simple example of a family that observes *Shabbat*. Those families who keep the *Shabbat* holy, refrain from work, and have a traditional Friday night dinner are firsthand witnesses to the fact that this is a wonderful way to achieve family unity and kinship. I personally know of many Jewish families who are not observant yet always celebrate a traditional Friday night dinner, because it brings the family together at least one day of the week amid all of their worldly pursuits. Furthermore, since *Shabbat* is a time of peace in which no electricity may be used, the television and radio are off and thus a family and friends can enjoy each other's company without the noise of weekday life. People can communicate and be entertained by each other's conversation and company without the need for an artificial stimulant to keep themselves interested in remaining together. *Shabbat* is not a time when a family watches a Woody Allen film together and then remarks what a lovely time they had together, not even realizing that they have barely communicated with one another. Rather, *Shabbat* is people time. As can be appreciated, this provides for much family unity and closeness.

Thus as a direct consequence of refraining from work on *Shabbat*, which is the central premise of the Sabbath, a family is rewarded with rest and the ability to focus on each other. Thus we see an intrinsic relationship between the reward of *Shabbat* and the *Shabbat* itself. The peace and quiet of *Shabbat* is not something foreign to the day of rest, but constitutes its very essence.

Another example may be drawn from the *berakhot* (blessings) that one is required to recite for every item of food consumed. Jewish law prescribes a blessing for every item of food eaten. Thus, when eating a fruit a Jew blesses "the King of the world who creates fruit of the tree," and when eating a vegetable, "the King of the world who creates fruit of the ground." The reason these blessings were instituted was so that one not take for granted everything God does on one's behalf, but rather appreciate and pay homage for everything that one has to eat. Our Rabbis felt it vital that the Jews learn to appreciate and acknowledge the goodness God performs on our behalf.

Thus, from a Jewish individual's earliest youth, he learns the all-important concept of saying "thank you" and appreciating the favors one does on his behalf. The importance of this lesson cannot be underestimated, for the greatest impediment to successful human relationships later in life is the lack of appre-

ciation one partner shows to the other. Any marriage counse-
lor can verify that the beginning of marital strife is when one
spouse feels that he or she is being taken for granted. Thus the
reward for the *mitzvah* of thanking God for the food one eats
is intrinsically related to the *mitzvah* itself. The *mitzvah* is to
thank God for his goodness, and as a direct result one learns to
be thankful, and is sensitized to acknowledge acts of benevolence and loving-kindness.

A slightly different variation on this theme of the reward of a
mitzvah being a direct and intrinsically related consequence
of the *mitzvah* itself, is found in Maimonides. In his introduction to the Thirteen Principles of Jewish Faith, Maimonides
writes:

> But the promises of goodness and likewise those of retribution
> which are enumerated in the Torah, should be understood in the
> manner in which I will now explain them, and it is this: God is
> telling us, "If you fulfill my specified commandments, I will then
> assist you with their further observance and completion, and I
> will remove from you all hindrances and impediments." For man
> is incapable of doing *mitzvot* when he is sick or hungry, or thirsty.
> Neither is he capable during times of war and siege. Therefore,
> God promised that he would remove all of these things, and that
> people will be healthy and content, until they are able to com-
> plete their tasks and thus merit life in the world to come. Thus,
> the purpose of the rewards allotted for the observance of the
> Torah is not so that the land should be fertile, and that people
> should live long and healthy lives, but rather that through all of
> these conveniences they should be assisted in the fulfillment of
> the Torah. Conversely if they choose to forsake the Torah, their
> punishment will be that terrible evils will befall them, thus seri-
> ously impeding their ability to dedicate themselves to the fulfill-
> ment of a *mitzvah*, as it is written, "[These ills will befall you]
> because you did not serve the Lord your God with joyfulness and
> with gladness of heart, by reason of the abundance of all things."
> And when one will fully ponder these words, one will find that
> that it is as if [the Almighty] is telling you, "If you have observed
> some of the commandments out of love and toil, I will assist you
> in fulfilling all of the commandments, and I will remove all of the
> hurdles and encumbrances. But if you forsake My commandments

out of passivity and apathy, I shall bring hindrances upon you which will prevent you from observing all of them. . . ."

What must be explored within this concept of the reward of a *mitzvah* being an intrinsic part of the *mitzvah* is why God found it necessary to do it this way. What would have been lacking had the reward for a *mitzvah* been similar to the salary earned by a laborer, in which there is no inner connection? It even seems that it is improper and degrading for a *mitzvah* to have a reward become an integral part of it.

The reason that an employer pays his employee a salary is not because of his benevolence or strange fascination with distributing his money. He pays his worker a salary simply because he wants a job done, and it will not be done unless there is something in it for the worker. But as far as the worker is concerned, the reverse is true. The reason why he is doing the job is to earn the salary, not because he cares for his employer's needs. In other words, to the employer the work is the end and the salary is the means to achieve the end. To the worker, however, the salary is the goal and the work is the means by which to attain that goal.

As far as Torah and *mitzvot* are concerned, however, the whole issue of which is the means and which is the end is confused when we say that the reward is an integral part of the *mitzvah*. Surely we cannot accept that a *mitzvah* serves as a means to a higher end. After all, a *mitzvah* is the will of the eternal Creator, and since "The Torah and God are one," "He and His will are one," then just as God cannot be said to be a means to a higher end, so too His will cannot be understood as a means to an end.

Clearly, then, we must dismiss the notion that *mitzvot* serve as a medium to the receiving of a reward. If in the case of an employer–employee relationship the work itself is what is of significance, how much more so does it apply to the Torah! Why then should God have instituted that the reward for a *mitzvah* should be part and parcel of the *mitzvah* itself? It seems to degrade the *mitzvah* by synthesizing the means with the end. Even if the reward had been a part of but ancillary to the *mitzvah* it would not have been as bad. But it appears that the reward is central to the *mitzvah* and is attached in an inseparable way.

If in truth the *mitzvah* is far more important than the reward, then the Jew should fulfill the *mitzvah* because it is a goal, an end in itself. Why then build the reward as a direct consequence and result of a *mitzvah*? It would seem to have been far better if the *mitzvah* could have been rewarded by something external and unconnected to the *mitzvah*, just as an employee is paid currency, say, for painting a house.

We must delve deeper into this difficult but fundamental subject of reward and punishment. By doing so we shall also shed light on the eternal and elusive enigma of human suffering.

3

THE LOWEST OF WORLDS
DESTINED TO BE
THE HIGHEST

In *The Wolf Shall Lie with the Lamb*, the first volume of this series on the Thirteen Principles of Faith, I discussed at length the purpose for creation, as found in hasidic thought. For the purposes of this present discussion, I will encapsulate the argument here.

The founder of the *Chabad* hasidic movement, Rabbi Shneur Zalman of Liadi, writes in his hasidic classic, *Tanya* (chap. 36) that "the Almighty desired to have a dwelling place in the lowest of all worlds." Although God created all worlds, both spiritual and physical, it was his profound wish to reside specifically in the lowest of worlds, our physical domain. And he desired that this world be transformed from a mundane and often profane physical abode, into a dwelling that would fit the residence of the supreme King of kings and Creator of the universe.

The need for every human being to have a place to call his home, including, as it were, the Almighty Himself, is explained by the Talmud with its pronouncement, "Every person who does not have a home is not a person" (*Yevamot* 63a). When one lacks a home, one may never "be oneself." One is constantly acting, speaking, and behaving in a fashion tailored to fit the expectations of family, friends, society, and so on. Thus without a home, while one may be a person, one always remains somebody else's person. But in the privacy of one's home, one becomes one's own person and is set free.

As can be readily appreciated, the more glorified and famous the individual, the more is expected of him in terms of morality and behavior, and thus the more he is required to comply with the limits of greatness. The greater the level of personal grandeur, the more one must give up being one's own person. No president of the United States can walk the streets of Washington whenever he desires, due to security and other considerations. Neither can he express his mind about another individual in public, without making the statement conform to the strictest rules of diplomacy. A president, and even more so a king, must present himself in a manner in which the people expect a leader to behave. However, in the privacy of his own residence the president can come to life in his own right as his own person.

If this be true of a mortal king of flesh and blood, who must conform to the expectations of his subjects, who, as human beings, are after all qualitatively equal to the king, how much more so when we speak of the King of kings, the Creator of the universe. As can be readily appreciated, God, who is infinite, bears no relationship whatsoever to even the highest spiritual worlds, which are finite. Thus it is clear that the Almighty cannot reveal Himself even in the spiritual worlds the way He is in his essence, but rather must contract and limit Himself. In the language of Jewish mysticism, God must "adorn himself in a garb which conceals his true nature" (*Zohar*, sec. III).

But all this needs no mention. Anyone can appreciate that it is impossible to fit an infinite number of chairs into a finite room. At the very least, the same would apply to God. What is truly amazing is that God desires, somehow, to have the full intensity of his infinite essence manifest in our physical world. God wishes to dwell in our world without any garb or attire that would alter his infinite presence.

This is the desire of the Almighty in His creation of our physical world. God desires a residence. Even in the higher, more spiritual worlds, God cannot be Himself, as it were. He cannot radiate his true light nor may He reveal His true essence. Even the lofty spiritual worlds are too shallow and minuscule in comparison to God's infinite Being. Thus, He must contract and condense his infinite Self when He radiates His light in the higher worlds so as to suit their consumption. God must be careful to "tailor" and limit Himself to suit the capacity of receptacles much lower than He. Thus all the spiritual world cannot serve as a home or residence to the Almighty. He cannot reveal His true self within it. It is impossible for the infinite God to radiate his full intensity in a finite domain. It would overwhelm the domain.

But in the creation of our physical world, what God desires is a residence. God desires somehow to have the full intensity of his infinite essence manifest in our physical world. God wishes to dwell in our world without any garb or attire that will modify or minimize the intensity of his true Being.

This desire of the Almighty will come to fruition only in the messianic era, when God will be revealed and radiate the way He truly is without any curtain or obstruction. As Rabbi Shneur Zalman writes in *Tanya* (chap. 36), commenting on the verse from Isaiah (30:20), "And your teacher will hide no more," he explains, "this means that God will no longer conceal Himself in any garment or veil. For in that time God will reveal himself the way He existed even before the Creation of the world."

This, in brief, is what we discussed in the previous volume, which dealt with Principles #11 and #12, namely, the belief in the coming of the Messiah, and the belief in the resurrection of the dead.

Now, one of the important questions relating to the creation of the world that Rabbi Shneur Zalman addresses is the question of identifying which element of the creation is most important: the spiritual world or the physical world? Which of the two realms is God's goal and purpose and which of the two is only the means by which to bring about or help achieve that goal? After lengthy discussion and debate Rabbi Shneur Zalman arrives at the conclusion that the essential purpose behind the creation is not found in the spiritual worlds but specifically in the physical realm. Using different proofs Rabbi Shneur Zalman concludes that out of the entire creation God desires the concealment and darkness that pervades our world, just as the Midrash says, "The Almighty desired that He have a dwelling place here in the lowest of worlds" (*Tanchuma, Nasso* 16; *Bechukosai* 3).

When we refer to this world as the "lowest," as we will do throughout this work, our reference is not to lowliness in a spatial or temporal sense. Rather, it is in reference to godly light and revelation, in which our world is judged to be the lowest when compared to the amount of spiritual light revealed in other worlds. God is most concealed in our world and is found only with great difficulty. The Almighty created an infinite number of worlds, just as our Rabbis commented on the verse *Ve'alamot*–"and maidens without numbers." The Rabbis explain that the word *Alamot* should be read *Oilomois*, so that the statement reads: And *worlds* without number. These infinite numbers of worlds are distinguished from one another by the amount of spiritual light that radiates within them. This also defines which of the worlds is higher in comparison to the others. To be sure, in the spiritual realm there is no such thing as a physical hierarchy of higher and lower. Rather those worlds that have more godly light manifest within them are considered to be higher, while those that have less godly light are considered to be lower. In this hierarchy of spiritual light, our world figures the lowest.

The lowliness of our world expresses itself in not just one but two ways: first, in relation to the contraction of God's light; even the godly light that does exist and radiates in our world, thus giving existence and life to all objects within the creation, is a very limited one compared to the godly illumination of the higher spiritual worlds. Second, in relation to the concealment of the light; even this very contracted godly light that our world does receive *cannot even be seen*: God is entirely hidden in our world. Rather, the light is concealed and hidden and is expressed only in a very minute way. Thus, in two important facets, both the quantity of godly light, and the revelation of godly light, our world finds itself in the lowest possible position in the spectrum of worlds created by the Almighty.

To better understand the difference between these two qualities just mentioned–*contraction* and *concealment*–we will use an example taken from our own world.

All existence within the empirical world subdivides into four categories: the mineral, the vegetable, the animal, and the intellectual. In each and every one of these categories there is a godly light that sustains the object's existence and constantly suspends its creation, thus keeping the object extant. If not for this spiritual force it would be impossible for these objects to exist for even a split second (as we shall discuss later in the chapter about creation *ex nihilo*). This godly light, which vivifies all four categories of creation, is not equal in each. Clearly, since the vegetable category possesses the ability for growth and development, something that does not exist in the inanimate category, it necessitates a qualitatively higher godly light for its sustenance than that needed by the mineral.

The reason the vegetable has the potential for growth and development, something not possessed by inanimate objects, results from the fact that the vegetable is a product of a higher godly light, and it is this godly radiance that gives the vegetable the ability to expand beyond its original state of being. The same applies with the animal kingdom, which has a qualitatively higher life force than that possessed by the vegetables. This too results from a higher radiance of godly light, which gives the animal the ability for movement, will, and spatial independence. The same is true with regard to the difference between the animal and the intellectual. A human being has rational, cognitive faculties, something not possessed by the animals, because it has a much higher form of godly light sustaining it.

The more we descend down the ladder of existence, beginning with the sublime virtue of the intelligence of man, and continuing down through the animal and then to the vegetable and the inanimate, the godly light received by each of these parties diminishes as well. It is impossible to generalize about or compare the godly life force that sustains a human being to that which sustains a stone. Whereas a human being has the faculties of speech, thought, desire, growth, development, and so on, a stone has nothing save its very existence.

Notwithstanding all of the immense differences noted above, the differences exist only with regard to the magnitude of contraction that the godly light contained within our world must undergo in order to bring about and sustain the existence of each individual category of creation, which is to say that only in the *amount of godly light that they receive* do the categories of existence differ. But when we speak about the concealment and hiddenness of that godly light that does exist in our world, we find no differences between the four categories of creation whatsoever. In this respect they are all equal. Just as an inanimate object does not manifest its true origin and source to an impartial observer, so too a human being expresses the same lie about it being an independent existence with no strings attached, and having no dependence on a Creator and Regulator of the world. In fact the entire creation and all of its subcomponents tell the very same story. From the inactivity of the stone to the swiftness of the deer, they both convey the misleading impression that they originate with themselves and that there is no Creator that sustains them.

Thus all of the immense differences that exist in the four categories exist only in respect to the *amount* of godly light that they possess. But with regard to the concealment of the light, that is, the godliness they radiate to the observer, there is no difference between them at all. They all hide God's light equally.

This analogy accurately expresses the difference between the concepts of contraction and concealment, which in both categories this world finds itself at the bottom of the ladder in the hierarchy of created worlds.

As far as the contraction of light, the life force that radiates and sustains the physical world is much more limited compared to the godly light that radiates in the spiritual worlds. For the spiritual worlds are far more godly and transcendent. The physical world is far inferior, without any comparison to the spiritual worlds. Therefore, even if there weren't a concealment of God's light in our world, even if the amount of godly light that is contained within our world were revealed with its greatest radiance, even then all we would see is an infinitesimal ray, so small as once again to put our world at the very bottom of the spiritual ladder.

As far as the concealment of light is concerned, our world appears to be "a palace without any ruler" (*Zohar*, sec. III). The godly life force that sustains our world is completely hidden to the extent that one could be led to believe that the world has always existed, as in the Aristotelian theory of the eternity of matter, or that the world and all its inhabitants have come into being through the world's own indigenous processes, as in the Darwinian theory of evolution. One may truly be led to believe from the concealment of godly light in our world that there is nothing that transcends material existence and has formerly created the world. This is not the case with the spiritual worlds, which, to the observer, immediately express the truth about their condition. They are no more than an extension and a radiance of God's light, just as the light of the sun that reaches the earth could never lie about its origin. For just as the light of the sun, the moment it is disconnected or obstructed from its source, disappears or vanishes, thus proving that it was never an independent existence without the sun, so too the spiritual worlds must be connected to their source and radiate openly the godly light that sustains them. They cannot be disattached.

We may now appreciate why it is that throughout Jewish mystical literature our world is constantly referred to as "the lowest world to which there is nothing lower." Nevertheless, it is specifically in our lowly, physical world that God has chosen to have His essence reside. God wishes that from our world a dwelling for Him should be created.

The concept of a dwelling is in complete contradiction to (1) a contraction or (2) concealment of oneself. Due to this fact it is our world that is far more complete and perfect in comparison with the higher worlds. How so? Taking our previous definition of a dwelling further, in *Hassidut* it is explained that the word *dwelling* has two connotations: First, when a person finds himself in his house he takes no precautions of how he should dress and how he should appear, as he does when he is outside in the public eye. It is only in one's home that one expresses oneself completely, be it intellectually, emotionally, and even physically in the choice of how one should attire oneself. Of course in public one is obligated to conceal or dress up one's true self, especially bodily, but also emotionally and intellectually. Thus, being at home or being outside is a complete reversal of affairs. It is for this reason that the Talmud states that "a man who does not have a home is not a man."

Thus, the word *dwelling* is a statement of one's true manifestation without any concealment or contraction. The second connotation of the word *dwelling* is that it expresses the fact that the individual finds himself at home totally and completely. A lawyer at the office only fills his chair partially. What the firm requires of him is only his legal talent, but not necessarily his character. Neither will his emotions be fully expressed, as they would at home. Thus, only one dimension of his being is present in the office. In one's business what is needed is one's ability to invest wisely and manage one's office. It is therefore one's managerial skills that are the focus of attention and not other human facets. But when one is at home where nothing in particular is the focus of attention and the individual finds himself at home not to fill a specific need or calling but rather because he chooses to be at home and this is where he belongs, he thus fills his home totally and fully. It is one's essence that is expressed and resides at home, not just a particular talent or facet. Thus the word *dwelling* also expresses the fact that a person finds himself at home completely and without any contraction. In other words, the word *dwelling* means a complete revelation both in quality as well as quantity. The individual is found completely in his home without any contraction and this fact reveals itself without any concealment or latency. We thus see that a dwelling is the very antithesis of contraction and concealment. A dwelling is the most wholesome revelation of a human being, impervious to any concealment of one's true character.

A fuller appreciation of the Midrash, which proclaims that "the Almighty desires a dwelling place in the lowest of all possible worlds," may now be obtained. The Almighty desired that specifically in our physical world He should have a dwelling. The word *dwelling* means that His godly light should be revealed without any condensation or concealment, but radiate with its full intensity and strength. And God also desired not just for an infinitesimal godly ray to vivify our world, but that His quintessence, the very matter of which God is, should be found in our world without any compression whatsoever.

This then is the true intention of the entire creation, that this world become a dwelling for the Almighty. This purpose is found specifically in our world where the word *dwelling* can assume its fullest meaning by counteracting the two factors that are the cause of the lowliness of this world. Thus, a dwelling could not be established in its most complete sense in the higher worlds where these two factors do not exist. All the higher worlds were only created for our world and serve as a medium for the perfection and elevation of this, the physical realm, the place where God's home must be made.

4

MAKING GOD THE HOST: THE CHOICE TO GIVE UP CHOICE

Thus far we have emphasized that the whole purpose of our fulfillment of *mitzvot* in this world and in essence the very reason for the creation of the world is that here in the lowest possible world, a world in which God and the origins of the earth are concealed, God can be revealed and recognized. And the more divine commandments that we fulfill, the more we bring God into our world. One cannot expect a king to reside in just any dwelling. Even the king's private apartments must be fit for a king. By fulfilling the *mitzvot* we transform the mundanity of the world into a holy abode. Thus, as we invite God to descend into our world, we wish for Him to feel as though He is at home, and not just visiting the home of a stranger. And this is the way God wills it. His intention was not to be a *stranger* in our world, but rather the householder and owner of the home. And the more godliness we bring into our world, the more at home He feels.

To illustrate this principle, let us utilize an anecdote of two individuals, one by the name of Reuven and the other Shimon. Reuven wishes to dwell in the home of Shimon, but Shimon is unwilling to allow him to live with him. Reuven, who is more powerful than Shimon, can easily enter and live in Shimon's house by force. Shimon cannot chase him out. If he does so, can it be said that Reuven *lives* with Shimon? Of course not. He may occupy the home, but living or residing in a house means that one feels comfortable in the home, to the point where one feels as though one is in one's own home. To achieve this objective one must be invited into a home and be made to feel as comfortable as possible by the owner of the home. Only then can one feel that this new home is truly one's own. Without the complete consent of the householder, Reuven may indeed be sharing a house with Shimon, but it is more like Reuven has chased Shimon from his house. And although Shimon might be living there and for all practical reasons the house belongs to Shimon, one cannot say that Reuven and Shimon coexist peacefully, comfortably, and warmly together, but rather that Reuven has imposed his will on Shimon and now occupies his home.

The same applies with regard to God's desire to dwell in our world. There are two parts to God's wish. First, God requires that not only the spiritual worlds be a dwelling for Him, but also this, the lowest of worlds should be also. This is accomplished by studying Torah and fulfilling God's *mitzvot*, in which He is enclothed. As stated earlier, God's wisdom and will are all one, and therefore studying the Torah and performing the *mitzvot* brings God into our world. But this is only one aspect of God's will. The second and possibly more important, is that the transformation of this physical world into God's home not be accomplished from above. In other words, it should not come about solely through the agency of God's power and might, that man agrees for God to enter and reside in his world because he is incapable of stopping him. Rather, God wishes that His residency in this world be brought about by man from below. God wishes the inhabitants of this world to invite Him into their world and do everything possible to make the Creator feel comfortable in their midst.

Here the importance of free will and free choice on the part of the individual comes into its own. Had it not been for the fact that man has free will and choice to do as he pleases, to either use this world to his own selfish advantage or to live in accordance with God's law and make this world a proper dwelling place for God, it would be as if God simply imposed His will upon us. God's residency among us would not be accompanied by any sense of invitation on the part of the earth's inhabitants. Thus, Maimonides writes in *Laws of Repentance* (5:3) that "this principal of freedom of will is a cardinal tenet of Judaism and serves as the very foundation for the Torah and all its commandments."

But even with freedom of choice, man only fulfills one of God's two objectives in creating the world. It makes the world a dwelling place for God, but it does not necessarily make this world God's home. The purpose is that God should feel so comfortable in this world so as to feel that this world is His actual home.

In this discussion, the reader should be drawn to a qualitative difference between our analogy of a householder and his guest, and the God–world relationship. In the analogy, how the host treats his guest will, in the final examination, effect only the *feelings* of his guest. For even if Reuven will *feel* completely at home in Shimon's house, the fact will remain that, in reality, the house still belongs to Shimon. No feelings or illusions on the part of the guest will alter that fact. He may be so comfortable that he feels that it is his home. But it still is not.

But in the creation of the world, God's intention is not only that the world become His, but that it be demonstrated that it always *was* His. God does not merely desire to *feel* at home, with the world, in reality, belonging to man. Although it appears as though the world and God are two divisible entities, thus necessitating the need for God to be invited into this world as a guest, in reality this is an illusion. And with every *mitzvah* we do we show more and more how everything ultimately belongs to God and is in fact godly. At the same time, and here is where things get really complicated, God wishes for the world to remain a physical world where godliness is concealed. The purpose of our observance of Torah and *mitzvot* is not to change this world from being the lowest of all worlds, but to preserve its material construct while infusing it with godliness. These two statements seem extremely contradictory and we will discuss them in the upcoming chapters.

Thus what can we do in order for God not only to be found in our world but to feel comfortable and at home? Jewish mystical thought maintains that in spite of the fact that the study of Torah and performance of *mitzvot* must be done out of free choice, it is nonetheless essential that this choice be exercised out of the individual's acceptance of the yoke of Heaven, and not for any other reason.

In *Tanya* (chap. 41) it is explained that when an individual studies Torah and fulfills the *mitzvot* because he loves God and wishes to draw closer to Him, the individual thereby relinquishes the ability to serve God out of subservience and nullification. Rather, this person worships God out of a personal desire to achieve communion with God. He thus cannot fully take upon himself the yoke of Heaven willingly, since he is too emotionally involved to act like a servant. Religion is simply too inspiring to this individual, so that it precludes the possibility of his being like a soldier who takes orders.

There are many ways to serve God, and it would seem as though this individual, who serves God out of love, would be missing only the virtue of subservience, but would be considered, nonetheless, to be a truly devout person. Yet, the *Tanya* says that this kind of person is considered as though he does not serve God at all!

The reason is that only when one serves God as a servant who has no will of his own, and executes the desires of his master without any ulterior motives, even good ones, is one considered "a servant of the Almighty." But when one studies the Torah and fulfills the *mitzvot* out of a burning love for God and a desire to be close to Him, then one is in essence serving oneself. Why does he serve God? Well, what else can he do? He has an unquenchable desire to be close to God, to the point where this yearning will give him no rest. And since the Torah and *mitzvot* are the only path through which to execute this desire, he studies Torah all day long and serves his Creator faithfully. But in essence, he is serving only himself. He follows the dictates of his passion and his heart. He feels he needs God. Others feel that they need a beautiful house and a Swiss bank account. But would they be considered as doing God's work? If not, then why should he? While it is true that worshiping God is holier than accumulating wealth, it does not change one's motivation.

Therefore, it is vital that the launching point for one's service of God be a simple acceptance of the yoke of Heaven. In its wake will follow a complete nullification of self and an acceptance of God as the absolute master of one's being. It is only then that holiness can reside in one's being and the individual can be elevated to something higher. Only through absolute nullification of one's ego, and not for any personal gain, does one become an empty vessel and thus a receptacle to God's presence. In the language of the *Zohar* (*Parshat Behar*): "A person must accept upon himself the yoke of Heaven before anything else. If in this he is lacking, no holiness can reside upon him."

Stated in simpler words, when a Jew serves God out of love, without any acceptance of heavenly sovereignty, in essence he is doing not what God wants but what *he* wants. He is fortunate in that his will and God's will are identical, and thus he acts in accordance with God's directives. Notwithstanding this, however, he is accommodating his own aspirations and pursues them through the fulfillment of Torah and *mitzvot*. Why can't this person become holy? Because in everything but deed this person is exactly the same as someone who pursues material and worldly pleasure. Both men are doing whatever makes them happy and whatever satisfies their personal desire.

Since this is so, we now must struggle to explain the fundamental importance of freedom of choice. In light of the above, it would appear far better for a human being to totally give up his freedom of choice and fulfill the Torah and its commandments out of a wholesale submission to God. It seems proper to weed out any personal initiative and participation in divine worship.

Here we must return to the point made earlier. The reason why it is essential that a human being retain his freedom of choice amid the need to subjugate oneself utterly to the will of the Creator, is because God's will in having a dwelling place on earth has, not one, but two objectives.

The first is that in order for God to have a dwelling on earth, He must be the absolute master over the dwelling. But the second aspect of that desire is that the transformation of the world into God's abode be done by the world itself, that is, by its inhabitants, through using their empirical faculties to invite God in and make Him at home. In order to fulfill this side of God's will, it is imperative that one have the freedom to choose. God does not wish to invade man's planet by means of a *coup d'etat*.

Rather, His desire is for man to choose to build Him a home through his own personal initiative and choice.

Thus the reader should not misconstrue our arguments and conclude that we are suggesting that freedom of choice is not essential in religious endeavor; it is. What we are saying is that the choice one makes to indeed fulfill God's Torah and *mitzvot* should never be due to one's personal needs and aspirations. Even if one has an aspiration to become closer to God, it still is selfish and smacks of self-preservation. Rather one should *choose to submit* oneself to the study of Torah and the fulfillment of *mitzvot* out of a recognition that God is the true master over the world and that He needs to reclaim the earth as His home. And through every additional *mitzvah* we are slowly transforming this world into a welcoming abode for the supreme Ruler of the universe, truly fit for a King.

In the upcoming chapters we will deal further with the examination of personal motivations and intentions in the service of God, and its relevancy to the promise of reward and punishment.

5

AN OBLIGATION
TO LOVE GOD

In his celebrated *Laws of Repentance* (5:1–3), Maimonides writes: "The choice is given to every individual. If he wishes to follow the path of goodness and righteousness, he has the choice. And if he wishes to turn astray to evil and be a wicked person, this too is his choice. . . . This [principle of choice] is of fundamental importance and serves as the pillar of our Torah and commandments, as it is written 'See that I have given to you today life and death . . . good and evil, and you shall choose good.'" Thus the freedom of choice constitutes one of the most fundamental tenets in the relationship between God and man.

On the other hand, we find throughout Jewish literature the need for one to completely and utterly nullify oneself to God's will and worship Him out of an acceptance of the yoke of Heaven. In the previous chapter we quoted from the *Tanya*, which states in the name of the *Zohar* that it is only the subjugation of oneself to God's will in the study of Torah and fulfilling of its commandments that is considered serving God properly. Without this premise one may become a great Torah scholar and perform all the *mitzvot*, but is not considered to be a true servant of the Almighty.

In the previous chapter we also discussed how if one's service to God is lacking in subjugation to God's will, one fails to address the second, and possibly more important, aspect of God's purpose in creating the world. God desired a dwelling place here in the lower world that entails, first, that the earth become his home, and second, that His residency in the world be established, not through His barging through the door and overpowering the earth's inhabitants, but by invitation. Only through the will of the people is God made to feel not only as a guest in this world, but also as its Master and householder. The purpose of the creation of the world is for God to feel, and for the entire creation to come to know, that the world belongs to God, that the illusion of the world being detached from God and an independent entity is false. We are not inviting Him into *our* home, but rather destroying the false impression that the world was ever outside God's domain.

And this is why serving God out of love is insufficient and one should approach God as a servant. There are those who recognize that in comparison to God, all is naught. Why should they run after cars and clothing when these items are ephemeral and shallow? God is eternal and truly superb. Thus, they awaken a love for God from within and have a burning desire to draw close to Him. Since the only means by which to do so is by studying Torah and fulfilling *mitzvot*, they become great Torah scholars and meticulously observe all the divine commandments. Is this not commendable?

Yes and no. What they are doing is worthy, but it is more like treating God as if He were a very important guest and they feel honored that such a guest wishes to dwell in their home. Therefore, they gladly invite Him in. Needless to say, they undoubtedly treat this important guest with utmost respect and kindness. Nevertheless the guest will always remain just that, a guest. The guest will never be the master over this home. Likewise, these individuals are not willing to give up what they want, *their* love and *their* desires. God fulfills their need for completion and self-attainment, so they worship God. But the most important element in the equation is not the *object* of their love, God, but rather their *need* for an object to love. Thus, just as an important guest makes his hosts feel special, so too God serves these people's purposes. In this respect, the Almighty is being used as a means to a higher end. As an object that satisfies the desires of those who worship Him, He is not a goal in Himself. Rather, He serves to comfort and satisfy man.

On the other hand, if God did not give us freedom of choice, and our subordination to God's will were a product of programming from the heavens, *milemaalah lematah*, this could not be considered as us inviting God into our home to be Master. Rather, it would be analogous to a dictatorial ruler forcing his way into his neighbor's home and setting up camp. It is therefore of pivotal importance that one's submission to God be a product of one's own choice.

The *choice* to nullify one's ego to God's will is referred to in the *Tanya* as "the beginning of all godly service, its most important element, and its source." It is explained in *Tanya* that serving God with this attitude is the only way that the observance of *mitzvot* can be called *avodah* (divine worship). Here we have the reason why *yirat Hashem* (fear of God) is so important in Judaism. (Fear of God does not mean that one fears divine punishment or retribution. Fear of punishment is best defined as love of self, or self-preservation, as we shall see later.) By *fear* we mean the absolution of self-interests and personal will, and embracing a higher will.

Love of God is the exact opposite. Whereas fear and submission to God emphasize the complete lack of existence and will on the part of the individual and the superimposition of God's will on the subject, love of God necessitates that there is a lover, *someone who is loving*. There is an entity outside of God who wishes to draw closer to His infinite presence.

But lest one be led to believe that love of God is undesirable, in the same chapter of *Tanya* where the importance of the fear of God is discussed Rabbi Shneur Zalman addresses the centrality of loving one's Creator. He writes as follows:

> Just as a bird cannot fly with one wing, [so too fear of God unaccompanied by love is insufficient]. For fear and love are two wings, as has been explained in the *Tikkunim*. Similarly fear alone is just one wing, and one's service cannot ascend on high with it . . . for there must also be the filial quality, in order to awaken, at least, the natural love that is hidden in his heart to become conscious of it in his mind. At any rate, to be aware of

the love of the one God in his thought and desire to cleave to
Him, may He be blessed. (*Tanya*, chap. 41)

Looked at superficially, Rabbi Shneur Zalman's pronouncement is a statement of the difficulty inherent in having one's
divine service ascend heavenward. In order to fly, a bird must
cause its entire weight to defy the forces of gravity and lift off
from the ground. This necessitates not just one wing but two,
in order to give it the extra thrust necessary to soar in the heavens. One wing, Rabbi Shneur Zalman seems to be saying, would
be insufficient since it would lack the power to lift the bird's
weight. Likewise, fear of God alone is insufficient, but one needs
the extra push heavenward that comes in the form of love.

In reality, though, the Lubavitcher Rebbe, Rabbi Menachem
Schneerson, explains that there is a much deeper meaning in
this passage from the *Tanya*. The flight of a bird is caused, not
just by having sufficient thrust through its wings, but by flap-
ping both of its wings *in opposite directions.* This means that
the need for a bird to have two wings is not only because one
wing is insufficient and lacks the energy necessary to propel
the bird through the air, but each wing needs a counteracting
force. Each needs something to negate its own activity and thus
cause the bird to soar forward. Even if a bird had two wings,
but on the same side of the body, or just one big strong wing,
the bird would flap over on its side or just go around in circles.
What is necessary is one force and another antithetical to it to
afford the bird stable flight.

The same applies in the human need for love and fear of God
to serve as "wings" elevating one's *mitzvot* Heavenward. The
need is not only so that one's divine service be sufficiently
empowered to ascend, but rather that there be two antithetical dimensions. The first, the complete nullification of one's will
to God as a servant who yearns to fulfill the every wish of his
master. And the second, the need for the individual to remain
existent while fulfilling God's will, so that one's divine service
be done with joy, vitality, and personal initiative.

These two contradictory movements—love and fear of God—
are a direct result of the two topics discussed above—freedom
of choice and an acceptance of the yoke of Heaven.

Thus we see how these two things constitute not only a foundation and introduction to the service of God, but also the very emotions and attitude with which the service should be approached. Torah and *mitzvot* must be done out of a love for God, thus preserving the personal dimension in godly service. But accompanying this, one's subjugation to God must be a result of God's wish for it to be so.

An example of the dynamics of this process is found in the writings of the *Ari*, Rabbi Isaac Luria, the celebrated fifteenth-century kabbalist. He states that just as when one, say, puts on *tefillin* in the morning, one must take upon oneself the positive commandment associated with the *tefillin*, "you shall bind them," likewise one must consciously take upon oneself the positive commandment of the Torah, "And you shall love the Lord your God." This means to say that not only is there an absolute need for love and fear of God, but that the love of God must be a product of the acceptance of the yoke of Heaven and the fact that God has instructed us to fulfill his commandments, including the heavenly imperative to love Him. Thus, this statement of Rabbi Isaac Luria that when one feels love for God, one must think about the commandment to love the Almighty, proves that the love should be a product not only of self-initiative, but also of the subservience and the subjugation one has to God's commandments.

Here we have an example of how in the love of God there are two contradictory and antithetical premises: one, the feeling of one's personal participation in the act of the *mitzvah*, and two, one's absolute nullification to God while performing the *mitzvah*.

This all-important concept is a central tenet in the individual's approach to godly worship, and we will discuss it further in the upcoming chapters. In the meantime, we will once again reemphasize the essential thrust of this chapter: The purpose of creation, to make a dwelling place for God in the lower world, necessitates that the dwelling be built by the (inhabitants of the) lower world itself, and that God be invited to make that domain His own. And this desire of God is enacted through two polar opposites—the freedom of choice on the part of the individual and the simultaneous subjugation of that individual, with love and fear for God, to the will of his Creator.

6

LOVE OF GOD IS TORAH, AND FEAR OF GOD IS *MITZVOT*

In the last chapter we discussed the need for both love and fear of God in the study of Torah and the fulfillment of His commandments. We explained how only through both these antithetical properties does one gain "wings" for one's divine service to be elevated and ascend Heavenward. We also explained that love of God is necessary so that there be personal participation and initiative in serving God, and that fear of God, that is, absolute nullification to God's will, is necessary so that we make the world into a home for the Almighty. It is just not good enough for God to *feel* at home, but complete nullification is necessary so that our world become God's home and He its Master. Through our absolute submission to the will of the Creator, we allow Him to inhabit ourselves and our world, and thus He is given a home.

We shall now proceed to explain how these two properties, love and fear of God, can be said to represent, generally speaking, the study of Torah and the fulfillment of *mitzvot*, respectively.

When studying Torah, it is insufficient just to mumble words. Rather, the wisdom of the Torah must be apprehended by human intellect. The importance of one's properly understanding the Torah that one studies is underscored by the fact that Jewish law maintains that if one fails to comprehend the por-

51

tion which one is studying, one cannot recite the special blessing for Torah study. Why is it so important that one actually comprehend what one is studying? Because the purpose of Torah
study is for Godliness to permeate the human system. Since the
Almighty and His Torah are one, when a person studies and
understands the Torah, then godliness unites and becomes one
with the individual. Conversely, if one fails to understand his
Torah study, then he fails to unite with God's wisdom, which
comprises the Torah.

This thought is expressed aptly in *Tanya* (chap. 5) where
Rabbi Shneur Zalman explains why the Torah is referred to as
the "bread" and "food" of the soul. Since the soul engages its
faculties of knowledge in order to apprehend the Torah, and
the Torah becomes enveloped and absorbed in the soul and
intellect of a human being, the Torah can thus be said to "nourish" the soul. He writes:

> For just as physical bread nourishes the body as it is absorbed
> internally in his very inner self, where it is transformed into blood
> and flesh of his flesh, whereby he lives and exists—so too, it is
> with the knowledge of the Torah and its comprehension by the
> soul of the person who studies it well, with the concentration of
> his intellect until the Torah is absorbed by his intellect and is
> united with it and they become one. This becomes nourishment
> for the soul and in turn life from the Giver of life, blessed be He,
> God himself, who is clothed in his wisdom and his Torah [ab-
> sorbed in his soul].

We thus see clearly that in order for God's dwelling to be
constructed by the "inhabitants" of the world itself, divine worship must permeate the individual. One cannot only pay lip
service to God's entreaties, but also must digest and internal-
ize their holiness. This, of course, cannot be accomplished unless one actually understands the Torah, whereby it unites with
one's intellect. For one just to read the Torah as one reads, say,
the book of Psalms, one is merely uttering syllables and words
that go over the head of the reader and leave no lasting impression. Therefore, although one may be performing a godly and
spiritual act, in no way does it unite with the reader and become
a part of him.

When it comes to *mitzvot*, however, the very opposite is true. *Mitzvot* are exactly what their name implies—godly commandments. A commandment is fulfilled with the intention that it is God's will and one is subjugating oneself to God's will. Thus, in the performance of a *mitzvah*, one may not necessarily comprehend or feel the spiritual transformation one is performing on the object, nor the fact that this object is serving as a medium for the godly light one brings into the world via the *mitzvah*. The objective behind a *mitzvah* is not the unification of godliness with the performer, but the subjugation of the performer's will to God. In the performance of *mitzvot*, it is the action, and the action alone, that is of supreme importance. Everything else is secondary.

It should be noted by the reader that our present discussion of Torah representing personal participation and initiative, and *mitzvot* representing absolution of self, transcends our previous discussion where love and fear of God represent self and absolution of self.

Whereas before our emphasis was on the *kind* of feelings, emotions, and intentions one should have while engaging in divine worship, here we are discussing what it is that actually constitutes, serves as the very makeup, of Torah and *mitzvot*. The fact is that the *essence* of Torah study is its transmission and absorption into human intellect. And the essence of the performance of *mitzvot* is capitulation and surrender of one's entire being to God.

Love and fear of God, on the other hand, constitute the *means* and *meditations* by which one should go about the study of Torah and the fulfillment of *mitzvot*. As mentioned above, it is vital that one have freedom of choice in serving God, but it must be the kind of choice that is governed by an acceptance of the yoke of Heaven.

Notwithstanding this, contemplations and dispositions of this kind are very far from the essence of what Torah and *mitzvot* are. Rather, the former serve only as the underpinnings and supports for the fulfillment of Torah and *mitzvot*. As such, it is essential that the study of Torah and fulfillment of *mitzvot*, notwithstanding their antithetical constructs, be infused with love and fear of God.

The reader should not mistakenly be led to believe, based on our present discussion, that the study of Torah need not be accompanied by fear and nullification to God, or that *mitzvot* need not be done out of a love for God and total involvement of self. Rather, our purpose is to emphasise that the *essence* of Torah study is about the need for man to be permeated with holiness, and that the essence of *mitzvot* is the need for man to abrogate his existence and needs in the presence of God, and become a chariot to His will.

To be sure, even when we speak of Torah being the transformation of self and *mitzvot* being the nullification of self, this is said in a general way. Speaking more specifically there is no doubt that Torah and *mitzvot* also encompass each other's faculties. This must be so, for if God's dwelling here on earth is to be complete, then the divine worship that builds such dwelling must be complete. Thus, if the study of Torah did not encompass some nullification of self, and conversely if the fulfillment of *mitzvot* did not incorporate individual participation, both would be lacking. They would be missing the pivotal, antithetical element that negates their own essence, as explained earlier. As a consequence, God's dwelling in the lower worlds would be incomplete.

That Torah study, while representing the synthesis of godliness with one's being, nevertheless must incorporate self-negation, is a recurrent theme in the Talmud. The Talmud in many areas goes to great pains to emphasize that while there must be intellectual participation in the study of Torah, and not just faith and devotion or the mere uttering of unintelligible words, nevertheless Torah study must be accompanied by exceeding humility. Case in point, in *Eruvin* (13) we read:

> Rabbi Aba stated in the name of Shmuel: "For three years the house of Shamai and the house of Hillel disputed a legal ruling. Each one claimed that the *halakha* followed their respective interpretations. Suddenly, a Heavenly voice was heard proclaiming: 'Both these and these are the words of the living God, but the *halakhah* follows the house of Hillel.' But, since both are the words of the living God, why did the house of Hillel merit that the *halakhah* be established according to their interpretation? Because they were calm and humble [and patient, *Rashi*] and in

their academy they would teach both their own interpretations
as well as that of the House of Shamai. Furthermore they would
always precede their own words with the words of the House of
Shamai."

The implications of this passage are astounding. If the whole
objective of Torah study is that it be apprehended in human
intellect, to the point where it becomes one with the human
mind, it should certainly follow that the conclusion of all Torah
debates in the form of a halakhic ruling be decided solely in favor
of those with superior intellectual and logical arguments! Here,
however, the halakhah followed the house of Hillel because of
their humility. The incredible fact that emerges is that humility
is the proper path to accurately apprehend the truth of the
Torah. As a heavenly instrument, Torah is not merely an intellectual exercise but an encounter with the Divine.

Let us also add that humility in the study of Torah is in essence far more important than in any other sector of Jewish
religious endeavor. For, as explained earlier, the need for the
complete acceptance of the yoke of Heaven in the fulfillment
of *mitzvot* is in order that holiness rest on the individual performer (*Tanya*, chap. 41). But in the study of Torah the need
for subjugating oneself to the will of Heaven is not only in order
for one's study to become holy, elevated, and spiritual, but also
so that one properly apprehend that which he is studying in
the first place. Humility brings in its path intellectual comprehension, which cannot be achieved when one studies arrogantly
and for the purpose of achieving fame as a scholar. This can be
understood logically as well. Just as when a vessel is full nothing can be added to it, so too he who is arrogant in the way in
which he goes about studying is "too full for the Torah to make
its impression on him" (Maimonides, *Laws of Character*). Humility in the study of Torah brings in its wake, not only holiness, but depth of understanding.

Thus we see how important it is that Torah study be infused
with two antithetical human impulses: promotion and participation of self, accompanied by humility and abnegation of self.

The same applies to the fulfillment of *mitzvot*. A *mitzvah* is
God's commandment and one is enjoined to execute this com-

mand without any recourse to personal observations or opinions regarding the directive. And yet, many of the Torah's commandments have reasons for their fulfillment, reasons that are easily comprehended by the human mind. In fact, all of the Torah's commandments are broken down into two categories: *hukim* and *mishpatim*, suprarational and rational commandments (as we shall discuss later at length).

But why was this necessary? After all, *mitzvot* are orders issued from "above to below," from God to the earth's inhabitants, and are not given with any recourse to our opinion as to their righteousness and/or necessity. Apparently, no reason should have been given by God. As can be well appreciated, the usual custom of a master is not to disclose the reasons for his instructions to his servant. If he did, he would defeat the entire purpose behind the dynamics of the relationship that exists between master and servant. A master issues a command, and the servant executes that command precisely because he is a servant. Clearly, then, God nevertheless gave us rational reasons for many of his commandments so that there would be a degree of human involvement in the religious worship.

So here, as in the case of Torah study, one enjoys personal participation in the fulfillment of a *mitzvah* in two ways. First, there is the person who fulfills the *mitzvah*, which gives one full participation in the service of God since one chooses to fulfill it. One must actually make the rational choice of taking upon oneself the yoke of Heaven and fulfilling the commandments. Second, since many of the *mitzvot* have reasons that are plainly grasped by human intelligence, the *mitzvot* unite with one's mind, just as with the study of Torah. Of course, it is not only the intellect that is affected by the *mitzvah*, but since the *mitzvah* is comprehended, one may feel for its fulfillment as well and thus there is emotional participation in the *mitzvot*. One can fulfill *mitzvot*, as is often the case, out of a burning desire and love for God, Judaism, and tradition. Thus, the whole of one's being is permeated with the godliness of the *mitzvot*.

To sum up what we have explained over the past two chapters: Jewish religious worship requires that human beings engage themselves fully in serving their Creator, which necessitates a total exertion of one's intellectual as well as emotional faculties in apprehending God. God wants *people* serving him, not robots. On the other hand, God requires that man nullify his very existence and will in the face of the Supreme Will. This antithetical human experience in serving God expresses itself in three ways:

1. In the preparation and pretext for the fulfillment of Torah and its commandments, which involves at once accepting the yoke of heaven while exercising one's freedom of choice. Or, as stated earlier, choosing to abandon oneself and subjugate oneself to godly service.

2. In the actual study of the Torah and the fulfillment of its commandments, which is done through love of God, which is a feeling of a personal participation in serving God, and by fear of God, which is an expression of subservience and negation.

3. In the essence and makeup of the Torah and *mitzvot* themselves whereby the Torah invites human participation since it must be apprehended within the mind, and the *mitzvot* deny the self and human participation since they enjoin man to lay aside his opinions and feelings and ultimately subjugate his will to God's. Conversely, in *mitzvot*, too, there is the intellectual participation through one's understanding the reasons for many of the *mitzvot*, and emotional participation through fulfilling *mitzvot* out of love and excitement. And Torah too embraces nullification of self since in order to understand the truth of Torah, one must first have humility and remain an open vessel to receive the Torah's wisdom.

7

ANSWERING THE ORIGINAL QUESTIONS: WHY REWARD AND PUNISHMENT IS CENTRAL TO JUDAISM

After the discussion in the previous chapters, it is now possible to return and answer our original questions about the nature of reward and punishment. The main question we asked, and what is vital to a deeper understanding of the Jewish worldview, is why Judaism is so emphatic about the existence of reward and punishment and its centrality to Jewish belief. It seems so out of character. The religion that demands so much honesty, sincerity, and unquestioned devotion on the part of man in his service of God simultaneously whispers in man's ear constantly that he need not worry about the sacrifices he is making in order to be an observant Jew since God will always recompense him for his effort. On the other hand, if he does not make those sacrifices he is told that he will experience a lessening of his material fortune, or even death. How can these two contradictory philosophies coexist?

What room is left for altruism if we are told so emphatically throughout the Torah that we will be rewarded for our efforts? Take for example the *mitzvah* of *tzedakah* (charity). Surely,

one of the most difficult things in life is to take that which you
have toiled and sweated for and simply give it away. Yet, this is
why the *mitzvah* is so commendable. One of the greatest ac-
colades that we can attribute to a human being is to label him
a "charitable person." Yet the Torah promises that in return for
giving charity one will be rewarded with wealth and riches, as
in the Talmud's exposition of the words *Aser Te'aser* ("You shall
surely tithe") (Deuteronomy 14:22). The Talmud comments,
"Aser bishvil shetisasher" ("tithe in order that you become
rich"). Now, if these are the promises being given to a person
who indeed has faith in the truth of the Torah, what possible
virtue can there be in being a charitable man? Is it now merely
for personal gain? Why must God reward man when the very
promise of the reward seems to transform what should be a religious act into an act of self promotion and preservation?

We also inquired as to why man must be rewarded if, by serving God, he is basically fulfilling the purpose for which he was
created. And does the promise of reward not contradict universal Jewish teachings on the subject that emphatically emphasize the need for man to serve God with no ulterior motive?

Furthermore, we asked why God is obligated to compensate
the Jewish people for fulfilling His *mitzvot*? Throughout the
Torah the Jewish people are constantly referred to as God's servants, not employees. If so, they deserve no reward since they
have not been commissioned for what services they are render-
ing unto the Almighty, but rather have been created for this
express purpose.

Finally, we asked why it is that the reward that the Almighty
grants for the performance of a *mitzvah* is directly related to
the *mitzvah*. Why is it that *"sehar mitzvah mitzvah,"* the reward for a *mitzvah* is the *mitzvah* itself? Could God not just
have given a general reward for the *mitzvot* without them being
specifically an actual outgrowth of the *mitzvah*? Why is it that
a *mitzvah* and its reward are intrinsically related to the point
where the reward is a direct consequence of the *mitzvah* performed?

In the previous chapters we have made a lengthy exposition
on the purpose of creation. We explained that the Almighty
desired a dwelling place in the lowest of worlds, our physical

domain. But He was not content merely dwelling in the world, He wanted to be revealed in that world. He did not merely desire to be present in the world, but also noticed and seen.

In other words, what God desires from our world is that it be revealed for all to see that, contrary to what appears to be the case, this world is in fact godly. Although it appears that we live in a mundane, material, even profane world, that may even have arisen spontaneously by virtue of its own indigenous processes, nevertheless it was God who created the world and it is God who resides in this world even more than all the higher worlds. Man's duty is to reveal, through the ongoing performance of spiritual acts, that God inhabits our world and that the world is in fact godly.

The entire historical process is but one long attempt for man to show, by virtue of his religious worship, that godliness is associated not only with those things that are overtly godly, such as spiritual worlds, angels, charity, and prayer, but that the physical world conceals a sublayer of holiness and godliness. God resides in our world and is concealed by what we call nature. But ultimately His desire is to be manifest in our world, and our job is to reveal him, as has been discussed throughout this work.

Thus, as explained above, man must not only submit himself to God's will, which actually constructs God's home on earth through the performance of *mitzvot*, but must do so willingly, which makes God feel as though He is invited into our world. This invitation allows God to feel comfortable, as it were, and not as though He has forced His will upon us and has commandeered our home. And this, in turn, allows for godly manifestation, the revelation of godly light in our world so that it is transformed from a purely physical domain into a godly one.

If man were forced into serving God, then the spiritual light of the *mitzvot* would not be absorbed by man or his world. Since man is being coerced into action, the godly light of the mitzvot just passes over him. Since he is being coerced, he is removed from the picture. His will is not being influenced by God's will, but rather the act of coercion says, "We are ignoring your will, it is of no concern to us." But what is vital is that godly light be manifest in the physical world, that God be seen to be resident in our world. For this to happen, the world must be transformed into a godly abode, which can only happen if the light of Torah and *mitzvot* permeates the whole of creation. In other words, God wishes to be unified with His world. He does not wish for creation to be seen as something independent and outside of His unity. This can only be accomplished if (1) the world subjects itself to God's will and (2) if it does so willingly so that man brings God into His world by virtue of his own initiative. This will ultimately occur in its most complete form in the messianic era when it shall be revealed for all to see the godliness inherent in creation, as stated by the prophet Isaiah, that "[in that time] the earth shall be covered with the knowledge of the Lord as the waters cover the ocean floor" (Isaiah 11:9).

But even in our own time we reveal the fact that the physical earth is godly, even to a limited degree, by using physical objects in the performance of spiritual deeds, in short, doing *mitzvot*. The fact that a physical object, such as cow leather, can be used in such lofty *mitzvot* as *tefillin*, is proof of the fact that indeed the cow leather has latent godliness. This is the reason generally that it is so important that we have physical participation in serving God. If there were no physical participation in serving God, then this would mean that the physical is unworthy in religious worship and that ultimately there is no godliness contained in physical things. If man could carry out his morning prayers without the use of *tefillin*, for instance, then this would have confirmed our intuition that the loftier things like prayer belong to God but not the material objects of the world, such as leather and animal skins.

It is also for this reason that fear of God and negation of self are insufficient. If Jewish religious observance were predicated only on the need for man to subjugate his will to God's will and remove any form of personal involvement, as it were, this would confirm that godliness was not within the human and that the only way he can become godly is to discard his material being.

But the obligation for one to harbor love of God and to affirm oneself in the service of God is confirmation of the fact that there is a part of God within every human being. The fact that

Judaism demands that man exercise his understanding and judgment, his pleasure and emotion, in the service of God is an affirmation of the fact that being human does not serve as an impediment to godliness, that the physical world is an extension, and not an obstruction, of the Divine.

Had there only been the concept of *mitzvot*, which as above, generally constitutes a denial of self and a submission to the word of God, and no Torah, which generally signifies man's participation in divine service, then there would be no avenue or means by which the physical world could manifest its inherent godliness. The physical would have always been left out.

But the physical is, in fact, godly. And this fact is reflected in four key areas of Torah theology:

1. In man's need to exercise freedom of choice in the fulfillment of God's will. This affirmation of the intelligence and the rational thought process of the individual in the service of God through the exercising of choice, as opposed to commandments that are fulfilled only because of subjugation of human will to the divine will, display how human faculties are absolutely natural in a spiritual environment and how they facilitate the execution of the divine will, rather than serve as an impediment, or obstacle, to the divine. Thus, the human mind is godly.

2. In the obligation to accompany all acts of divine worship with love of God, and not just fear of heaven. This participation of human emotion is representative of the fact that a divine act is actually enhanced, and not stifled, by the fervor of human emotional involvement. Had there been emphasis only on fear of heaven, this would have confirmed that man can only exist in a spiritual environment by minimizing, retracting from involvement, to the greatest degree. But the obligation to love God confirms that human emotional involvement serves as a window to embracing the divine. Thus, the heart too is godly.

3. In the fact that all of Judaism comprises not only *mitzvot*, which bid man to surrender his will to God's bidding, a denial of self, but the *mitzvot* counterpart—the Torah. The Torah, which must be apprehended in human intelligence and engage man's intellectual faculties fully, serves as the ultimate expression of the spirituality of all the human faculties: thought,

speech, and action. Man is obligated not just to understand the Torah, but to speak the Torah and perform its commandments. Thus, the human body is holy.

4. In the fact that virtually all of the Torah and *mitzvot* concern themselves with physical objects and everyday life. The fact that virtually no *mitzvah* can be performed without the aid or the direct involvement of a physical object is a testament to the latent holiness contained within material existence. And in most cases the physical object not only facilitates, serves as a medium, for a divine act, but actually constitutes the act itself. This is seen most clearly in the fact that as a result of utilizing a physical object, such as cow leather, for the performance of the *mitzvah* of *tefillin*, the physical object retains its holiness even after the event and is heretofore regarded as a *heftzah shel mitzvah* (a holy object). Thus, the entire physical world is holy.

And here we have the reason that the doctrine of reward and punishment too enjoys such centrality in Judaism and even serves as one of its thirteen cardinal tenets. The fact that every time we perform a *mitzvah* we receive a physical reward demonstrates that Torah and *mitzvot* have not only a spiritual dimension but a physical one as well. Godliness permeates the world to such an extent that whenever someone performs a godly act there is a natural, physical outcome. Every time a *mitzvah* is performed there is a direct consequence in the physical world and every spiritual undertaking has a physical corollary. Every spiritual act not only has a physical counterpart, but even more so, has a direct effect on the physical world since the two are absolutely united.

And in what way is that outgrowth manifest? How does it affect our world? In either bringing God closer and making him more revealed, or in making Him more distant and thus detracting from the world. As explained above, every time a human being fulfills a *mitzvah*, he is bringing God closer to our world. He is creating unity between the physical world and the divine. And this unification is manifest in the fact that there is a greater abundance in physical prosperity.

For example, every time man gives *tzedakah* he is promised greater wealth. But what is the connection between a holy, spiritual act and receiving more money as a result of this act? It is this: by giving charity this individual has brought God further into His world and this is manifest in a greater abundance of material reality; his money, his wealth, actually grows. The direct consequence of bringing God closer is that material wealth increases as well.

Anyone can appreciate that by performing a *mitzvah*, a godly act, we bring about an increase in spirituality, in godly light. We recognize this and readily accept it. Our mistake, however, is that we believe that this only affects the spiritual worlds. We believe that as a result of our *mitzvot* we cause a swelling of spiritual illumination. In truth, however, as explained above, being that the physical world is also godly, albeit not yet revealed, a *mitzvah* therefore causes a swelling in the physical world, in physical possessions as well. Just as one becomes holier as a result of a *mitzvah*, so too he becomes richer, because a *mitzvah* affects the spiritual and the physical equally— they are not different, and they are not separate. They are both godly, and they are both one.

The same applies as a result of committing a sin. When one sins he brings about a distancing of God from His world. A sin minimizes God's involvement with His world and this too has its direct correlation in our lives commensurate with the enormity of the sin. It brings about a minimization of our own earthly involvement, of our own earthly possessions. Just as committing a sin lessens the godly light in the spiritual worlds, so too does it minimize God's involvement in our world and thus minimizes any abundance of material objects. Thus, if a person commits the ultimate distancing of God from His world, bloodshed, which God says He despises, the result is that he is punished with losing, not just some of his innocence and spirituality, but his physical life as well. The gap that *he* has created between God and the physical world manifests itself in the individual who brought this about, who likewise becomes distanced and less attached to the physical world. It is not a case of measure for measure, but the exact consequence of his very own action not only manifests itself in the world, but has a direct effect on physical reality.

Another example: We recite thrice daily in the *Shema* God's warning:

And it will be, if you will diligently obey My commandments which I enjoin upon you this day, to love the Lord your God and serve Him with all your heart and with all your soul, I will give rain for your land at the proper time . . . and you will gather in your grain, your wine, and your oil. Take care lest your heart be lured away, and you turn astray and worship alien gods and bow down to them. For then the Lord's wrath will flare up against you, and He will close the heavens so that there will be no rain and the earth will not yield its produce, and you will swiftly perish from the good land that the Lord gives you.

Why should the rain be ceased and the Jews driven from the land of Israel as a result of their sins? The answer is that their sins cause God to be less involved in and less connected to His world. And when God is less involved, automatically the physical world is deprived. Just as there is less spirituality and holiness if God is driven from the world, so too there is less of the physical, since the physical is also godly. Thus, there is less rain and no produce. And ultimately, the perpetrators are not *punished*, but *affected* by their deed. Since they caused God to be removed from the land, the direct result is that they too will lose their connection with the land. They will be driven from the land of Israel.

Likewise, if they follow God's law and bring God closer to His world, cause God to be more involved with His world, the direct result is physical prosperity, or in other words, an increase in physical success and abundance—more grain, more wine, more oil.

To sum up, bringing God closer to His world as a result of fulfilling His commandments brings in its wake an increase in physical abundance. The physical is directly increased as a result of closer proximity to the Creator and increased godliness. And the farther God retreats from this world results directly in a lessening of physical prosperity and abundance—simply because they too are really one. Both are part of God. And thus, the more spirituality and holiness increase, the more the physical increases. And conversely when spirituality and holiness decrease, the physical decreases simultaneously.

No wonder then that the epoch of the Messiah, an era when godliness and holiness will reign throughout the land, is associated with promises of great material abundance, an end to death, war, and disease, and an increase in joy, peace, and prosperity. The two are intrinsically connected. In the messianic era when God's unity with the world will have reached its zenith, when it shall be revealed for all to see how our world is in fact an extension of God, so too there will be a perfection in the material world. Just as God's spiritual light will reach its fullest and most revealed intensity, the same will be true of the physical world, which is also a part of God. It will be perfect.

It is based on this understanding between the increase of godliness and a commensurate increase in physical reward that the Lubavitcher Rebbe explains an enigmatic passage in the commentary of Rashi on the Torah, which in turn is derived from the Midrash on *Bereishit*. On the words "And Jacob dwelt in the land of his father's sojournings, in the land of Canaan" (Genesis 37:1), Rashi comments, "Jacob desired to dwell (*leisheiv*) in peace, but there sprang upon him the troubles of Joseph. The righteous desire to dwell in peace; the Holy One Blessed Be He said, 'It is not sufficient for the righteous that which is prepared for them in the world to come, but they seek to dwell in peace (also) in this world!'"

The Rebbe asks how could it be that Jacob, who was so devoted to God's will that along with the other forefathers he is called "the chariot," suddenly concerns himself with a desire to be rewarded with peace and an end to his troubles? Did someone so devoted to God not recognize that what's important in this life is hard work and constant striving to execute God's will, not peace and an easy life?

What the Rebbe explains, however, is that Jacob, unlike his predecessors Abraham and Isaac, achieved more than any person before him in uniting the spiritual with the physical worlds. The efforts of Abraham and Isaac primarily affected the higher, spiritual world of *Atzilut*, emanation, but Jacob, who established a permanent godly people on earth, largely synthesized the material and spiritual worlds. He therefore desired that the effects of this union be so complete that his spiritual acts and devotion to God yield the automatic by-product of physical success and prosperity.

Jacob's request for bliss and peace had nothing to do with a desire to be compensated for his devotion to God. Rather, it had everything to do with his desire to be close and attached to God. Jacob desired that he and his *mitzvot* achieve so high a state of union with God that they have an automatic effect on the physical world in general, and his personal life in particular. If in truth he had served his Creator faithfully, then the automatic outcome should have been a peaceful and prosperous life.

So, the meaning of receiving a reward is not that God *compensates* man for doing His bidding. Rather, every spiritual act has a physical corollary as well, which is what we see to be the reward. And when someone performs that spiritual act there is a natural physical effusion. Every spiritual deed when performed has a spontaneous empirical expression and tributary that is the natural manifestation in the physical world of the godly act.

Thus, the fact that there is a physical reward and punishment is not degrading to Judaism or belittling to man's motivations. Neither does it compromise man's integrity, sincerity, or religious devotion. On the contrary, the fact that there is a physical reward serves to demonstrate the truth of Torah and *mitzvot* even in the physical world. Because it shows that in keeping Torah and *mitzvot* there is a physical effect on the world, there is an automatic outgrowth, a manifestation in the physical world, in the form of a reward or punishment to either increase or diminish man's presence in the physical world. His possessions are either added to or subtracted from. This has a direct bearing on the truth of Torah in the physical world. It shows that the Torah is not merely "in the heavens," but is firmly ingrained on earth. It demonstrates not merely the relevance of Torah to earthly life and activity, but its oneness with human life and man's dilemmas. The word of God is not a foreign or alien presence on earth, but part and parcel of all created existence.

Had there been no reward and punishment, that is, no direct physical counterpart to a spiritual act, then this would be an indication that there is no fusion between the physical world and the spiritual world, that they are two distinct and separate entities. It would be as if the spiritual and physical worlds are completely independent of one another and one has no bearing on the other. But the fact that one is rewarded with a physical remuneration illustrates how very much intertwined the physical and spiritual worlds are. It is the illustration par excellence that indeed the physical world is godly and there can be no justifiable demarcation between the two as one being holy and spiritual and the other mundane. Rather, the only difference that can be said to exist between the lofty spiritual worlds and our lowly earth is that in the higher worlds God is present and visible, but in our world God is just as present but is concealed and hidden.

The question we posed above regarding charity betrays a superficial understanding of divinity. We asked why is it that as a result of a spiritual act, like giving charity, one receives a material reward. Does this not compromise altruism? Does this physical reward not contaminate or pollute the spiritual side of the mitzvah? This question can only be asked if we see the physical and spiritual as being antithetical, even contradictory realities. Nobody seems to question the notion that a *mitzvah* brings an increase in holiness and godliness. What people cannot seem to accept, however, is the notion that a *mitzvah* can bring in its wake an increase in material possessions, health, or wealth. And why is this so hard to accept? Because no matter how many times we hear it, people steadfastly refuse to accept that this world is in fact godly, a part of the Divine. It doesn't look the part, so we reject its underlying spiritual nature. And if we were to embrace this concept, we would have no problem not only accepting but also predicting that for every *mitzvah* we will be rewarded automatically with physical prosperity, and for every sin we will be punished with a decrease in our material existence.

This is why reward and punishment serves as a fundamental tenet of Judaism. The world was created for God to have a home in the lowest of worlds, the physical domain, which necessitates man bringing God into this world. Man must demonstrate through his actions that godliness is not foreign or contradictory to material existence. Thus man is instructed to use the physical world to serve God. But even this might have been dismissed as merely forcing God upon the world. Doing a *mitzvah* might have been interpreted as taking a physical object and, in spite of its coarse physical properties, forcing it to be used to worship God. But every action man commits either in accordance with God's will or the reverse demonstrates that godliness is not being forced onto the world. Rather, the world is godly. Man is not even making it godly. Rather, man is manifesting the latent godliness of the earth, and thus physical objects can be naturally employed in serving God.

The fact that Judaism teaches that one should not serve God with the intention of being rewarded, such as in *Ethics of Our Fathers*, "Do not be like servants who serve their master for the sake of receiving a reward," or in the words of Maimonides, "One should not say: 'I hereby am fulfilling the commandments of the Torah and studying its wisdom in order that I should receive all of the blessings which are enumerated with it,'" does not in any way contradict what we have said above. What the Rabbis of the *Mishnah* and Maimonides mean to say is that one should not be superficial or silly enough to believe that we serve God because we will benefit from it. One should not be so shallow as to abuse the concept of reward and punishment by believing that God must entice man into worshiping Him with promises of personal gain. If one does serve God with these motives, they will have missed the whole point of reward and punishment.

Reward and punishment, as above, demonstrates the unity between God and the world, as well as the unity between God and man. Yet, if someone serves God out of promises of personal reward, he is thereby demonstrating that what God wants and what man wants are totally different. God and man are not unified and the proof is that man will only embrace God's will if it serves his personal interests. It is a statement of "God has His will and I have mine. They are not the same. But, if doing what God wants will allow me to do what I want, then I'll do it." And it is this type of attitude that our Sages warn us not to embrace. Through the fulfillment of Torah and its commandments, man must come to know the absolute consonance between his will and God's will.

This also answers the question we asked as to why Jews should receive compensation for their religious worship if they are not considered to be hired employees. Throughout the

Torah the Jews are referred as "servants," not workers. Furthermore, the Jews are said to have no identity outside of being God's people and being created to serve His will. Why then should there be any remuneration for their activities?

The answer is that the receipt of the reward does not contradict, but rather demonstrates precisely the fact that the Jews are united with God and have no identity outside their identification with God. The fact that every spiritual act the Jews perform has a direct physical outcome is proof of the fact that God and the Jewish people are one. Therefore, their status as servants, as loyal and humble attendants to the will of their Master, is specifically confirmed by the fact that every time the Jew draws closer to God through the execution of a divine dictate, the physical side of the Jew is increased. He grows through his closer association with God, since he is an attached servant who is affected both spiritually as well as physically by his proximity to his Master.

8

THE AGONY OF INNER TENSION: SELF-NEGATION VERSUS AFFIRMATION

For the final two chapters of this first section, we will return to the conflict spoken of above, the constant tension between affirmation and negation of self. We discussed how within Judaism there is the constant need for the antithetical embrace of promotion and affirmation of self on the one hand, as in the case of exercising one's freedom of choice, harboring love for God, and studying Torah, and negation and absolution of self on the other hand, as in the need to accept the yoke of heaven, harbor a fear for the Almighty, and execute divine commandments irrespective of our understanding of them. These antithetical emotions also apply to reward and punishment, reward being promotion and participation of self, and punishment being negation of self.

In truth, however, upon careful examination one discovers that this conflict of self versus nonself, or the passive versus the active, is not confined to Judaism alone. It can be found in everyday personal trauma. We witness how all of life can be subdivided into a conflict where man must decide when to be passive and when to be aggressive, when to assert oneself and when to stand by the sidelines, when to be a participant and when to be an observer. Philosophers and lay people alike speak often of the agony and torment of life, the fact that life is fraught with tension and indecision. This conflict is found throughout all the major world disciplines, whether it be called yin and yang, whether it is called in the kabbalah *ilah v'alul*, or *ratzo veshuv*, or whether it is the Greek concept of contraries. The point is that this tension is universal, and Judaism maintains that this is because it reflects a real and universal dialectic, one which originates in the Godhead itself. God has both finite and infinite characteristics, both transcendent and immanent features. Thus Descartes' view of the transcendental God and Spinoza's arguments of the immanent God may both contain valid arguments.

Are these two strands irreconcilable? No, rather they are essential for human creativity and perhaps for life itself; life is a struggle amid the tensions between self and what is beyond the self, between the microcosm and macrocosm. Hence, we all speak of peace being found only in the grave after 120 years, for in life there is little peace and harmony. But what exactly is the nature of this conflict?

Life is difficult because man is in a constant state of flux. Man is as if pulled by two extremes, one pushing him to assert himself and the other prodding him into a state of passivity. We seek to maintain a balance, we cherish the middle ground. But maintaining this balance is not always easy. According to Maimonides (*Hilkhot De'ot*), finding the balance between the two polar opposites of apathy and extreme indulgence is the key to success in life and bliss. Of all the tension that we experience throughout life, this is the most prominent, the most all-inclusive, and the most difficult to reconcile.

This dynamic tension is found in virtually every area of human life. Take, for example, the doubts that are always found within human relationships. Basically, there are two people trying to come closer together but never knowing when it is proper for them to be more assertive in their relationship and when to be more passive. When, for example, a woman should allow herself to be swept off her feet, but also when to stand up for herself and prevent someone from taking advantage of her. In fact, the very conflict that is being waged in contemporary society between modern-day feminists and more traditional women is this question: Is the woman's role to be more aggressive and to compete in a man's world, or to be content with the more passive role that has always been assigned her as befits traditional expressions of femininity? But the same applies to the man who engages in a relationship. He must balance when to assume his traditional role of being the one who initiates and times the stages of romance with the desire not to crush and totally dominate the woman he loves, lest he create a totally one-sided relationship. In this context, the conflict can be described as one of dependence versus independence.

This carries over into one of the major conflicts of contemporary society: the war between the sexes. Whereas once the line that separated men and women seemed to be defined in terms of the man being the conqueror who leaves home every day in pursuit of his bounty and the woman remains complyingly at home, things have now changed. Women are no longer content with a passive role and are demanding, and earning, the same right to ambitiously and aggressively pursue wealth, power, career, and fame. Similarly, whereas it was once casually assumed that men are the ones who pursue a relationship and "conquer" a woman, today it is perfectly natural for the opposite to take place. The question is whether or not there is any virtue in passivity, and if there is, who will embody it. Perhaps it is time for the men to be more passive since women are growing more aggressive.

The same type of conflict applies in the child–parent relationship where the child must on the one hand be nurtured into maturity by his parents, which first involves a very lengthy, mostly passive phase. But, as time passes the child must emerge from the cocoon of parental supervision and become a man or woman in his or her own right. But the exact balance is most important. Being too independent too early can scar the child for life. On the other hand, being overly receptive to parental guidance and help can render the child an emotional invalid. Likewise, the parent too must learn not to be overly dominant, either by spoiling the child or being too strict and demanding. The parent must be responsive to a generation gap and the needs of the younger generation. On the other hand, if the parent acts overly passive the child will not receive the attention or guidance he needs and the result will be either an unloved or bewildered adult. Here the conflict can be described as being one of responsibility versus freedom: the need for a parent to actively assert him or herself and take responsibility for the child, and the need for the parent to be more passive and allow the child latitude for personal growth. The same applies when a parent is older and dependent on his children. The child must decide at what point he is a child and must care for his parent in need, and at what point he is an independent being who needs his or her freedom. For example, will caring for one's parent at home disrupt the privacy of one's immediate family and anger one's spouse?

The same conflict applies in the context of a more global interpersonal relationship, such as that between a leader and his people. On the one hand a leader must be aggressive and seize the initiative in pulling his people into greater achievement and better times. But simultaneous with this, he must remain passive and responsive to their needs, lest he become just another despised dictator and autocrat. Here the conflict can be described as autocracy versus responsiveness.

The same applies to a political leader who must know how to balance diplomacy and pleasantries with war and action. While usually diplomacy should be the first steps taken in a conflict between two powers, there is no question that sometimes this is a gross error, as in the appeasement of Hitler by Chamberlain. It is just as important for nations to know when to be hostile and aggressive as for them to know when to be docile and sympathetic.

The same type of conflict is also found in a soldier or warrior and the responsibility he feels toward his country. He finds himself battling personal urges for self-aggrandizement and promotion versus the genuine needs of his people and compatriots in battle. At what point should he remain passive and just follow orders, just like any good soldier, and at what point should he break loose of orders and distinguish himself through great displays of courage and valor? This conflict can be described as one of (personal) honor versus duty.

The same applies, on a somewhat less glorious plane, in the employer–employee relationship. Where does an employee draw the line between being strictly an employee whose first loyalty is to the company and to fulfill the desire of his employer, and being an aggressive and ambitious young graduate who demands promotion and greater rewards for his services? Many an employee has had to grapple with this difficult dilemma, not being quite sure what is the proper time for demanding a raise and similar advancements in career. Similarly, the employer must also learn to balance the legitimate demands that he can make of his employees with accommodating their personal aspirations for success and achievement, which may sometimes be outside the interests of the company.

Another key area where this conflict applies most succinctly is the one that usually precedes the conflict found in the business relationship, and that is in the teacher–pupil relationship. A disciple is someone who serves as a receptacle for someone else's knowledge, and thus is in an almost entirely passive role. As I used to be told in *yeshivah* (rabbinical training college), a good student is not someone who has a good mind, but someone who has a good bottom. It is someone who can sit and listen. All the brains in the world cannot compensate for lacking a desire to learn.

But there is another side to being a student. The student can only progress if he both feeds on an elder's wisdom and develops his own innate ability for comprehensive and analytical thought. The pupil must not only learn from his teacher, but emulate him as well. He must aspire to be his *own* teacher, and this entails learning to challenge and question the ideas of his master, in a word, to assert himself more. But a proper balance must be struck. Similarly, the teacher himself must not only be aggressive in his dissemination of knowledge to his pupil, but must also be responsive to the individual needs of each pupil, lest he become an insensitive and uncaring teaching machine. A balance must be struck. Here the conflict is personal development versus acquiescent absorption.

In *yeshivah* one of the biggest conflicts we faced was that of absorption and self-development versus dissemination and devotion to others. On the one hand, the whole purpose of being in *yeshivah* was to gain knowledge and devote all of our time to study. On the other hand, the Torah goes to great lengths to emphasize that one who studies only for himself, who does not share his learning with others, is selfish and worthless. So what should one do? Every moment of aggressive study brings self-development and an enhancement of knowledge. And every moment of denying one's needs and devoting time to others brings a sometimes well-needed redemption to the intense focus on self. Here the conflict can be described as being between the individual aspirations and peoplehood, between the rightful needs of the individual and the necessary obligations to the community.

This same conflict is found in the relationship one shares with oneself. Within our minds there is a constant battle being waged over when to be satisfied and content with what we have, and when to desire more and set about achieving it. This conflict, which dramatically reflects the passive versus aggressive tension, can be described as being one of contentment versus ambition. On the one hand a person should be thankful for what he has, and content. On the other hand, without energetic ambition, without setting one's sights very high, man would aspire to no great heights and mankind's achievements would be negligible. But blind ambition leads to megalomania and self-destruction. One must attain a proper balance. One must know when to buy and when to sell. One must know when it is proper to be envious of one's friend's success and when to be content with one's own achievements. One must be capable of balancing the happiness and satisfaction that comes with achievement with feelings of ambition for those things not yet achieved. Ultimately, this conflict is portrayed in the greatest opposites of all: life and death, life being man at his most active and aggressive, and death representing man at his most inactive and passive.

But perhaps more than in any other relationship, this dynamic conflict between assertion and denial of self is most acute in the God–man relationship. The conflict exists on all levels of religious endeavor. For instance, there is the constant conflict of tradition versus innovation and creativity. On the one hand, man must be responsive to God's calling as has been transmitted through the generations. On the other hand, religion itself must be sensitive and responsive to each individual age and adapt accordingly, without however compromising its essence. A very difficult task indeed.

I see this conflict constantly, particularly in matters of prayer. Inquisitive Oxford students ask me why we must recite the exact same prayer thrice daily. I have had people insist that they think it would be far more pleasurable to them, as well as desirable to God, if they were to grab a guitar and go out into the field and sing a song of thanks to God, rather than recite the traditional Hebrew incantations found in the prayer book.

Then there is the age-old dilemma in the God–man relationship over when to accept God's commandments and when to question and challenge. If one feels that a specific commandment is irrational, uninspirational, or even unspiritual, is he permitted to object or question? Can one voice a moral objection? Or, if one feels that he would achieve closer communion with God, or get "turned on" to Judaism through methods not prescribed by Judaism, is it permitted? At what point is man permitted to legitimately break free of the tight reins of religious devotion and assert himself? To be sure, God has made it clear that He does not enjoy being served by obedient robots. But neither does He wish for man to cast off the yoke of Heaven and invent his own religious tenets.

This same conflict carries over into the most unresolved and painful of all religious disputes: the question of suffering. If one is witness to a gross miscarriage of justice, such as the slaughter of one million innocent children in the Holocaust, does he have the right to question? Is he still a devout Jew if he does? Or must one accept God's actions blindly and unquestioningly in order to be righteous? At what point does man remain silent and accept what he is witnessing as the will of God, and at what point does he cry out that this tragedy seems to contravene the very rules and laws that God has Himself laid out in the Torah, and the promises God has made to the Jewish people of His love for them and His being a compassionate and forgiving Creator? If we always remain silent, while we may be preserving our faith, we run the risk of becoming insensitive to human suffering on the whole. One must maintain a balance.

And finally, as discussed in detail above, there are the conflicts within Judaism itself that, on the one hand, argue emphatically that man possesses freedom of choice and that religious worship is meaningless if man does not exercise that freedom, but on the other hand demand that man subject himself to divine rule. Judaism wishes for man to *choose* to abandon his freedom

of choice, to choose to be a servant of God. How can the two
be reconciled?

Then there is Torah and *mitzvot*. Torah, as discussed above,
in that it embraces man's higher cognitive faculties, is a repre-
sentation of man's active involvement in the God–man relationship. But *mitzvot*, in that many are suprarational and even those
that are rational are supposed to be fulfilled simply because they
are the will of the Divine, are an expression of man's passivity
and acquiescence in his relationship with the Almighty. We also
mentioned how both Torah and *mitzvot* incorporate elements
of the other. But how is the devout Jew expected to reconcile
these antithetical constructs of Judaism and the demands it in
turn makes on the believer?

In Jewish mysticism there is an important concept known as
"ratzo-veshuv," the desire of the soul to depart the body and
its duty to remain within the body. This is the conflict of the
soul as it is pulled between two realities: its acquired earthly
domain, and its lost heavenly reality where it basked in the glory
of the Divine Presence. On the one hand, the soul has a constant striving to leave the body and return to its source. It shuns
the material world and is pulled, as if by a magnet, to the glory
it has lost. On the other hand, the soul understands that the
purpose for creation, and the purpose for its descent, is to give
life to the body and work to transform this world from a profane haven into a domicile for the King of kings. Thus, every
time it lunges forth toward heaven thinking to abandon the
body, it must remind itself of its mission and return to earth. It
is for this reason that the soul is likened to a flame that flickers
constantly. It is in a constant state of excitation and expansion
followed by contraction

On a slightly less mystical plane, each of us experiences the
same conflict in the form of being torn between materialism and
spirituality. There are times when all we care for is a new car,
a new house, or beautiful clothing. Then suddenly, these same
desires seem vain and unsatisfying and we find ourselves yearning for higher things.

As a rabbi I have often found congregants appearing spontaneously in synagogue. They are not regulars and have no special reason to attend. When asked what they are doing there,

they often respond, "I just felt like it." I have had the same experience with students in Oxford who ask to study something Jewish with me, or be given some reading material, simply because they "feel like doing something Jewish." They have been moved to engage themselves more fully in the exploration of their tradition, but without any tangible or identifiable cause.

Needless to say, these moments of inspiration are largely ephemeral. They rarely last or lead to anything more meaningful, and yet they reflect a tension that lies at the very core of our being. Are we spiritual beings with a body, or material beings with a soul? What came first—the soul or the body?

Notwithstanding how insignificant some of the above conflicts may seem, they still deny us a sense of confidence and peace. We seem hybrids embodying antithetical gravitational pulls, one away from ourselves, and the other toward ourselves. A resolution of the conflict, if one is at all attainable, is drastically needed. A deeper understanding of this conflict, as shall be explored in the next chapter, will help afford a solution.

9

THE DUAL NATURE
OF GOD: MASCULINE
AND FEMININE WITHIN
THE GODHEAD

P art of the understanding of the nature of this conflict and its resolution is to recognize that it is all-encompassing. This dualism in man in the form of the passive and the aggressive is reflected in every aspect of creation. All of creation subdivides into donor and developer or donor and recipient. Take for example, the very first things that God creates at the beginning of the world: heaven and earth. Thus, at the very onset of creation, well before the advent of Adam and Eve or their animal counterparts, the Creator had already introduced into His creation the components of male and female, or what might also be called donor and developer. The heavens would shower water and bounty onto the land, which the land would in turn transform into lush greenery bursting with life. The heavens would provide the necessary life-giving substance in potential form, which would later come to materialize via the reception and subsequent development on the part of the earth. Later, this conglomerate trend of a two-part world continued with the creation of male and female life beginning first with animals and eventually culminating in the creation of man and his counterpart, woman.

But even inanimate objects reflect this dualism. The inanimate world can be said to be composed of, in the language of the Kabbalah, "vessel and light," or, in more contemporary language, a receptacle and something put into that receptacle. For example, liquid must be contained within a bottle, wheat only grows in a husk, radio waves must be received by a dish, and information must be stored in a book or in the mind. In short, everything in the world consists of one thing that fits into another. Stated in other words, the two main divisions in the empirical world are benefactor and recipient: one object that encompasses another.

For the benefit of a visual aid, the world can be said to consist of circles and lines. The circles represent the containers, that is, that part of the world that receives and develops. The lines represent that part of the world that gives and is encompassed by the circles. The lines serve as the potential for something that is later developed by the circles.

This is described in the Kabbalah, Jewish mysticism, as the tension between male and female; women represent the passive, infinite dimension of God and can therefore give birth to children, and men represent the masculine, more finite element of God. These differences are said to be evidenced even in the anatomical makeup of men and women whereby males represent a line that has a beginning and an end, thus being finite—*kav* in the kabbalistic vernacular; and women represent a circle (or receptacle), which possesses no beginning or end—*igul* in Kabbalah, the infinite. This conflict or discrepancy is what leads to their attraction and union.

The mystery of the need to fragment the inhabitants of creation into male and female, line and circle, donor and developer, has eternally perplexed philosophers and theologians of all denominations and creeds. How could the monotheist who believes and devoutly proclaims the oneness and indivisible unity of God reconcile that belief with God's pluralistic creation? The ways of God are meant to emulate His being and if He is One, then the world at large, and especially man, who was created "in His image," should be uniquely singular as well. If the intention was to facilitate procreation, then surely in His infinite wisdom the Creator could have caused the world's inhabitants to reproduce via asexual means, self-procreation and the like. Why then is the world so divided? Furthermore, why is it that even within clearly definable elements of the empirical world as to which is the donor and which the developer, such as male and female, do each incorporate elements of the other so that each is really a hybrid?

For instance, while men are surely recognizable biologically as the donors, there is no question that they incorporate elements of passivity, as discussed in the previous chapter. Men also perform the function of developers on occasion as well. And while women are anatomically developers, they are also donors in that they raise, support, and nourish their children and in the process give them a great deal. In short, although things seem to be clearly and neatly definable into one of the aforementioned categories, they also incorporate antithetical elements as well.

Man erroneously tends to view the world as a separate and independent entity divorced from God's all-encompassing unity. God is not readily seen in this world and the mistake of dissociating Him from His creation is easily made. Notwithstanding this inconsistency in man's perception, the purpose of the Creation was to demonstrate, not to compromise, the unity of the Creator. To this extent, our mundane and physical world, whose very existence seems to negate that unity, was chosen as the showcase, the very arena, for this display of unity. A manifestation of the eclectic nature and dualism that exists within the Godhead and affords a deep and penetrating understanding of the Creator.

We all understand that God is infinite. We accept that this must be so, not only because a God who is not all-powerful is most unimpressive, but also because this is the very definition of a God: an omnipotent, omniscient, all-powerful Being infinitely higher than man or any other life form. Theologians and laymen alike will go to great lengths to protect the notion of God's infinity. It is a doctrine that few are willing to compromise. We even look scornfully at the gods of Greek mythology who are flawed with human traits of lust, anger, vengeance, greed, and are often easily manipulated and outsmarted by other gods.

While all of these attitudes may indeed be accurate, the problem with them is that they are incomplete. Part of God's infinity is His unequaled ability to contract Himself, in other words, to make Himself more finite. God has the ability to be not only very, very big and mighty, but also very small and meek. And this should come as no surprise to the reader because, on the contrary, if He lacked this ability He would not be infinite. Being all-powerful means being able to be as large as one wants and as small as one wants as well.

To illustrate this concept, imagine a great physics professor who is charged with teaching a group of nursery children quantum mechanics. The fact that on a daily basis he teaches great intellects the theories of physics in his laboratory at the university is impressive. It indicates that he has a most impressive mind that can tackle all questions thrown at him. He is bright enough never to be stumped even by the most intelligent of students. Yet if he can only teach university students and not little children, then his intellect and his grasp of the subject is very limited. If he cannot invent a simple teaching method, perhaps a story or table by which to convey the essentials of the theory, if he cannot divest the theory of all its mathematics and equations, then he doesn't understand the theory fully. However, if he can contrive lively anecdotes, stories, and allegory to describe the theory to the extent that even small children with extremely limited intelligence can grasp the theory, then the professor is truly a genius. The ability to limit and condense, and constrain oneself is drawn from the highest levels, not the lowest. The same principle holds true in today's consumer electronics boom. It is specifically those companies with the most impressive engineers and most advanced technology that are able to miniaturize mobile telephones and Walkmans that also sell the most.

Or take for example the incredible leaps being made in modern computing. What is amazing about a microprocessor, for example, is not only the millions of calculations that it can perform per second, but the size of the chip. To fit so much in so little borders on the infinite.

God is so powerful, so unrestricted, that He can even limit Himself and become finite (although even then the constraint is more of condensation, and He remains latently infinite all the same). For instance, in the Torah there are many command-ments that are known as *hukim* (suprarational laws). The rea-son for their observance is not known to man. And most peo-ple are willing to accept this because, after all, how could a mortal man fully apprehend the infinite Creator? It is therefore surprising that people do not realize that just as the *hukim* reflect God's infinite nature, which is inaccessible to man, the many *mishpatim* (rational commandments), which are acces-sible to man, reflect God's contracted, or ability to be finite, nature. God is endowed with the ability to make His intrinsic will so small that it can even fit into and be absorbed by man's limited intelligence.

God has a dual nature. God is both infinite and finite, and what is truly remarkable about this duality is that both occur simul-taneously. When God limits Himself to the point where He can communicate with man, for example, although it appears that He is now very small and finite, in truth He is able to con-tract Himself to such a degree only because He is unlimited. Nothing can prevent Him from becoming or doing anything He desires.

Taking the analogy of the professor a step further, it will be recognized that even while the professor is telling fables and tales in order to teach quantum theory to the children, he re-mains even then a profound intellectual. It would be inaccu-rate to say that now that he is telling nursery rhymes and sounds like a two-year-old that he has actually become a two-year-old. On the contrary, because he is a great genius he is able to con-descend to the children even at their level and relate to them at their intellectual plane. And not just relate to them but even convey to them the deepest discoveries of physics. So, the per-son dealing with the children is not a professor who has become a two-year-old, neither is he merely a professor who is acting like a two-year-old. Rather, he is a professor who, *due to the fact that he is a professor*, is able to act like a two-year-old, and even his ability to conceal his great intelligence while behav-ing this way does not compromise his intellectual stamina and aptitude, but rather reinforces it. On the contrary, it is because of the fact that he understands the subject so well that he is able to behave the way he does.

The same is true of God. Because He is infinite He is able, for example, to contract Himself and create a finite world. For in truth, He is not so much contracting Himself as condensing and concealing. And even the ability for this concealment arises from God's infinite nature.

Understanding this concept is elementary in the overall approach to understanding Kabbalah and Jewish mystical teachings. It is the secret of truly apprehending the nature of "*tzimtzum*," one of the most fundamental and recurrent themes found in kabbalistic and hasidic literature. It is only by applying the concept of *tzimtzum* that one is able to understand how the Creation of the world comes about.

Drawing upon the explanation of *tzimtzum* given by Rabbi Immanuel Schochet in his work *Mystical Concepts in Chasidism* (Kehot Publications, 1971), we will delve further into a deeper explanation of the concept of *tzimtzum* that will facilitate a truer understanding of the dual nature of the Godhead.

One of the basic theological problems is concerned with the seeming enigma of reconciling God with the universe: How can there be a transition from the infinite to the finite, from pure intelligence to matter, from absolute unity or oneness to multifariousness? Moreover, how do we reconcile the divine creation or bringing about of the universe and its multifarious parts with the eternal and inviolable absolute perfection of God, of whom Scripture affirms "I the Eternal, I have not changed" (Malachi 3:6)?

Creation is often explained in terms of a theory of emanationism: by means of a progressive chain of successive emanations from higher to lower the finite evolved from the infinite and matter evolved from spirit. But this suggestion as it stands is insufficient. To speak of a causal evolutionary process of successive emanations merely begs the question but does not answer it. For regardless of how long this chain of causal evolutions may be, there always remains some relationship, qualitative as well as quantitative, between the effect and its cause. Just as in a material chain the links are interlocked, connected, and interrelated—retaining a basic relationship between the first link and the last one—so, too, would it be in a gradual process of causal evolution. Thus, since the beginning of the chain of emanations is God, the Infinite, the aspect of infinite is never really cast off. Had the worlds descended from the light of the infinite according to a gradual descent from grade to grade by means of cause and effect, this world would not in such a case have ever been created in its present form—in a finite and limited order.

In a gradual evolution and causal process, "The effect is encompassed by the cause, in relation to which it is essentially non-existent. . . . Thus, even numerous contractions will not avail to there being matter as dense as earth by way of an evolution from the spirituality of the abstract intelligences, nor even (that most subtle and diaphanous type of matter) of the angels" (*Igeret Hakodesh*, sec. 20). As Rabbi Shneur Zalman writes in his work, *Likkutei Torah*: "The creation of the worlds is not by way of a development from cause to effect . . . for even myriads upon myriads of occultations and evolutions from grade to grade in a causal process will not avail the development and coming into being of physical matter—not even the matter of the firmaments but of an evolution from spirit. Rather, it is the power of the blessed *En Sof* (Infinite), the Omnipotent, to create . . . ex nihilo, and this is not by way of a developmental order but by way of a 'leap.' "

Hence, that something nondivine and finite should come about necessitates there being in the process of emanation a "radical step," a "leap," or a "jump" *(dilug, kefitzah)* that breaks the gradualism and establishes a radical distinction between cause and effect; a radical act of creation. Only after that has occurred can we speak of an evolutionary process culminating in finite and material entities. And this principle is at the root of the doctrines of *tzimtzum* and the *Sefirot* introduced by the Kabbalah (and elaborated upon in Hasidism) to solve the problem of creation.

The word *tzimtzum* has two meanings: (1) contraction, condensation; and (2) concealment, occultation. Though both these meanings apply in our context, the second one does so more than the first. For the doctrine of *tzimtzum* refers to a refraction and concealment of the radiating emanation from the Godhead, in a number of stages and in a progressive development of degrees, until finite and physical substances become possible. This intricate theory is first treated in detail by Rabbi Isaac

Luria. The basic works of his system all begin with an exposition of *tzimtzum*. Rabbi Shneur Zalman partly deals with it in *Tanya*, more extensively in *Shaar Hayihud Veha'emunah*, and above all in *Torah Or* and *Likkutei Torah*.

Prior to creation there is but God alone. God as He is in Himself is called *En Sof* (the infinite), He that is without limit (end). Of God as *En Sof* nothing can be postulated except that He is *En Sof*: "High above all heights and hidden beyond all concealments, no thought can grasp You at all . . . You have no known Name for You fill all Names and You are the perfection of them all" (*Tikkunei Zohar*, Introduction: 17a–b).

In a mystical way, rather difficult to explain, there is a manifestation or self-revelation of God *Or En Sof* even before the act of creation. This manifestation is called *Or En Sof* (the Light of the *En Sof*), and we speak of this Light as equally omnipresent and infinite. This distinction between *En Sof* and *Or En Sof* is extremely important and must be kept in mind. For when speaking of *tzimtzum* and the *Sefirot* we relate these to the *Or En Sof*, the Light and radiation, rather than to the Luminary and Radiator (*Ma'or*), the *En Sof*.

When it arose in the divine will to bring about the world and the creatures, the first act in the creative process was to bring about space in which the divine emanations and, ultimately, the evolving, finite world could have a place to exist. This primordial space was brought about by a contraction or withdrawal and concentration of divinity into itself: the omnipresent, infinite Light of the *En Sof* was withdrawn into Himself; that is, it was screened, dimmed, hidden, and concealed, and where it was dimmed, where this occultation and concealment of the Light occurred, an "empty" place, a "void" (*makom panui; hallal*) evolved into primordial space. This is the act of the first *tzimtzum*, the radical act of *dilug* and *kefitzah*, as it were; an act of divine self-limitation, so to speak, as opposed to revelation. However, this does not mean that the *hallal* is literally empty and void of all divine radiation, that the divine presence is literally and totally withdrawn therefrom. Such interpretation would suggest an illegitimate ascription of spatiality, and hence corporeality, to the Infinite, and would violate the principle of omnipresence affirmed in the most literal sense by Scripture and tradition.

The *hallal* is metaphorically spoken of as a void, in relation to that which is "beyond" or "outside" the *hallal*: outside the *hallal* there is a full manifestation of the *Or En Sof*, while inside the *hallal* the Light is concealed. The *En Sof*, the Luminary (*Ma'or*) whence the Light issues, is totally unaffected by *tzimtzum*. *Tzimtzum* relates only to the Light of the *En Sof*. Moreover, even in the Light per se there is no real change whatever; it is neither reduced nor removed but merely concealed. Even this concealment and occultation is strictly relative, relative to the void and its subsequent contents, without—strictly speaking—affecting the Light itself in any way. Moreover, in relation to the void there is not an absolute and total withdrawal; some residue or vestige (*reshimu*) of the Light remains in the *hallal*.

Despite all these qualifications and the metaphorical interpretation of the withdrawal of the Light, this first act of *tzimtzum* is a radical "leap" *(dilug)* that creates the possibility for a gradual process and evolution of emanations to take place and to culminate in the creation of finite and corporeal entities. The principal purpose of *tzimtzum* is to create a *hallal* in which the divine creatures would be able to exist and subsist as opposed to becoming dissolved in the divine omneity. The infinite radiation of the divine Light having been dimmed and concealed, as it were, will now no longer consume and nullify the contents of the *hallal* in the way, for example, that a spark is totally consumed and nullified in the flame itself, or the way the light of a candle would be totally absorbed and nullified in the very intense light of the sun.

In the second phase of the creative process an overt ray or radiation of the divine Light is made to beam into the primeval space of the *hallal*. This thin ray or "line" *(kav)* irradiates the *hallal* and is the source of the subsequent emanations; it is both the creative and the vivifying force of the creation; it is the immanence of God in creation while the concealed Light is the all-encompassing transcendence of God taking in all creation. However, the *kav* itself also undergoes a series of numerous, successive contractions and concealments. Each of these contractions and concealments makes it possible for a successively lower stage of creation to take place, ultimately culminating in the lowest stage of creation represented by this finite, material, and pluralistic world. It is via this *kav* that the process of successive emanations and causal development takes place. Unlike the first *tzimtzum*—which was by way of *dilug* (leap)—this development and evolution can be spoken of as gradual and causal.

To summarize, *tzimtzum* is

> something in the nature of an occultation and concealment of the flow of the light and life-force so that only an extremely minute portion of the light and life-force should irradiate and flow forth to the lower beings in a manifest way, as it were, to be vested in them and influence and animate them so that they may receive existence *ex nihilo* and be in state of finitude and limitation (*Tanya*, chap. 48). . . . "There is, thus, no change whatever in His blessed Self but only for the created entities which receive their life-force . . . through a process of gradual descent from cause to effect and a downward gradation by means of numerous and various contractions (*tzimtzum*) so that the created entities can receive their life and existence from it without losing their entity. *These* tzimtzum *are all in the nature of "veiling of the Countenance"*(Hester Panim), *to obscure and conceal the light and life-force . . . so that it shall not manifest itself in a greater radiance than the lower worlds are capable of receiving.* Hence it seems to them as if the light and life-force of the Omnipresent, blessed is He . . . were something apart from His blessed Self. . . . Yet in regard to the Holy One, blessed is He, there is *tzimtzum*, concealment and occultation that would conceal and hide before Him and "the darkness is even as the light"(Psalm 139:12), as it is written, "Even the darkness does not obscure from You . . ." (Psalm 139:12). For the *tzimtzum* and "garments" are not things distinct from His blessed Self, Heaven forfend, but "like the snail whose garment is part of its very self" (*Genesis Rabbah* 21:5). [*Tanya*, chap. 21]

What this all means in practical terms, as explained above, is that in the Godhead there exists both an infinite and finite dimension. The finite nature is referred to as God's masculine side, as it were, or in kabbalistic terms as "*zah*," and the infinite side is referred to as God's feminine side, or in the language of the Kabbalah as *"malkhut."* It is only when these two aspects of the Godhead unite, masculine with feminine, *zah* together with *malkhut*, that the creation of the world takes place. This union, known in Kabbalah as *"Yihud zun,"* signifies the contraction, or *tzimtzum*, of God's infinite side into a more finite dimension, enabling the Creation of the worlds. Thus, the infinite and the finite come together, as it were, which, as explained above, indicates that they never really are different. Rather, the ability to contract and limit Himself arises from His being infinite and all-powerful.

But what is of great significance in this discussion is the knowledge that within the Godhead are contained both masculine (finite) and feminine (infinite) dimensions. And the reason for the finite being referred to as the masculine and the infinite as the feminine can be readily appreciated.

The miracle of life expresses how the masculine has the power to initiate a process, but the feminine, once that process has begun, possesses the ability to produce something from nothing, or at the very least, the closest possible equivalent to Creation *ex nihilo* that can exist in the empirical world. In childbirth, one begins with a microscopic egg that, when fertilized by the male seed, develops into a full-grown child complete with "248 limbs and 365 sinews." The same applies with a tree that grows from a tiny seed. After a seed (the masculine) is planted in the ground (the feminine) and a process of birth is initiated, the earth produces a massive hulking tree complete with roots, fruit, and bark, all from a tiny seed—something from (almost) nothing. This incredible feat can only be brought about through an infinite source and it is for this reason that the feminine resembles God's infinite ability. On the other hand, the masculine symbolizes God's ability to restrain and contract Himself, which initiates a process of birth. Without this initial contraction, there can be no worlds, for everything would be dissolved in God's infinite presence. Thus, this contraction, the masculine side of the Divinity, initiates a process of Creation and birth, just as the masculine does in the physical world as well.

Long before anyone could accuse the Rabbis of making the following statement just in order to appease disgruntled feminists, our Sages taught that women have their source in the infinite side of God, while men emanate from the finite side of God.

Everything in this world is a reflection of the higher worlds and everything that exists in our world does so because it has a spiritual counterpart. It was God who created our world and because the world is an extension of the Creator, it reflects his nature. Thus, just as God possesses both finite and infinite, donor and developer, masculine and feminine traits, as it were, our world too subdivides into these categories. The masculine aspects of our world reflect God's ability for finite contraction and the feminine reflects God's ability for infinite expansion.

Although the two are antithetical, in truth they derive from the same source, as explained above. The purpose in creating this world was for the world to serve as a showcase for divine unity. The purpose is for man to demonstrate that in reality both the infinite God, and the finite world which He created, are one. We must demonstrate through our actions that God and His world were never separated, that the masculine and feminine are united to form a single whole.

In unity there exists many differing degrees. Two independent entities may unite, yet all the while remain autonomous, and even harbor animosity to one another. The peace treaty between Israel and Egypt, or Israel and the PLO, stands as a classic testimonial to this phenomenon. But true unity can only exist when two individual items become synthesized and orchestrated together as one through a process of mutual fusion, to the extent that each item becomes the half of a single whole. Amid this scenario does the Creator desire for male and female to come together and unite as one. For "one" to in turn give rise to and equal "one" is hardly a special feat. But for two separate beings to unite and, notwithstanding their own individuality, equal "one" is an astounding achievement. For male and female to unite and give birth to a child is a demonstration par excellence of how two separate entities, while being fragmented and dissociated, may nonetheless combine to equal "one." It is also a manifestation of the fact that in truth they were never really divided. Although it appeared that they were two distinct entities, the fact that they can have a child together shows that in truth they were always a single essence separated, however, into two bodies.

The applicability of this analogy to the Creator and His world is self-apparent. In this respect, it may be appreciated that the association between husband and wife is unique and substantially greater and more intense than all other forms of unity found in the empirical world. But this is the kind of unity God wishes to achieve with His world. No wonder then that the love of God for the nation of Israel is so often described in the Bible as that of a husband for his wife. The Almighty wishes to be so revealed and apparent in this world that all will see that God and the world have always been one; it is only that until now God has been masked by the facade of nature. But with this mask removed, the purpose of creation will have been achieved. The longed-for unity between the infinite and finite qualities of God will have been reached. The infinite, One, unified Creator will be openly revealed in the finite, pluralistic, multifarious world that He created and that is being sustained by His infinite power. As we recite thrice daily at the conclusion of every prayer service, "And God will be King over the entire earth and on that day the Lord Will be One and His Name One" (Zechariah 14:9).

The above sounds like an impossibility and a contradiction in terms. How could the finite and infinite coexist? How will there once again be complete unity within the Godhead? But this is not a contradiction nor is it impossible. In fact, it has a precedent in the physical world. Up to the time when the Holy Temple in Jerusalem was destroyed, the holiest place on earth was the "*Kodesh Hakadashim*" ("the Holy of Holies"), the innermost sanctum in the Temple. It was there that the holy ark, which contained fragments of the original tablets given to Moses by God Himself, was kept.

The Talmud relates a fascinating episode concerning the ark. The Holy of Holies was a perfect square in area, twenty cubits by twenty cubits. The ark, which rested in the center of the room, was ten cubits long, together with its protruding staffs used for carrying it. Thus, when one would measure from the tip of the staff to the edge of the room, one would expect to find five cubits on either side. But instead, what one discovered upon measuring was no less than ten cubits on either side, which meant that although the ark was indeed sitting in the room and occupying space, it nevertheless could not be measured as occupying any space. As the Talmud states, "It could be measured, but it would not occupy any space" (*Mishnah Middos*). Thus, one had an instance of the finite and the infinite merging as one in a revealed plane. This was achieved within the Holy of Holies because this was the site chosen for the manifestation of the glory of God on earth. This was also the reason for its extreme holiness and why the High Priest could enter the room only once a year. It was by far the most sublime manifestation of godliness on earth, far greater than any miracle or other supernatural intercession in the affairs of nature.

Nevertheless, even this kind of manifestation is insufficient. God requires total revelation in which it will be seen not only how the finite and infinite are fused as one, but how behind this fusion lies the Creator. In the words of King David in Psalms, "My heart and my very flesh will sing to and praise the Lord" (Psalm 84:3). God desires that man find Him from the mundanity of everyday existence. This is where God lies. No wonder then that the numerical equivalent of the word *tevah* (nature) is *Elokim* (God). It is not to convey that God is nature, and nature is God, as in the Spinozan, pantheistic sense, but rather that nature is a *part* of God, but not the totality of the Creator. This unity will be achieved ultimately only in the messianic era. In that time, godliness will be revealed and will pervade all the earth. The *tzimtzum*, or concealments, that today mask God's presence in the creation will be removed "and the earth shall be filled with the knowledge of the Lord as the waters cover the ocean floor" (Isaiah 11:2).

Now, although that time has not arrived, it is incumbent upon man to strive to bring about this epoch. And it is for this reason that, as discussed at length above, man seems torn asunder by innate forces of passivity and aggression operating within him. Just as the Almighty Himself wishes the forces of finite and infinite to be reconciled in a messianic epoch, so too man feels this tension, since he is created by God and reflects and emulates the Creator's being. Man knows no rest, he knows no peace. He feels within him a deep sense of discomfort because of his antithetical impulses. He longs for orchestration and cohesion. He longs for *Moshiah*.

Man is created in God's image and just as God possesses these dimensions, man possesses them too. Just as this takes place on a macrocosmic level with God, so too it takes place on a microcosmic level in the world of man and on different planes. But where in God they are unified, in man they seem to oppose each other and man spends all of his life seeking harmony. This is similar to how men and women spend their lives seeking out each other, looking for their lost halves as well. We all seek satisfaction and completion. And on a more personal level, man looks to reconcile the antithetical impulses lurking within him. This gives him no rest, and indeed is designed as such. For just as God will only be truly unified in the messianic epoch, so too only then will man know peace and harmony. *Thus man must aspire and work toward a messianic destiny. This is man's goal and crowning achievement.* Only in the messianic era will there be unity between choice and submission, love and fear, Torah and *mitzvot*, assertiveness and passivity, male and female, donor and developer, reward and punishment, promotion and denial of self, God and his world, and finally between man and himself.

It is also for this reason that Maimonides immediately follows up the Principle #11 of the essentials of Jewish faith, the one dealing with reward and punishment, with Principle #12, the obligation to await the coming of the Messiah. One is dependent on the other. Once man comes to realize the dynamic tension and forces operating within all levels of existence—within the Godhead, the Universe, Creation, Judaism, the sexes, and within himself—he looks for reconciliation and achieving the purpose for his creation. He looks for a resolution and synthesis. He seeks a messianic redemption and epoch. He seeks a reconciliation of the cosmic forces that have been operating from time immemorial and that have sustained the world and driven man to higher and higher levels of achievement and served as his source of creativity until he is able to reach the ultimate achievement—making God One once again, as He was (and still is but in a concealed manner) prior to the creation of the world.

It is also for this reason that one of the principal prophecies associated with the messianic era is that of a world of peace and harmony. This was not merely a promise that there would be no more war, but rather a promise that there would be no more inner tension and confusion in man himself and that everyone would find comfort and confidence from within. Man would finally be rid of all his insecurities because he would then be truly one. He would no longer be plagued by indecision and confusion, but rather muster all his forces to pursue a single uncompromising path of goodness. The messianic era is also a promise of a time when God will be at harmony with His world because there will no longer be any tension between the One, indivisible God, and His finite world, whose inhabitants are now so seemingly independent of Him that they could even act in contradiction to His will. For in that time it will be manifest to all "that the earth is the Lord's" and all of the world's inhabitants will act in accordance with the divine will from whence they derive.

II

THE PROBLEM OF SUFFERING: RECONCILING THE BENEVOLENT GOD WITH THE EXISTENCE OF EVIL

Overview to Part II

To Challenge
the Divine

The collective suffering of the Jewish people as a nation began in Egypt. There they were herded together like so many oxen and horses whose only reason for existence is to do someone else's work. Israelite babies were cast alive into the Nile river, and suckling children were used in place of bricks if these were not produced quickly enough by the Jewish slaves for the architectural edifices that they were forced to build for Egypt.

God saw this unjust suffering and decided to rescue them from the cauldron that was Egypt. He handpicked Moses as the agent through whom the deliverance would come about. What was this man's reaction to witnessing the suffering of his people? How did the great lawgiver respond when he saw the awful misery of the Jews? Was he patient, in the knowledge that whatever their sufferings at present, they were soon to be freed? No. After having been appointed redeemer by the Almighty Himself, Moses offered a complaint. This is recorded near the beginning of the Book of Exodus, and is significant because it is the very first mention in the Bible of a challenge to divine justice. Moses is sent by the Almighty to demand the Jewish people's release from Pharaoh, with the result that not only does Pharaoh refuse to free them but in addition he orders that the Jewish slaves should not be given straw to build bricks, but should be required to fill the same quota per day. This invites a sharp response from the Egyptian prince turned Jewish prophet. "And Moses returned unto the Lord and he said, 'Lord, why have You dealt ill with this people? Why is it that You have sent me? For since I came to Pharaoh to speak in Your name, he has dealt ill with this people; neither have You delivered at all Your people.'"

Whereas the word *Islam* means "submission to God," and Christianity advocates faith above all else, the word *Yisrael* means "he who wrestles with God." In Jewish thought there is recognition of the existence, sometimes even the need, for dual purposes that sometimes appear to contradict each other. For example, a child who misbehaves is warned by his parents to behave himself. Yet even while offering a reprimand, the parents fully understand that it is natural, even desirable, for a child to act in this way. In fact, if the child sat lifeless and still throughout the day just gazing into the air, his parents would take him to a child psychiatrist! In a sense, therefore, the role of the child is to misbehave, and the job of the parents is to correct and maintain discipline. Each party carries out his role legitimately, although they conflict.

The same paradox is evident in the relationship between God and humans. That relationship too involves contradictory responses, both of which are appropriate and justified. God's task is to steer the world in the way that He sees fit, for whatever reason. As human beings, it is not our role to concern ourselves with God's affairs and to offer rationalizations for other people's sufferings by saying, for example, that they carry an internal, albeit latent, good. Why God brings suffering upon mankind, and especially upon the righteous, is something that we currently cannot comprehend. And the truth is, it is none of our business. The moral imperative beholden upon us when witnessing the suffering of another individual is simply to cause it to cease, not to attempt to understand it ourselves or to explain it to others. And if it is something over which we can have no control, such as an incurable illness or a powerful aggressor such as the Nazis, against whose force our defiance will do little, then it is our obligation to lift our heads heavenward and launch vociferous protest against this miscarriage of justice, even though it may appear to be divinely sanctioned. We must pray, plead with, and pressure the Almighty to intervene and to end this senseless and undeserving suffering being visited upon our brothers and sisters of the human race.

The real challenge that should be posed to God upon witnessing a child with leukemia, or a collective holocaust, is not, "Please God, explain to us why this happens and how it fits into Your overall plan for creation?" but rather, "Master of the Universe, how could You allow this to happen? Was is not You who taught us in Your Torah that life is sacred and must be preserved at all costs? So where is that life now? Was is not You who also promised that the good deserve prosperity, and not pain? Where is that promise now? By everything that is sacred to You, I demand that this cease, and that the person recover, immediately!"

This response should not be misconstrued as a heretical rebuke to the deity, nor as a rejection of divine providence, because we are not contending that God does not know what He is enacting, nor maintaining that nothing positive can result from suffering. Rather, our statement is this: "Master of the Universe, is this really the only method by which You can achieve Your aims? Surely You, who are of infinite power and intelligence, could devise some alternate means by which Your will can be carried out for the benefit of mankind without the accompaniment of so much pain? We believe that somehow this pain must be to our benefit, and that You are a good and just Creator. But You are also all-powerful; would it not therefore be possible for You to bring about this desired end in a less painful pill?" We desire not only spiritual good, but physical good; not only hidden goodness, but revealed goodness, in the plain sense of the word.

Take, for example, someone who visits a dentist. He complains about the needle the dentist uses to numb the tooth, yet it is he who has paid for the treatment in the first place! What the patient is really saying is this: "I accept that your poking my gums with the needle is for my own good. But after all these years, has medical science, with all its impressive progress, not developed a means to numb a tooth without pain?" And the same thought applies here: whatever good we as individuals, or the world in general, might receive from suffering, could it not be brought about in a painless, joyful manner?

To the many who argue that all human suffering is a punishment for sin, and in particular, view the Holocaust as a divine visitation in response to the wholesale assimilation of German Jewry, I ask, what magnitude of arrogance must you possess to condemn six million victims, none of whom you ever knew or even met, and to affirm that they deserved to be punished? And what of the one million children who were not even of culpable age? Are these people privy to some divine communication regarding the actions of these millions that the rest of us are not?

It is not for us to challenge the fierce anger and pain of the victims of tragedy when they refuse to observe divine precepts and display anger toward God. It would be far better to learn from the beautiful and sensitive teaching found in the *Ethics of Our Fathers*, which bids us never to judge a man until we have endured his hardships. It is no wonder that so many survivors of the Holocaust find the shallow reasons and justifications offered by so many religious thinkers sanctimonious, patronizing, and offensive.

Indeed, what is so tragic about those who argue that suffering is a punishment for sin is that by rationalizing thus, they dignify death. Judaism, however, sees death, illness, and suffering as aberrations in creation that were brought about through the sin of Adam in Eden (not to be confused with the Christian doctrine of original sin and the spiritual fall of man). Man's mission is not to make peace with suffering and death, but rather to abolish them from the face of the earth for all eternity by joining God as junior partners in creation. By using physical tools such as studying medicine, giving charity, and offering help in times of need, as well as by using spiritual means such as protesting to God against injustice and demanding that He correct the flaws of the world, we help to usher in an era where only goodness will prevail over the earth. It is in this context that I maintain that a doctor who struggles to cure AIDS, even in the pursuit of vanity and fame, has actually done more to answer the riddle of suffering than a clergyman who has reconciled himself to the fact that some people just have to die, and that it is all for a divine good.

Thus, rabbis and clerics who try to give spiritual meaning to the Holocaust miss the point. Our job as humans is not to give meaning to aberrations, but to abolish them from our planet. Human beings are commanded by God to occupy themselves with life, not death. Our energy must be dedicated not to explaining hurt and pain, but to fighting it. And in this respect there is no answer to the problem of suffering, but there is a *response*, because positing an answer means being reconciled to the problem. Responding not by remaining passive or adopting an acquiescent religious obedience but instead by fighting with every fiber of our being ensures that we shall be harbingers of redemption rather than prophets of doom. As long as we can explain why people can be gassed, or why people die of miserable illnesses, the pain associated with these losses will be mitigated. And that is not meant to happen. As human beings we have a responsibility to thunder against the heavens and demand the total cessation of all human misery. In this respect, we must use our pain not to look for reasons, but to demand the messianic era. Our efforts should not be employed in questioning, for example, why innocent Israeli soldiers die in battle; we must rather search for a *real* and lasting peace. We should not seek to understand why an event happens, but must instead endeavor to prevent it from ever happening again.

For those who argue that challenging God is sacrilege and most un-Jewish, let them learn from the giants of Jewish history. What was their response upon witnessing injustice and suffering? When God came to Abraham and informed him that he was about to crush Sodom and Gomorrah, cities that Abraham himself knew were deserving of punishment, did Abraham bow his head and accept divine judgment? No! Although these were cities that the Almighty Himself had described to him as "exceedingly evil and filled with transgression," Abraham nevertheless pounded with his fist and demanded from the Creator, "You are the Judge of the whole earth. Shall You not practice justice?" (Genesis 18:25). What magnitude of courage would have been necessary for a mortal man to challenge the supreme King, unless Abraham felt that it was for this, the exclusive promotion of life, that he was created?

Similarly, the first reference cited above in Moses's complaint to the Almighty, "Why have you let so much evil come upon this people? Why is it that you have sent me?" (Exodus 5:22), shows clearly how Moses responded to the suffering of the Jewish people. He did not ask God to *explain* what good the Jews received from their enslavement. He was not interested in rationalizations, nor did he seek to uncover the cosmic whys and wherefores. Rather, he demanded that God bring an *immediate* end to their suffering.

In the same vein, when informed by the Almighty that He intended to devour the Jewish nation for their sin of the golden calf, Moses responded in one of the most eloquent and courageous supplications ever recorded in defense of human life: "If you do not forgive their sin . . . blot me out, I pray you, from the Torah which you have written" (Exodus 32:32). Where in the history of apocalyptic literature does a human admonish the Master of the Universe to remove his name from a divine work, so that he will not be associated with the terrible deed of failing to save the victims (Rashi's interpretation)? Can one even begin to fathom the enormity of Moses' request? And yet Moses understood that as a human being his foremost obligation was the enhancement and preservation of life. The taking of life is only God's domain. And finally, after the debacle with the spies, when God threatens, "I will smite [the Jewish people] with pestilence and root them out," Moses again challenges the wrath of heaven and demands clemency.

My argument is not simply that this response is proper because it was practiced by Moses. It was the Almighty Himself who precipitated Moses' entreaty, as is explained by the classical commentaries on God's statement to Moses, "And now [Moses] leave me so that I can devour [the Jewish people] immediately" (Exodus 32:10). Moses had not yet even begun to speak, yet the Almighty commanded him not to interfere! The explanation is that God was hinting to Moses to open his mouth and defend the Jews, and not to accept the terrible fate that He had decreed for them.

Our role as human beings therefore is never to reckon with God's reasoning, but rather to promote those values that He conveyed to us as being supreme. In this respect, the very definition of evil is to meddle in those areas that are reserved strictly for the divine and are off-limits to humans. God gave permission, and furthermore the obligation, for human beings to take up the study of medicine, for example, so that they might pro-mote life. That is a human affair and a legitimate human domain. But the taking of life is not, nor is the justification or reconcil-iation of the loss of life.

It is here that we can appreciate the importance of demand-ing the advent of the messianic era and the final redemption. All those who refuse to clamor for the Messiah are, de facto, accepting the world for what it is. By not demanding from God that the world return to its original state of perfection, we simul-taneously embrace the world with all its ills and accept that such is life, things are just imperfect, and we must learn to live with it. But as Jews we retain an eternal belief that "death shall be defeated." We were never intended to adapt to the hardships of life, but are meant to call out to the Creator and demand a world where no child would ever go hungry because there would be abundance for everyone. And no parents would be bereft of their children because disease would be permanently eradicated from the earth. Never were we meant to learn to cope with life's imperfections, nor even to triumph above them in the face of adversity. Rather, our first preoccupation must be, in the words of the *Aleinu* prayer that we recite thrice daily, "to perfect the world under the sovereignty of the Almighty." Judaism's preoccupation is with the heavens, and not with the earth. We are not interested in the mysterious, esoteric reasons for suffering, but rather with its destruction.

It is in this context that I will maintain throughout this work that there is no good to suffering at all and that, as I shall dem-onstrate, death and suffering never had a place in the original cosmic plan. There is no good that can be achieved through suffering that cannot come about through overt goodness. Whatever good we as individuals, or the world in general, may receive from suffering, the same can be brought about in a pain-less, joyful manner. I believe this, in sharp contrast to the many people, and particularly the very religious, who maintain that the whole purpose of suffering is for our good. I have served as a rabbi to some of the brightest and most accomplished young minds anywhere in the world for the past six years, and I have yet to find one student who is better off because he has suffered than he would have been had he not suffered. This is not to say that suffering cannot afford some wonderful human character traits. In fact it can sometimes engender compassion, charity, generosity, determination, and selflessness. However, in my experience it just as often leads to bitterness, resentment, hardness, and pessimism. Whatever the positive consequences that may indirectly come out of suffering, the good that a stable, nurturing family life provides for a young student always transcends these by far.

Having made these preliminary comments as an overview, we set about discussing the problem of suffering in detail, penetrating the surface of this most difficult and enigmatic of subjects with the aid and illumination of classical hasidic thought.

10

FLAWED THEORIES
OF A LESSER GOD

N o study of the religious outlook on reward and punishment would be complete without addressing the problem of suffering. In the case of this particular work, it
is even more pertinent due to the subject matter. For this book
is a hasidic approach to the concept of reward and punishment,
and *Hasidut*, true to its overall worldview, which is totally
devoted to the belief in godly supervision of all earthly activities, sees reward and punishment in its most basic form as a
statement of the total involvement of God with His creation.
The fact that reward and punishment exists lends credibility to
the belief that God's primary attention is focused not on the
angels, but on man; not on the Garden of Eden, but on earth.
Thus a thorough understanding and acceptance of the concepts
of reward and punishment serves to draw man closer to God
and enable him to feel that he enjoys a unique place in God's
creation.

But the problem of suffering eats away at this conception. If
the world really is godly, then why is gross injustice woven into
the fabric of this world and everyday life? By examining the
problem of suffering through the eyes of *Hasidut*, we intend
to bring the reader to a deep appreciation of how God is
intimately involved in every aspect of our world, and offer a truly
Jewish and somewhat novel response to the eternal problem of
suffering. This and the following chapters are in no way meant

to be an exhaustive study on the subject. Rather, the purpose is to extend the issues already being covered with the intention of emerging with new insights into this most important subject.

The problem of suffering is one of the most vexing and as yet unsolved problems ever to confront man. How can we reconcile an all-powerful, all-merciful God with the existence of grotesque pain? Moreover, how can we justify the notion of God's active participation in all aspects of life when often He seems to stand by as a passive onlooker as man aches and grieves? The question is indeed almost as old as mankind itself. To rephrase the question: How can we affirm the validity of a sincere religious commitment in a world where we ourselves have witnessed such prevalence of gratuitous, gross evil? The problem goes beyond the issue of the suffering of the innocent and beyond the question of the suffering of the righteous. It involves the fundamental issue of whether there is any higher moral order at all operating in the universe, and whether or not God is truly attentive to the call of man.

There is a name given to the entire study of the reconciliation of the benevolent God with evil—*theodicy*, a hybrid of the Greek words for God and justice. The word is a technical shorthand used several ways. Theodicy is a shorthand for the problem of evil in the face of God. It is also a shorthand for a formulation of a resolution of the problem of evil. A common definition of the word theodicy is "a defense of (the justice and righteousness of) God in the face of evil."

Some of the themes that arise as part of the theodicy dilemma are the following: If God is omnipotent, omniscient, and all-merciful, why does gross evil befall the innocent, for example, infants? If God is all-merciful and omnipotent, why does evil exist at all?

But theodicy is not necessarily a problem for all religions and faiths. Even those who share a common religious tradition are affected differently by the problem of evil. Different systems of thought and their adherents have different thresholds at which the issue of evil becomes a serious philosophical problem. But theodicy is particularly problematic for monotheistic religions proclaiming a God who is all-powerful and all-good.

While this clearly encompasses all the major Western religions, the problem of theodicy particularly plagues Judaism. This is first and foremost because the Jews have suffered more than any other people, and second, amid their suffering, more often than not, they have emerged with their faith shaken but intact. Thus, more and more study had to be devoted to the problem of why suffering greeted the Jews everywhere they traveled amid their faithfulness to God's covenant.

Even more specifically, theodicy is especially problematic for hasidic Judaism. Jewish mysticism in general, and the founder of the hasidic movement, Rabbi Yisroel Baal Shem Tov, in particular, have emphasized, more than any other system of religious thought, how God is in control of all things in the universe, from the biggest and the grandest, to the smallest and most insignificant.

Once when the Baal Shem Tov was teaching this doctrine to his students, he walked over to a small leaf that had fallen from a tree. Underneath the leaf was a tiny worm. "You see, my students. If the leaf had fallen with its underside facing the sun, the worm would have died." With this he emphasized how the direction taken by a falling leaf was under God's constant supervision. The same is true whether or not there is a worm on the leaf, or any other tangible way of discerning why this would be of significance to the Almighty. So hasidism cannot hide behind doctrines of God's noninvolvement in worldly affairs.

Because of this, our dealings with the problem of suffering will take place within the larger framework of Jewish mystical thought. Theodicy has been treated by all too many as somewhat independent of other philosophical and religious issues, and consequently some formulators of theodicies have been operating in a total vacuum. It is our belief that any attempt to solve the problem of evil must conform to a commonly accepted religious philosophy. However, the problem is of such magnitude that we may have to modify some of our basic philosophical assumptions. *Hasidut* in any case has ample experience in turning popularly held conceptions of God and our world right on their head.

The gamut of Jewish responses includes the grossly sardonic. Elie Wiesel tells the story of a small group of Jews who were gathered to pray in a little synagogue in Nazi-occupied Europe. Suddenly, as the service proceeded, a pious Jew who was slightly mad—for all Jews were by then slightly mad—burst in through the door. He listened silently for a moment as the prayers ascended, then slowly said: "Shh, Jews! Do not pray so loudly. God will hear you. Then He will know that there are still some Jews left alive in Europe."

This story synthesizes two theodicy themes: a non-Jewish theodicy of a God turned evil, and a fundamentalist Jewish theodicy of God punishing all Israel for its transgressions.

Both of these are problems for both the believer and the non-believer. In the mind of the latter it stands as a major obstacle to a religious commitment. Even if he were to believe, who would like to worship a God that can be so cruel or unyielding, a God who is swift to exact punishment from the innocent as well as the guilty, a God who seems more involved in devising the most torturous forms of punishment than in leading the sinners back to a path of righteousness? For the former it sets up an ongoing internal tension to constantly challenge and cast doubt upon the validity and value of his faith.

If we were to place the impressive weight of evidence testifying to the existence of God in one scale, it would be outweighed for many by one thing, and one thing only: the existential tragedy of suffering, the burden of human misery, from which none are free. Untold sensitive men and women claim to have had their faith shattered on the hard rock of the persistence of evil in a world allegedly created by a good God. And while I personally take issue with this statement on the matter of abandonment of faith, I do of course accept that the problem of evil can create a terrible strain in our relationship with God. I take issue with the claim that people have lost their faith because of one tragedy or another due to the fact that faith, by definition, cannot be refuted. Faith is something suprarational. We speak of a "leap of faith." If someone sees God or knows of His existence beyond the shadow of a doubt, what faith is necessary? So faith, as something that transcends intelligence, cannot be refuted. No happening in the world can, by definition, stop our power to believe. But, what it can do is alter what we thought we *knew* about God. Holocaust survivors who in great fits of emotion describe the hell that they have experienced and then question the existence of God are really saying, "He may exist, but I don't want to have anything to do with Him. Before the war I was under the impression that God cared about justice and was sensitive to the suffering of man. Now, I no longer believe that."

Thus, the Holocaust and other tragedies like it have dealt our relationship with God a serious blow. If Judaism is to exist as a living fountain, to attract new adherents and comfort those who have always been true to its traditions, then its theological formulation must be able to handle all challenges satisfactorily. Judaism is a comprehensive theological and social discipline demanding internal logic and consistency. Internal contradiction cannot be tolerated.

In addition, human suffering poses a threat to the overall and most important claim in religion, namely that there is a benevolent God who seeks a dialogue with every created being, who cares and listens, who is attentive to our prayers, and is a personal God. When a human being is afflicted with some incurable illness, or when war snuffs out the life of the young, then one of the fundamentals of Jewish belief must fall. Can we still accept that God is all-powerful and causes everything that happens in the world, and that God is just and fair, so that the good people are rewarded and only the wicked are punished, when those who are good wallow in agony?

Immanuel Kant pointed out that if it is arrogant to defend God, it is even more arrogant to assail Him. Yet the Jew in particular, and religious man of reason in general, has always grappled with cosmic whys. It is in part this grappling for authenticity that distinguishes religious man of reason from religious fanatic man, moved by intense uncritical devotion, who is untroubled by reason.

In his excellent book *God and Evil*, David Birnbaum lists the traditional Jewish theodicies that have been offered by various thinkers and emanated from various sources throughout the ages as an answer to the problem of suffering. Many of these theodicies appear in related form in non-Jewish traditions.

The Torah is not a history book, but a book of instruction. When it recounts for all of eternity the differing dialogues between the Almighty and the giants of Jewish history like Abraham and Moses, it is instructing us to emulate their response, as we shall shortly explore. But before embarking upon our lengthy response to the problem of suffering and in an effort to demonstrate the shortcomings, blatant contradictions, and general inviability of many of these traditional responses to suffering, I present the list of conventional Jewish theodicies as listed by Birnbaum.

Group I. *Finite man cannot comprehend infinite God's ways.* The underlying implicit theme of this group is that the universe is somehow better with apparent evil in it. Finite man cannot understand infinite God. God's ways are inscrutable. God has His ultimate purposes known to Him. Man must have faith in God's justice. God's ways will be made understandable to us in the next world.

Group II. *Man is punished for his sins, failings.* The iniquities of the fathers are visited upon the sons ("vertical responsibility"). Man is punished in this world to increase his reward in the world to come. There is no suffering without sin. All men are imperfect and sin in some way. Suffering is due to evil deeds or neglect of religious observance.

Group III. *Hester Panim: hiding of the divine face:* a temporary abandonment of the world, a suspension of God's active surveillance. This concept is almost never applied as a general response to theodicy, but rather as a response to a particularly catastrophic series of events.

Group IV. *Other mainstream traditional responses regarding the suffering of the tzaddik (saintly individual) in particular.* "When permission is given to the angel of destruction, he makes no difference between righteous and wicked." "The righteous man should have acted more forcefully in promoting righteousness or interceding for his people." The *tzaddik* is held to a much higher standard. A *tzaddik's* suffering is atonement for all the people. The righteous will get their reward in the world to come. There are some merits for which God rewards in this world, and there are merits for which God bestows reward in the world to come. The *tzaddik* is "gathered in" prior to the appearance of great evil.

Other mainstream traditional responses regarding man in general. In recompense for his suffering, man will receive his reward in the world to come; man suffers in this world to purify him and clear his slate for the world to come; sins are forgiven through suffering. The individual is punished along with the rest of the community for communal sin ("horizontal responsibility"). The sin of Adam brought suffering upon the world. This is the concept of *yissurin shel ahavah*, tribulations of love, to purify man, to ennoble man, to chasten man, to raise man to a higher level, to test man, through suffering comes redemption, to increase man's reward in the world to come, to provoke man to reflect on his inadequacies and propel man to develop his potential. The process of divine justice takes time and man must have patience. Man is responsible for sin and suffering, not God. Suffering is a discipline, warning man against sin. Suffering keeps man from committing the sin of *hubris*. Suffering lessens the physical pride and selfish nature of the individual. Divine Providence is linked to piety and intellectual attainment, the absence of either leaving man vulnerable to evil. Nature is morally neutral. *Hashgachah* (Providence) does not apply to acts of nature.

Group V. *Freedom of man.* Implied in this group are self-willed constraints on God's intervention to protect man's freedom. Man's freedom must be protected, even at the expense of suffering. Suffering is an indispensable spur to human aspiration and achievement. Suffering pushes man over the brink to rise up against oppression, to demand freedom.

Group VI. *Kabbalistic responses.* The complex kabbalistic response to evil incorporates the following concepts in combination: *tzimtzum*, breaking of the vessels, dualities. These are esoteric concepts that will not be discussed here.

Group VII. *There currently is no answer.* However, the lack of an answer is held not to be a fatal flaw in the overall theology. We have no answer currently, but the answer will be clarified in the messianic era.

The fact that well over twenty major theodicies appear in various forms throughout Jewish literature reflects great dissatisfaction with any one existing theodicy. Clearly, each of the above has a gaping hole that offers the sufferer little consolation and none can really said to be fully tenable. How then is man meant to respond as he bears witness to human misery? If and when the Almighty, whom we believe actively controls our universe, visits calamity, death, and destruction on man, how should we react?

Although traditional theologies of all faiths have been aware of the potential danger of reducing God's attributes, and have attempted to protect the status of the deity, of late new and radical attempts have been made to resolve the God and suffering dilemma from a nontraditional perspective. The scarlet thread that runs through all of these attempts is that one or more of the traditional attributes of God's omniscience, benevolence, or omnipotence have to be deleted or seriously curtailed. For the purpose of introducing and expounding upon the hasidic doctrine of God's involvement with Creation, we will briefly explore some of these new theories.

Published in 1981, *When Bad Things Happen to Good People* was a runaway best-seller. After the tragedy of losing his only son to progeria, a rare aging disease, the book's author, Rabbi Harold Kushner, was inspired to write a book that heals for "everyone who has been hurt by life." The book is written sensitively, and in it Kushner, a conservative rabbi, emerges as a man of great compassion and extraordinary humanity. The central premise of the book, however, is very controversial. It is a radical departure from a traditional view of God and His interaction with His world.

Kushner begins with a study of Job, the classical biblical text on suffering. He argues that everybody in the book of Job would like to believe three things simultaneously. First, that God is all-powerful and causes everything that happens in the world. Nothing happens without His willing it. Second, that God is just and fair, so that the good people are rewarded and only the wicked are punished. And finally, that Job is a good person. But with the loss of all of Job's possessions and the death of his family, one of these three propositions must be dropped. We know that Job is a good and righteous man. So why is he suffering?

Forced to choose between a good God who is not totally powerful, or a powerful God who is not totally good, Kushner chooses to believe only in God's goodness. He retains the latter two premises and drops the first. This becomes the central theme of his entire book. Kushner's central premise is that God is not all-powerful and thus cannot be held accountable for the things that go terribly wrong in this world.

> Bad things do happen to good people in this world, but it is not God who wills it. God would like people to get what they deserve in life, but He cannot always arrange it. . . . From that perspective, there ought to be a sense of relief in coming to the conclusion that God is not doing this to us. If God is a God of justice and not of power, then He can still be on our side when bad things happen to us. He can know that we are good and honest people who deserve better. Our misfortunes are none of His doing, and so we can turn to Him for help. (pp. 50, 52)

But Kushner does not accuse God of observing other people's suffering idly like an innocent bystander. To him this would also be cruel and barely discernible from a God who actually causes suffering. Rather, he argues that there are certain things that are simply outside of God's ability:

> God wants the righteous to live peaceful, happy lives, but sometimes even He can't bring that about. It is too difficult even for God to keep cruelty and chaos from claiming their innocent victims. (p. 51)

Once God has established the laws and orderliness of nature, there is nothing he can do to alter its course. God intended nature only to be a blessing, but he cannot stop its side effects and unintended consequences.

> But the unchanging character of these laws [of nature], which makes medicine and astronomy possible, also causes problems.

Gravity makes objects fall. Sometimes they fall on people and hurt them. Sometimes gravity makes people fall off mountains and out of windows. Sometimes gravity makes people slip on ice or sink under water. We could not live without gravity, but that means we have to live with the dangers it causes. Laws of nature treat everyone alike (p. 66). . . . The earthquake and the accident, like the murder and the robbery, are not the will of God, but represent that aspect of reality which stands independent of His will, and which angers and saddens God even as it angers and saddens us. (p. 63)

This is also how Kushner interprets major tragedies and atrocities visited by one human being on another. The Holocaust was not something God could prevent. One should accuse God neither of sending Jews to the oven as a punishment for their sins, nor of refusing to intervene while the Nazis gassed half of Europe's Jewish population. God would certainly have done something had he possessed the ability, and we "have to believe that the tears and prayers of the victims aroused God's compassion, but having given Man freedom to choose, including the freedom to choose to hurt his neighbor, there was nothing God could do to prevent it" (p. 92).

Kushner's theodicy is born out of his theory which maintains that real evil is better defined as chaos. Although God ordained for the laws of nature to follow a specific pattern, nevertheless there is still an element of chaos lurking within them that God is unable to control. Once the laws of nature were set in motion, the world becomes like an unstoppable machine that runs on its own. God cannot intercede. It is outside His capability.

A change of wind direction or the shifting of a tectonic plate can cause a hurricane or earthquake to move toward a populated area instead of out into an uninhabited stretch of land. Why? A random shift in weather patterns causes too much or too little rain over a farming area, and a year's harvest is destroyed . . . These events do not reflect God's choices. They happen at random, and randomness is another name for chaos. (p. 61)

No matter what stories we were taught about Daniel or Jonah in Sunday School, God does not reach down to interrupt the workings of laws of nature to protect the righteous from harm. This is a second area of our world which causes bad things to happen to good people, and God does not cause it and cannot stop it. (p. 66)

Accordingly, the divine creative process involves not so much bringing a new world into existence from nowhere, but rather taking an existing chaotic matter and giving it orderliness.

[At creation], God began to work his creative magic on the chaos, sorting things out, imposing order where there had been randomness before. He separated the light from the darkness, the earth from the sky, the dry land from the sea. (p. 59)

Kushner creates the impression that before creation some huge blob of matter, a chaotic matter, but matter nonetheless, existed. He ignores the question of the origin of that matter:

This is what it means to create: not to make something out of nothing, but to make order out of chaos. A creative scientist or historian does not make up facts but orders facts; he sees connections between them rather than seeing them as random data. A creative writer does not make up new words but arranges familiar words in patterns which say something fresh to us. (p. 59)

But Kushner wants to have his cake and eat it too. Although he does not hold God responsible for the evil of this world since it is outside God's ability to prevent it, he does credit God with all of the orderliness and good things that do exist in Creation:

First of all, God has created a world in which many more good things than bad things happen. We find fires and disasters upsetting not only because they are painful but because they are exceptional. Most people wake up on most days feeling good. Most illnesses are curable. Most airplanes take off and land safely. Most of the time, when we send our children out to play, they come home safely. (p. 145)

Kushner also credits God with giving us the comfort and perseverance that get people through the pain of tragedy.

God may not prevent the calamity, but He gives us the strength and the perseverance to overcome it. Where else do we get these qualities which we did not have before? The heart attack which slows down a forty-six-year-old businessman does not come from God, but the determination to change his lifestyle, to stop smoking, to care less about expanding his business and care more about spending time with his family, because his eyes have been opened to what is truly important to him—those things come from God. God does not stand for heart attacks; those are nature's responses to the body's being overstressed. But God does stand for self-discipline and for being part of a family. (p. 148)

Kushner understands that many will want to reject the God that he proposes because of this god's uselessness. After all, of what good is a God who cannot interfere with the workings of creation or prevent people from suffering? Kushner advises all those who cannot accept this miniaturized God to think of all the ways in which God does make our lives easier.

[To those who ask,] "If God can't make my sickness go away, what good is He? Who needs Him?" God does not want you to be sick or crippled. He didn't make you have this problem, and He doesn't want you to go on having it, but He can't make it go away. That is something which is too hard even for God. What good is He, then? God makes people become doctors and nurses to try to make you feel better. God helps us be brave even when we're sick and frightened, and He reassures us that we don't have to face our fears and our pains alone. (p. 136)

Seemingly blind to the philosophical inconsistencies of his theory but quite aware of the theory's unkosher and nontraditional orientation, Kushner recognizes that amid his belief in God,

I do not believe the same things about Him that I did years ago, when I was growing up or when I was a theological student. I recognize His limitations. He is limited in what He can do by laws of nature and by the evolution of human nature and human moral freedom. I no longer hold God responsible for illnesses, accidents, and natural disasters, because I realize that I gain little and I lose so much when I blame God for those things. I can worship a God who hates suffering but cannot eliminate it, more easily than I can worship a God who chooses to make children suffer and die, for whatever exalted reason. Some years ago, when the "death of God" theology was a fad, I remember seeing a bumper sticker that read "My God is not dead; sorry about yours." I guess my bumper sticker reads "My God is not cruel; sorry about yours." (p. 140–141)

But Kushner is not the only Jewish thinker who would propose a theodicy, or solve the problem of suffering, by leading us to believe that God is not intimately involved in the course of history and everyday events. Nor does it take a non-Orthodox rabbi to renunciate, albeit more subtly, God's intimate supervision of the world's affairs. Increasingly, this is an attitude being advanced by more traditional Orthodox Jewish theologians as well.

Thus we find that one of the attempts respected by Orthodox Jewish scholars as most accurately embodying an authentic Jewish response at reconciling the occurrence of the Holocaust with the just, benevolent God is that offered by Eliezer Berkovits, quoted by British Chief Rabbi Jonathan Sacks in *Tradition in an Untraditional Age*. Berkovits rejects the notion that the Holocaust is unique among tragedies suffered by the Jewish people. The problem of *tzaddik vera lo*, the "righteous who suffers," is one as old as Abraham. "Shall the Judge of all the earth not do justice." The answer given by what Berkovits calls tradition, applies to the Holocaust too. God, in giving man the freedom to choose to be good, at the same time necessarily gives him the freedom to be evil. God teaches us what goodness is. But He does not intervene to force us to be good or to prevent us from being wicked. Berkovits emphasizes that God is powerful not through His interventions in history but through His self-restraint.

Berkovits quotes the interpretation of the verse "Who is a Mighty One like You, O Lord?" (Psalm 89:9), given by the Tannaitic teacher Abba Hanan. "Who is like you, mighty in self-restraint? You heard the blasphemy and the insults of that wicked man [Titus, who destroyed the Second Temple], but You kept silent!" In the school of Rabbi Ishmael the verse "Who is like You, O Lord, along the mighty (*elim*)'" (Exodus 15:11) was amended to read "Who is like You, O Lord, among the silent ones (*illemim*)," since He sees the suffering of His children and remains mute. Berkovits maintains that the central religious paradox is that God leaves the arena of history to human freedom, and therein lies His greatness. So when human beings perpetrate evil it is they who are to blame, not God, who must necessarily restrain himself from interfering in human events so that man might retain his freedom of choice.

Berkovits then proceeds to deal with the crucial question arising from his theodicy. Where do we witness God in history? Of what use is a God that refuses to intervene? To whom are we praying with our supplications? Berkovits answers: God reveals His presence in the survival of Israel. Not in His deeds, but in His children. There is no other witness that God is present in history but the history of the Jewish people.

Hence the demonic character of the Nazi project. The final solution, says Berkovits, was an attempt to destroy the only witnesses to the God of history. The ingathering of exiles after the Holocaust, and the creation of the state of Israel, revealed God's presence at the very moment when we might have despaired of it altogether. The rebirth of the state came at a moment in history when nothing else could have saved Jews from extinction through hopelessness. The miracle that testifies that God exists is that the people of Israel exist.

Hence we have yet another theory promulgating God's receding into the seventh heaven in order not to disturb man's affairs. While the God of Berkovits is not as weak as that of Kushner, ultimately it doesn't make much of a difference. Both see God's participation in world events as scant and minimal. Kushner sees the extent of God's interaction with our world as being there to give us the fortitude and courage to continue even when the chips are down, and Berkovits sees God's interaction confined to the *overall* survival of the Jewish people. Thus the God of Kushner and Berkovits is a transcendent one in the classical Cartesian tradition—a God who lives more in the heavens than on earth.

Both of these arguments are severely flawed, in more than one way. But for our purposes, we shall only deal with refuting the perception of a transcendent and detached God that they put forth. By doing so, we shall also set the stage for demonstrating the deep hasidic approach to the problem of suffering. In the next chapter we shall spell out the Jewish mystical explanation of how our world came into existence, and how it continues to exist. This shall, of itself, destroy all notions of a transcendent God who does not interact within His creation or supervise all of the world's events from the greatest to the smallest, from the highest, loftiest reaches of the heavens to the anthills and beaver dams on earth.

11

THE NATURE OF NOTHINGNESS: THE NEED FOR GOD IN CREATION

Y ou shall know this day and take to heart that the Lord is God in the Heavens above and on the earth below; there is none besides Him" (Deuteronomy 4:39). This verse from the Bible expresses how the knowledge of the oneness and unity of God is not something instinctive to human knowledge. Rather it is something that we *must come to know* and take to heart. Man is instructed to ponder the unity of God via observation and reflection. Much of hasidic thought is dedicated to this goal: bringing man to a realization of how our world, against all appearances, is united with God.

The question that initiates the whole discussion of the unity of God is this: How can we indeed say that "there is nothing besides Him" when we see the world existing, at the very least, alongside God as an independent entity? What does it mean that "in the Heavens above and on the earth below" there is nothing besides God when our eyes bear witness to the fact that the world consists of millions of different creatures that exist outside the unity of God?

Seemingly, the first step in understanding the unity of God is to see and accept that everything that transpires in this world is an integral part of God's plan in creation. Nothing comes into being and no event comes to pass independent of God's will—everything serves a higher cause. If events were to take place for any reason other than the fact that God willed them, this would mean that they are outside the unity of God. But, since God created everything for a purpose and all of creation is a necessary part of God's plan, everything can be said to be within the unity of God. The meaning of the verse above, "There is nothing besides God," would then mean that since God is the Creator, everything we experience and everything we see in our physical world is a detail in God's plan, an object of God's creative power. Thus, all living things receive their existence from God, and nothing in the world can be said to be independent, since it is God who created and is overseeing all that happens.

On this level, the answer to the question of how God is one amid the existence of a multifarious world is this: All of creation is of secondary nature and is subordinate to God's will. The world may indeed exist, but this poses no inconsistency with the unity of God since God created it and it does not exist independently nor possess its own laws or nature. God dictates its laws and determines its nature. So, the world, the universe, does exist, but it thanks and is indebted to God for that existence. It simply wouldn't be, would never have been, without God.

This level of divine unity can be compared to the actors and the director in a play. If someone were to question why the director gets the credit for a fantastic production, is it not true that the production consisted of many actors who brought the production to life? The answer would be that the director takes the credit because although there were many actors, *they only did what the director told them to do.* In fact, it was the director who auditioned them and brought them into the production in the first place. Thus, we feel justified in subordinating and accrediting the entire production to one individual—the director.

So, too, on this level of thinking God takes the credit for being solely existent, and the principal existence, since everything follows His command and was brought into being to execute His Will. But closer examination of God's unity will show that this explanation is insufficient.

It is not sufficient to say that God is the original existence. He is, He was, and He always will be, while the rest of creation emanates from God and didn't always exist and this makes God unique. To reconcile the unity of God with the existence of creation by saying that the world is a subordinate entity is superficial and shallow because this does not fit the true definition of unity. Unity means that two objects that appear distinct and separate are really one. It does not mean that the the two objects are *to be considered* as one since the latter is so much less important and follows the lead of the former. Unity is not achieved by taking two distinct items, labeling one the principal, and subordinating the latter to the former.

To truly understand the meaning of God's unity, we must know what we are up against. If it is the creation that is posing the incompatibility with God's unity, we must define what creation is.

The word *creation* and the act of creation indicate that there was a need for something to be created out of total nothingness, and that this thing that was created had no existence prior to its coming into being. This is the true meaning of creation—the emergence of something from nothing, the technical term for which is creation *ex nihilo*.

Many think of the world before creation as a lifeless, shapeless, unrecognizable mass of material. Some think of a palpable darkness, while others simply call the precreated world a primordial mass or chaos. To them, God's creation of the world involved giving life, shape, color, and character to this characterless mass—in short, putting things in order. This is exactly what Kushner believes, as quoted earlier:

> [At creation], God began to work His creative magic on the chaos, sorting things out, imposing order where there had been randomness before. He separated the light from the darkness, the earth from the sky, the dry land from the sea. . . . This is what it means to create: not to make something out of nothing, but to make order out of chaos. A creative scientist or historian does not make up facts but orders facts; he sees connections between them rather than seeing them as random data. A creative writer does not make up new words but arranges familiar words in patterns which say something fresh to us. (p. 59)

This is a superficial understanding and severe misrepresentation of the true definition of creation. The Hebrew term for creation is *bara* (as in the verse *"Bereishit bara . . ."*), which means "to bring into being." "To bring into being" denotes that prior to that act of creation there was *no* being, there was no existence, there was *nothing*. When God "created" the world He brought into being an existence from something that was nonexistent. Creation connotes that God called forth the world's existence from an absence, an abyss, a total void of darkness and nothingness.

In fact, the word *bara* is a verb that is used in Scriptures exclusively with reference to divine activity. Thus it is explained by the major Jewish biblical commentators as referring to producing something out of nothing (*yesh me'ayin*), creation *ex nihilo*. As Nachmanides comments: "There is no expression in Hebrew for producing something from nothing other than the word *bara*—created. Never in the Bible do we find *bara* as describing man's activities because man cannot *create*. Because *bara* does not mean to give life, or shape, or color, or form— but to bring into being. This means that the moment before creation it simply wasn't, it had no existence at all. By stating, 'In the beginning God created Heaven and earth,' the Torah is out to convey that somehow that which did not exist came to exist" (Commentary of Nachmanides on Genesis 1:1).

Before God created the world in six days the world was nonexistent. What reigned in its absence was absolute nothingness. But the Almighty through his infinite energy performed what to man is unfathomable—creation *ex nihilo*. Man cannot, even in the deepest recesses of his mind, understand nothingness, let alone the *emergence* of something from nothing. Amid an absolute vacuum of existence and empty space God brought into existence a pluralistic, diverse, and complex creation. When God said "Let there be light," light was called into existence from nothingness. When God said "Let there be a firmament," this too was called into existence from an utter void.

From this it should be obvious that the creation differs greatly from the average physical product of man's labor. For example, when a carpenter takes a rough and coarse block of wood and through his craftsmanship and skill cuts, sands, and polishes it into a beautiful mahogany table that is sold at a high price in the market, he hasn't *created* anything. The same block of wood with which he started remains a block of wood, although it now has a different appearance and form. The carpenter has refashioned, enhanced, and beautified an existent block of matter. But the carpenter introduces no qualitative change or property into the block of wood that it did not possess previously, but rather enhances its appearance and use. Had the carpenter never come along and never redesigned the block of wood it would have remained peacefully unmoved in its natural environment. So too, an artist can put paint on canvas or give form to a lump of marble, and then walk away. The painting will remain as will the statue even though the artist has now disengaged himself. The marble will not slip back to its original shape, nor will the paint drip off the canvas and back onto the palette. Both will retain the shape, form, and character given them by their respective artists.

But when one takes *nothing* and gives it character, what is there that can possibly retain the character given to it? What is the *it*? What is going to maintain the shape that one has created or the property that one introduces? The *it* is a nonexistent it and therefore there is nothing here to maintain the shape, the character, or the properties one provides. This is totally dissimilar to the artist above who begins with a substance and reformats the already existing substance.

Close your eyes for a moment and see yourself as Francis Ford Coppola, directing the classic movie *The Godfather*. In front of your eyes, Marlon Brando is bringing the character of Don Vito Corleone to life. You watch him as he dispenses instructions to his Mafia henchmen. Suddenly you scream, "Cut." Marlon walks over to you and asks, "How was I? Was I convincing?" You respond, "Wait a second, what happened to Vito Corleone? You're not him, you're Marlon Brando!"

Marlon is mystified by your question. "What do you mean?" he asks. "Vito Corleone doesn't exist. I was *acting* the part. And so long as I continued acting, the character was continually being sustained. But the moment that I stop acting, Vito Corleone ceases to exist, not just now and just immediately, but retroactively as well. Because I am creating him, calling forth his existence into life, I must do so constantly. The moment I stop, he ceases to exist, instantly, because his existence is not real. It is an illusion that I create by acting the part constantly."

The same is true of God's creation of the world. Had God started with some existing matter, and merely reformed and refashioned it according to His liking, it could be sustained without His active involvement. But because He started with nothing, He must constantly suspend and animate the world if it is not to revert to nothingness.

Thus, when the Torah states that "In the beginning God created Heaven and earth," we are to understand that in the beginning God gave existence to nonexistence, and therefore it would be ludicrous to assume that after God gave the world existence, He can now move on to other things and leave the world to exist on its own. God cannot leave the world to itself, with the world retaining its existence, shape, and any other property or character it possesses. This cannot be because there is nothing there that can retain any shape. God started off with nothing and must constantly maintain the world's existence because it is simply not possible for nothing to become something. It must be sustained constantly. Hence, the very idea that God created the world and it exists as an independent entity is misguided. It is a misunderstanding of the nature of creation. It is also a misunderstanding of the truth of existence. The simple reality is that God exists and the universe does not, because it cannot maintain its own existence. Because it cannot become responsible for its own existence, it cannot take credit for its own existence, even now as it exists. Taking nothing and making it into something means that the something that has now been created really remains a *nothing* and only appears as a *something* because it is being sustained and suspended by an outside source.

Here Kushner's fallacy of creation is exposed. Creation cannot be compared to a scientist or historian who orders facts. Scientists and historians begin with an existent subject or material, they do not create it. Scientists do not bring elements into being and historians do not create history as they write. Both analyze existent matter. But God creates universes and calls them forth into existence from utter nothingness. Kushner himself totally ignores the issue of whence derived the matter which God formed and ordered. Thus it is stated, "Our [human] actions bear no resemblance to Yours, Oh Lord," for whereas God calls forth and sustains the existence of a previously nonexistent entity, man merely gives new shape or form to an existing matter already created by God. Man is the Johnny-come-lately who merely changes the properties of a world that already exists through the active grace and benevolence of God.

In hasidic thought an appropriate example of the above is provided. Suppose a person throws a stone into the air giving it, temporarily, the nature of flight and lightness, rather than the heaviness and immobility that is intrinsic to the stone. This imposed nature, this given talent, of lightness and movement does not take hold in the stone. The stone cannot acquire this talent permanently. In short, it cannot learn to fly. And although one has helped it to fly and given it movement, it cannot retain what one has given it. And notwithstanding the number of times one causes it to fly, it will still not absorb this quality that one is attempting to confer upon it. What is possible is that so long as one continues to carry the stone by the power and the momentum of the throw, the stone will continue to act against its nature. But as soon as one's influence fades, the stone immediately reverts to being a stone like all other stones, because it never changed.

This, in fact, is what happens every time we throw an object and cause it to whisk through the air. We transfer onto that object the energy previously stored in our muscles, which enables the object to counteract the forces of gravity. So long as that energy acts upon the stone, it will fly. But when friction and other sources of resistance overpower the transferred energy, the stone will fall to the ground. This all happens because it is the energy that makes the stone fly, and the consumption of that energy that makes it fall. The stone plays no part in the flight.

Notice that when a baseball comes crashing through our window, we don't get upset at the baseball. Our immediate, intuitive reaction is to say "Who did that?" In other words, although one sees a baseball or a stone, one thinks of a person, because stones don't fly and baseballs can't move on their own.

People throw stones. The stone brings to mind not a unique stone that is different from all other stones, but the bad behavior of a juvenile delinquent. When one sees a stone going past one's window, one is not witnessing a flying stone. The stone flying through the window should properly be described as a *flown stone.* The stone was *flown* past the window, it didn't fly. Someone *flew* it, but it cannot fly. And even while it is flying through the air, it is not flying but *being flown.* A flying baseball conveys nothing more than the absolute need for someone to have caused it to fly through the window. The baseball remains a blameless and amoral object.

Now, if a stone that, after all, does exist and possesses its own intrinsic nature and properties, cannot be given even one added dimension or talent, how much more so that something that has no existence at all, no properties to speak of, no nature, and is utterly nothing, cannot retain anything new either? God cannot come along and institute the laws of nature into creation, because what or who abides by these laws? That which doesn't exist? Can we properly refer to our world as an independent entity? Can we say that its true nature has now been formulated and exists on its own? Can we say that the creation that was called from nothingness has become an independent existence and now is a *something*? Obviously not. Our creation, which began as nothingness, is being retained as something not through its own intrinsic nature but through God's constant creative force, which acts upon it and sustains it, just as the stone flies through the air via the human energy that constantly forces it upward.

So here we find that the oneness of God and the fact that the world does not pose an inconsistency with God's unity is much greater than the fact that He was the original existence and all other existence is secondary. It isn't even secondary. It isn't existent. It is being *existed.* And even while it is being existed it would be wrong and improper to describe this world as a world that exists, because worlds don't exist. Worlds are not. The fact that you are sitting and reading these lines and the fact I am writing them does not constitute proof to the fact of our existence, but rather it is a proof to the fact that we are *being existed.* The practical difference between something that exists and something *being existed* can be gained from their being destroyed.

The question was once asked of a child, "If God wished to destroy the world, what would He do?" The child responded innocently, "Well, He would burn it." But the questioner returned, "What would He do with the ashes?" "Wash it away with an ocean of water," responded the child.

"But what would He do with the water?"

"Vaporize it with an intense inferno."

"What will He do with the water vapor, clouds, and rain that result from the evaporation of the water?" asked the questioner, and on and on. The dilemma is readily apparent.

In truth, if God desired to destroy the world it would not necessitate a new action on His part, He would simply *stop creating it*. There would be no need to smash it, grind it, crush it, or burn it. If for a moment God would lose interest in this world, there would be no world. There would not be a pollution problem from the destroyed world's leftovers. There would be no ashes and no rubbish to clean up. There simply would be no existence. If God ceases to create the world this moment and the next moment and the next, then there would be no world. The nature of flight imposed on the stone will completely disappear when the influence of the thrower is gone because that nature is being imposed onto nothing and therefore has to be constantly repeated from outside the system. So creation has to be a constant ongoing act on God's part. God must create and sustain the world every second. Should he stop for even a second there would be no existence and no world.

The same is true of Marlon Brando acting the part of Don Corleone in our previous example. If the actor wishes to kill off the character, there is no need to have Don Corleone shot to death by other gangsters in real life. Rather, Marlon Brando need do nothing more complex than ceasing to act in order for the character to be destroyed.

It is for this reason that every morning in our prayers we praise God for being He "who in His goodness renews each day, continuously, the work of creation." The same applies to every hour and every second.

When disasters are discussed in the Torah, when times of

trouble befall the Jews, it is described as God turning His face. Why the use of this particular expression? Turning the face implies that there is some kind of relationship, some interaction between oneself and another person. But the relationship has become strained, therefore, one chooses not to face his counterpart directly. One cannot bear to look him in the eye.

Likewise, God's wrath is described as turning His countenance from us. In a time of trouble the Torah says, "God has abandoned you in that He has turned His face from you" (Leviticus 26:17). Thus, the relationship that was once pleasant is now harsh and painful. But to leave, to totally disassociate Himself from His world would be impossible. For if God were to abandon His world, this would not be a punishment for there would be nothing left to punish. If God would leave the world it wouldn't create a global disaster—there would no globe. There would be nothing. The world's demise would not be a slow tortuous process, but instantaneous. If God would stop creating the world there would be no world—nothing—just as matters stood before creation.

12

THE "CUSTOMS" OF NATURE

To further emphasize the difference between *existence* and *being existed*, we must distinguish between the very important concepts of *gilui hahelem* (revealing something hidden) and *briyah yesh me'ayin* (creating something from nothing). Briefly stated, an artisan who takes a piece of clay and molds it into an earthen cup has only revealed the hidden potential of the original clay, while one who throws a stone through the air has introduced a new dimension onto the stone, albeit only temporarily.

To explain: As described above, when an artisan takes a block of silver and makes it into a beautiful *kiddush* cup he has not changed the essence and true nature of the silver whatsoever. What he has done is merely change its shape and form. He started with a block of silver that was either square, round, or without any particular shape, and now introduced a new shape to his liking. But we can in no way say that this shape is something totally new to the silver. Already in a hidden form the silver possessed the potential to take upon itself and retain any shape given to it by someone who would mold it. Since clay, gold, silver, and all similar materials possess the the ability to be molded into any form, this indicates that in truth the material already contains, in potential form, an infinite amount of shapes. It can retain a shape imposed upon it because it holds within it a potential for millions of shapes.

Stated in other words, the only thing that happens when silver is banged into a specific shape is that its hidden potential for assuming that specific shape, or any other shape, has been translated from the potential into the actual. Although we can't see those infinite possibilities, this is due to the fact that the shape that the silver now retains conceals the potential for the material to assume another shape. But the very fact that we can take this block of silver and bang it into a beautiful cup means that the potential for that shape has always been in the silver and even when it becomes a cup it still retains the potential to be banged into some other completely different shape. Since all these shapes are already present in a potential form, by giving new shape to the silver and the silver retaining that shape no new dimension has been introduced to it at all. Rather the artisan is "revealing the hidden" from within the silver.

But when someone takes a stone and throws it into the air we cannot say that the potential for flight was previously hidden in a lifeless object like a stone. When seeing a stone thrown into the air no one would say that the ability for the stone to fly was always hidden within the stone and now the thrower has merely revealed a heretofore hidden property of the stone. Rather, the individual who threw the stone, who transmitted energy onto the stone from his own muscles, has now introduced a totally new property and new dimension to the stone that is causing it to fly. And while this imposed property may be ephemeral, it still does temporarily exist. Thus, this is not a case of revealing the hidden but rather creating a new dimension within the stone. It is not only the form or the shape of the stone that has been changed, but its very nature has been altered.

It is for this reason that the while the silver vessel does not need the ongoing interaction and attention of the artisan, the stone needs the energy to push it into the air and defy gravity constantly. In other words we may refer to "revealing the hidden" as *creating something from something* while bringing about a new property in an object may be referred to as *creating something from nothing*. When something is created from something else, all new properties were already present and what is needed is only for them to be manifest and translated from potential to actual. But when something new is created, when something must be created from total nothingness, it must be sustained constantly because the property was not present before but has been introduced as a complete novelty.

It can now be readily appreciated, since it is not the nature of nothingness to become something and it was God that brought nothing into existence, that He must do so constantly. If He were to withhold His creative effort for even a single instant the world would revert to what it was previously and what it is now without God, nothing. Therefore it cannot be argued that the world in any way is an independent existence but rather totally dependent on God's sustaining utterance.

This truism is conveyed in the very way in which the Talmud speaks about the laws of nature. In a discussion about why God does not interfere more often in the world's affairs and prevent people from sinning, the Talmud responds that God wants the world to run by its natural order. But the expression used is *Olam ke minhago Noheg*, the world behaves according to its *custom* (nature). This is the expression used by the Talmud whenever it discusses the world's everyday natural order. What is fascinating about this expression is the use of the word *minhago*, which literally translates to custom, rather than nature.

What the Talmud is saying is that the decrees and laws of nature really aren't laws at all. Rather, they are customs. Nature is basically a nonexistent entity and it is being existed only for the part that it plays in God's plan. Therefore when we talk about the properties of nature we refer to them as the world's customs. It is customary for water to run downhill; it is customary for fire to consume; it is customary for that which is heavier than water to sink. These are all customs, not laws.

The word *nature* when understood from a Jewish perspective means *habit*. This is referring to our own habit. Those things that we witness regularly are what we refer to as nature. Since we are in the habit of seeing the sun rise daily, we refer to it as a natural phenomenon. But those things that we are unaccustomed to witnessing at regular intervals are what we call a miracle, or the intervention of God in nature. But the truth is that the natural event is just as unreal and irrational as the miraculous event. Neither has a cause or explanation as to why it occurs. The phenomenon of a tree growing out of a seed is just as wondrous as the splitting of the Red Sea. But because we witness the occurrence constantly, we call it nature. We call something a law only when it behaves in a certain pattern repeatedly. It is the *repetition* that makes it a law, and not because there is something in nature that forces it to behave in this way. Therefore it isn't really a law at all but is more appropriately described as a custom.

Therefore, if we were to ask a highly qualified scientist who had never seen water before to analyze a bottle of this colorless substance and publish his results, there is nothing in the water from which the scientist could deduce that if the water were released from the bottle it would flow downhill. The number of tests he would perform on the bottle would be insufficient in informing him how the water would behave once it was released from its container. The only method by which the scientist could learn the properties of water is via direct observation. Without observing the behavior of the water under differing circumstances, the scientist could not predict its behavior. Every physicist today gains a knowledge of matter by conducting experiments and recording observations. It is based on these observations that predictions are made.

But this phenomenon is most surprising. One would be led to believe that if the nature of water is to flow downward, there would be something *within* the water which causes it to behave this way and that this element of water could be discovered through careful analysis. We would thus be able to predict the behavior of water through chemical analysis rather than observation. Yet this does not happen. No matter how well one analyzes or examines water, one cannot make any educated assumptions about the water flowing downward because there is nothing in the water that says that it must flow downward. The same is true of every law of nature.

Another Torah reference for nature conveys the same thought: *hukei hateva* (laws of nature). The word *hukei* in truth does not translate just as "laws," but as a particular kind of law. There are certain laws in the Torah that are reasonable and logical and are called *mishpatim*. There are also laws in the Torah that are suprarational. They carry with them no tangible explanation.

These are called *hukim*. While we shall discuss the differences between these laws in a later chapter, for our purposes now we note that *hukei hateva* translates as the irrational law of nature. The laws of nature are the kind for which there is no rationalization or explanation. We abide by that law only because it is a law and is repeated constantly. But we have no logic or validation for the existence of the law. So, with the use of this expression the Torah is out to convey, as before, that there is no such thing as nature, but rather observable repetitious events whose only rationalization is the fact that we witness them occurring on a regular basis, and can therefore predict their future behavior based upon past observation and experimentation.

To use contemporary scientific vernacular, the physicist today refers to the natural order of things as a behavior pattern, or a repetitive pattern. That's all it is. One cannot inquire as to why water flows downhill. The fact that this is so is an observation and not a law. Why does one observe water running downhill? Because it does. What makes water run downhill? Nobody knows and our ignorance is not a product of our lack of sophistication. No amount of sophistication or scientific erudition will ever give us that knowledge because there is nothing present that can be known. There is no "why?"

Stated in other words, it is the behavior that defines water and makes it what it is. And if we were to inquire what it is which is behaving, the answer would be: nothing. This is the entire idea behind creation. Creation is something that exists only in terms of observation. But beneath the surface there is no substance or existent matter. Creation is nothing but a behavior pattern.

If we were to ask a scientist to define a chair, he could not merely say "a piece of wood." To say the table is wood is not a very scientific statement at all. Nor would he respond that it is a collection of molecules, nor atoms, because particle physics can today break atoms down still further than that. His answer would be that the table is an observable behavior pattern. The scientist will also not state with certainty whether the chair will be present tomorrow. His reply to such a question would be "probably." Probably, not certainly. It is the law of probability, or Heisenberg's famous principle of uncertainty, that makes it impossible for the scientist to predict with any confidence that this chair will be present tomorrow.

The religious or suprarational question that the scientist ignores is this: Once you describe physical existence as merely observable behavior patterns, what is it that is behaving? What is behaving in this fashion, the electron? Again, the answer is nothing. The world was created out of nothing. The behavior pattern exists but there is nothing there to behave. It's not that there is first a substance and then one gives this substance a behavior, temperament, nature, or properties. We begin with a behavior and if it behaves long enough, fast enough, and consistently enough, then it is defined as an existent object with intrinsic properties. It becomes an object from its behavior. And although the fact of a behavior pattern without something to behave does not make any sense at all, this is the very definition of creation. In the beginning God *created* the world. He didn't shape it, form it, enlighten it, paint it, color it, teach it, bend it, or fix it. He *created* it. Thus, there is no such thing as an existentially independent world. When God said, "Let there be light," He created the behavior of light. But what is it that is behaving like light? Nothing. And when God said, "Let there be grass," it meant "Let there be the behavior of grass." But beneath this behavior is a layer of nothingness.

13

WHEN NATURE BECOMES A MIRACLE

T he Talmud relates a story in which Rabbi Shimon bar
Yohai came to the study hall and found the hall dark.
He inquired of the students who were sitting idly in the
dark, unable to study, as to why they had not lit the candles.
They replied that they had no oil. He then asked them what they
did have and they replied vinegar. Rabbi Shimon bar Yohai then
instructed the students to place the wicks into the vinegar and
to light it. Confounded, the students replied that vinegar does
not burn. How can we take a nonflammable liquid and make it
into a candle? Rabbi Shimon responded, "He who told oil to
burn will tell vinegar to burn as well." They placed the wicks
into the vinegar and the vinegar was consumed.

Superficially this is just another story of a miraculous event.
But with this story the Talmud is out to convey much more than
a mere story. The Talmud is out to teach us that it is no more of
a miracle for vinegar to light than oil. For vinegar to burn is
equivalent to oil burning because there is nothing about the oil
that necessarily makes it flammable, or about the vinegar that
necessarily makes it inflammable. Rather, usually we observe
how God tells oil to burn and so it does. And usually God does
not tell vinegar to burn and so it does not. But in this particular
case when there is no oil, Rabbi Shimon says that God will tell
the vinegar to burn and it will burn as readily and as naturally
as oil since both vinegar and oil are constantly being created
and sustained.

So when we talk about miracles versus nature all we are saying is that when God gives behavior to a nonexistent world He does so consistently and that's why it's called nature. When we observe a consistent pattern we call it nature. And what does nature do to us? Nature conceals from us God's involvement with the world. When we see that which God repeats often we forget that God is doing it, we forget about God and we begin to worship the reality of what we are seeing. We speak of indigenous laws of nature, which are in reality constantly being suspended by God. And that is the beginnings of idolatry.

Idolatry does not begin when you take a statue, you give it a certain shape, and then you bow to it and kiss its feet. It begins when you believe that there are those things which exist outside the agency of God; that is the beginning of idolatry and that is the result of what we call nature. Nature means the habit of seeing things happen. What is a miracle? A miracle means when God is acting, as involved as He always is, not even more involved, just as involved in making things happen, in being the only existence in the world, only this time He's allowing that fact to show, the fact that He is making it happen. That's what we call a miracle.

Two important conclusions emerge from this entire discussion. The first pertains to our definition of godly intervention in nature and the distinction we normally draw between nature and miracle. The second pertains to God's unity after creation.

In the case of the former we can say that basically there is no difference whatsoever between *nature* and *miracle*. Both are manifestations of continual godly involvement, supervision, and creative power. The only distinction that can be made between them is the rate of their occurrence. For the Jews coming out of Egypt, watching the Red Sea split when Pharaoh was in hot pursuit of them was no greater a miracle than the fact that every time we stick a seed into the ground a tree bearing luscious fruit grows forth.

In fact, if the Red Sea were to split every day at precisely 3:30 P.M., it would still be a magnificent occurrence and tourists from around the world would flock to see it. But no one would see any divine manifestation in the occurrence since it is regular. The splitting of the Red Sea would be nothing more grand than the Old Faithful geyser in Yellowstone National Park. No one can deny that this geyser is very impressive to witness. About 10,000 gallons of hot water plus billowing steam are ejected at one eruption. Its fountainlike columns reach heights of about 170 feet and stand for approximately four minutes. But do any tourists who witness this dramatic event walk away with new-found faith and inspiration in the God of history? Of course not. And why? Since it erupts "faithfully" at regular intervals on a daily basis, we are accustomed to its pattern and thus do not define it as a miraculous occurrence.

In illustration of this concept *Hasidut* quotes the statement of the *Hakham Tzvi* who says, "In reality nature is nothing more than miracles at regular and therefore predictable intervals." Human nature is such that witnessing wondrous events on a regular basis with precision timing is referred to as nature. But in reality there is no difference between the ongoing phenomenon of what we refer to as nature and a one-time-only miracle. The everyday events that occur around us are no less amazing. Let us be honest enough to admit that if trees did not exist and someone came along with a tiny seed and told the people around him that he is going to put this into the earth, of all places, and a few months later this tree will now bear fruit, surely everyone would call the man a lunatic. But because we witness this amazing occurrence on a regular basis, we call it "nature."

So if a person is almost run over by a car but is saved at the last second, is this a miracle? It is a miracle if it helps him see and accept that God regulates and controls everything in the world. If it doesn't help him see this truth, then for all practical purposes it is not a miracle, although the occurrence certainly involved God's intervention. From a purely human perspective, a miracle demonstrates overtly that God intervenes in man's life. Thus defined, the only accomplishment of a miracle is to take us out of the habit of nature. A miracle helps break us out of the habit of thinking that nature operates through its own indigenous processes and with its own momentum. This breaking of habit in turn brings us to the appreciation that we are indebted to God for everything that we have in life. Whatever we possess, and all good things that come our way through life, should bring us to offer God thanks for them, the same way we would thank a human benefactor for any favor he did for us.

No individual should be led to believe that his good fortune, his good luck, is responsible for his blessings or that left to its own devices, the world, by its nature, would have to provide for him. For example, imagine a small farm community in which there has not been rain in quite some time. All the crops are dying and the local farmers are all desperately awaiting the irrigation of their cash crops. Suddenly and unexpectedly, a rainstorm comes thundering through the village and saves all of the fields at the very last moment. All of the farmers gather in the local synagogue to offer prayers of thanks to God for saving them from ruin.

Now imagine one farmer stepping out of the crowd and refusing to offer thanks together with his colleagues. He complains that he has nothing to thank God for. After all, God did not make it rain for him specifically. Rather, it rained on the fields of the village, and as long as it was raining in the village generally, then it was impossible for his fields not to be irrigated in the process. So not every individual within the village must offer thanks. God is not singling him out. In fact, he complains, the very opposite is true. It would take a special miracle for God to make it rain on all four sides of his fields but not fall on his fields as well. Therefore, when God does allow it to rain on his field it is not necessarily because God wants him to earn a livelihood, but because his field is in the middle of all the other fields upon which it is raining.

But the fallacy in the farmer's argument is clear. Who says that the nature of rain dictates that everything in its path must get wet? In fact, who says that rain has a nature at all? Rain, like everything else, is an observable behavior pattern and it behaves according to what God conceives. And if God wishes for it to rain all around the other fields without watering this farmer's field, this can happen just as easily as the field indeed being irrigated. As a matter of fact, it could even rain on the farmer's head without him getting wet. There is simply no law that dictates that rain must be wet. It is rather our observations, after the fact, in which we have witnessed that water is indeed wet that leads us to predict that in the future it will be so as well.

The latter conclusion, that pertaining to God's unity, is radically altered as a result of the above discussion. The continued emphasis in the Jewish faith on the unity of God, "the absolute oneness of God," "the indivisibility of God," are not statements that are meant to negate the possibility of a deity other than God or to contradict the potential for a being of God's awesome might and power. No thinking person would naturally have been led to make such a gross misjudgment in the first place. Rather this concept of God's unity comes to reinforce that the entire creation, which to the naked and untrained eye appears to be an independent existence, is misleading and false. Even those who believe that God has created the world can argue that now that the world is already in existence it no longer needs God's constant interaction and providence. The concept of unity of God brings us back from even that type of idolatry.

Idolatry in Judaism is the belief that any existence, even that which was once created by God, now exists outside His unity and is independent of His being. There are no two absolutely existent entities so that one might say there is God, and *then* there is the world. Rather, God is the primal Cause who suspends and animates all antecedent effects. There is only God and then there is the world that, if not for God, would not be. This is the meaning of God's proclamation in the Torah, "I am God, I have not changed." This is a statement about God in relation to His creation. God says that in His unity there is no difference between before the creation of the world and after. Just as it is clear that before God created the world there was no independent existence other than Him, the same thing applies today even after the creation of the world. Since the world is constantly being suspended and sustained by God, the world is not an independent existence. It is completely dependent on God. Thus it is not outside His unity and God has not changed.

To follow up our analogy of an acting company at the beginning of this chapter, this level of divine unity can be compared to the characters in a play in comparison with, not the director, but the playwright or screenwriter. In the case of the director, it was he who took existing characters and instructed actors how to enhance their already existing role. He started with an existing plot and added dramatic effect to it. But the playwright is far more unified with his play than the director. The characters within the play only exist so long as the playwright *keeps on writing*. Not only are the characters nonexistent before the playwright invents them, but even while he is writing they are still fictional characters, and they act out their destiny only so long as the playwright adds another chapter to his play. If he stops the play in middle, the characters literally cease to exist. Their lives and destiny come to an abrupt end. And if the playwright decides to destroy one of the characters in the play, he need not have the character shot, knifed, or kidnapped. All he has to do is omit him from the play. So the characters in the play and the storyline of the play itself are intrinsically unified with the mind that invents them and sustains them.

We gather a unique glimpse of this in Kurt Vonnegut's *Breakfast of Champions*, where the author decides to "go down" into the pages of his book in order to meet his favorite character. At this point in the book, the favorite character, Trout, is sitting at a bar, calmly nursing a drink. Suddenly he is overcome by a tremendous feeling of anxiety and apprehension. He senses that something is about to enter the room—something not only "awesome," but so powerful that "he cannot possibly face." That something is the author. The author describes how even every reaction of Trout to his presence is, of course, dictated by himself, the author.

> Trout was the only character I ever created who had enough imagination to suspect that he might be the creation of another human being. He had spoken of this possibility several times to his parakeet. . . . Now Trout was beginning to catch on that he was sitting very close to the person who had created him. He was embarrassed. It was hard for him to know how to respond, particularly since his responses were going to be anything I said they were.
>
> I went easy on him, didn't wave, didn't stare. . . . I wrote again on my tabletop, scrawled the symbols of the interrelationship between matter and energy as it was understood in my day: $E=mc^2$. It was a flawed equation, as far as I was concerned. There should have been an "A" in there somewhere for Awareness— without which the "E" and "M" and the "c" . . . could not exist.

Even as real human beings are not mere letters on a piece of paper, we need the same awareness. To say that anything happens in our world without God making it happen is idolatrous. It is ascribing significance to something for which God should take the credit. (And while there is no question that man has absolute freedom of will, this does not contradict all of the above for while man does have the power to choose *how to act*, he does not have the choice to determine *what will happen to him*. God controls that, as we shall see at length in a later chapter.) To say that a leaf moves because the wind causes it to move, even if one admits that it is God's wind and God's leaf, is idolatrous because it is giving the wind significance, power, and ability well above and beyond what it has, and thus it is idolatrous.

There is another fundamental outcome of this absolute knowledge of the unity of God and an awareness of how it operates that affects our everyday lives. Usually, religious obligations are undertaken by people in a very unexciting and sluggish manner. It is as if we have no choice in the matter. We would have preferred to have been doing something else, but what can we do? We are like servants who are forced to do our master's bidding because we are weaker than our master. But when one understands with a firm conviction that there is no such thing as existence outside God's unity and even one's own existence is nothing but an extension of that unity, then one automatically feels not as if he is a separate entity who has been overtaken by something that is far more powerful than himself, but rather as part and parcel of God's unity. We go about fulfilling God's will not out of a feeling of coercion, but because we feel ourselves to be a part of it.

This awareness in turn allows us to feel liberated from the temptation of outside society. When we forfeit going to the beach on *Shabbat* in order to keep the *Shabbat* holy, we don't feel as if we have been coerced to give up an exciting experience. Rather, we understand that since the world is an actual part of God, the only thing on earth today is *Shabbat*. There is not *Shabbat* and a beach, there is only *Shabbat*. The beach too must rest on *Shabbat*. One feels "free" from the temptation to contravene God's will, not in bondage or enslaved by our inclination to pursue our own agenda.

Now we can see how the theodicies of Kushner and Berkovits, who argue that the evil that exists in our world is due to God's nonintervention, are severely flawed. If God indeed had a hands-off approach, regardless of whether the cause for that noninvolvement is as Kushner says, due to God's impotence, or as Berkovits says, to God's unwillingness to intervene, the result is still the same. Nothing could happen and nothing could exist. If God were to distance or detach Himself, not only could good or evil not exist, but nothing at all could exist. The world simply would not be. We must therefore tackle this most difficult of all questions, the reconciliation of the merciful, benevolent God with the existence of gross and unjust evil, from another angle.

14

THE CASE FOR AND
AGAINST THE EXISTENCE
OF EVIL

There is something comforting, almost soothing, to be learned from the discussion in the previous chapter. The fact that the maintenance of the world's existence necessitates God's constant involvement in the world's affairs means that we are never outside God's care and nothing ever transpires except for a purpose. It is important for an individual to recognize that everything that transpires in this world is part of a greater plan. The entire world was created so that it could be rectified and transformed by the Jewish people with the aid of all the nations of the world. Rashi makes this abundantly clear in one of his first comments on the Torah. Commenting on the word *Bereishit* (In the beginning), Rashi breaks the word into *Beit Reishit* (two beginnings). The world was created for two things: "For the Jewish people who are referred to as a *beginning* and for the Torah which is referred to as a *beginning*." The world was created for the Jews to utilize the Torah in elevating the world and to spread the knowledge of godliness and goodness among the nations of the world. It is clear then that everything that takes place in our world is guided by divine providence and is designed to help us execute the purpose of creation.

It is for this reason that the Baal Shem Tov stated emphatically that everything a Jew sees or hears should be taken as a lesson and a guiding light in serving one's Creator. The very fact that one sees a given event is not coincidental but divine providence. An individual is guided along a path in finding and witnessing this happening so that he could extract a lesson and a principal that can be applied to the service of God.

This utilization and application of events can come about in one of two ways. At times a person witnesses an event that undoubtedly serves to enhance his religious commitment. I shall never forget how as a young yeshiva student in Jerusalem I once went to the Wailing Wall at about midnight. There, amid the stillness of the night in one of the wall's corners was a man who was visibly neither Israeli nor an observant Jew, whose sparkling suit was drenched with tears. He cried and cried without abate. Thinking that the man was in desperate need of help, I had the chutzpah to interrupt him and ask if I could be of help, was he okay, was a relative ill? He shook his head and answered in a perfect and nonaccented English, "I'm crying because I don't feel that I have any right to be at this wall." This small encounter made me reexamine the sincerity of my own Jewish commitment and goodness. Did I have a right to go to the wall?

But at times a person comes across a happening that seemingly has no connection whatsoever to Judaism and has no godly design. On the contrary, a great many experiences may serve as obstructions and disturbances to one's religious devotion. This can come in the form of seeing a religious individual behave immorally, or one can have a bad experience in the synagogue. I remember one individual who had married outside the Jewish community, who stopped attending synagogue after he was evicted from a synagogue for not paying for his seat on Yom Kippur. More often than not, however, those experiences that serve as impediments to man's devotion to God involve suffering. It may be personal suffering or someone else's suffering, but the issue is still the same. How can God allow this to happen? The following chapters will deal with the hasidic approach to answering this paramount question. It is a uniquely Jewish response in that it incorporates the dynamic tension that makes up the God–man relationship. While these remarks are not meant to be exhaustive on the subject, I hope that it will be a good start and help to soothe some open wounds.

The most common approach taken by theologians with respect to suffering is to interpret suffering as punishment. Taken at face value, this approach is terribly flawed and portrays God not only as a sadist, but even as worse, petty. The Master of the Universe is seemingly disturbed by man's trifling crimes to the point where He visits upon him in return massive retribution. But we shall nevertheless make some preliminary remarks about punishment.

Judaism cannot be said to be totally immune from sentiments of suffering resulting from sin. As we expressed in the very first pages of the book, one of the Thirteen Principles of Jewish Faith proclaims that for every *mitzvah* we perform we are amply rewarded and for every misdeed that we commit we are appropriately punished. This belief in justice, that the world is not merely a jungle where people can do as they please without their evil ever catching up with them, is not exclusive to Judaism. The truth of the matter is that whether or not one is observant, or a believer, devout or secular, we all have a deep-seated conviction that there is justice in this world. How many of us, after all, would feel comfortable with the notion that no suffering was brought upon Hitler after his unspeakable crimes?

The idea of justice is not only confined to the Jewish classroom where young children are taught that if they wear *tzitzit* and a *yarmulka*, God will watch over them. And it is not only confined to the superstitious who refrain from blasphemy because they fear God's retribution. Rather, this is a concept felt universally. When a child sees someone stealing a toy from a department store and asks his parent, "Why do we have to pay, when he doesn't?" the parent's response is that he will get caught. The parent teaches the child that at the end of the day crime does not pay. And what does that mean? There is not other way to define it other than to say that justice dictates that if you are good you are rewarded and if you are bad you are punished. Don't people still tell their children that if you are a good child everything will turn out well, but if you are bad you will only make yourself miserable? People who make no claim to belief or faith in God still renounce crime because eventually one gets trapped in one's own schemes. A popular social metaphor says,

"Don't do the crime if you can't do the time." At the core of our very existence we maintain that good people deserve success whereas bad people deserve to fail. And it bothers us when things don't go according to this plan.

Rabbi Manis Friedman tells the story of a woman whose husband, much to her disappointment, was getting more deeply involved with Judaism. She claimed to be an atheist and objected to his pursuit of nonsensical observance. But one day, her older brother, who by all accounts was a good man, had a heart attack and died. He was forty-seven years old. The woman could not make peace with what had happened and wandered aimlessly asking, "Why him?" At one point she was confronted by Rabbi Friedman who said to her "I don't understand where you, the atheist, come to ask such a question. What do you mean 'Why him?' The doctor explained to you why he died. He showed you the diagram. He explained how the heart works and how the arteries can get clogged. Your brother was a wonderful man and a good brother. But he had a bad heart. You know all of this. So why do you keep saying 'why him?'"

Obviously the woman was not interested in medical details. If her brother was a good man then why did he die? If her brother was a rapist or a murderer she would not be walking around asking the same question. But what kind of question is this? Whether we wish to admit it or not, the question of "why me" is a religious question. A secular individual cannot ask why me, or why him. A true atheist, if there is such a thing, cannot ask *why* somebody dies. He can only ask what made him die, or how did he die. But questions of why can only be asked by people who believe that there is higher order at work in the universe and people's lives are not ruled by chaos.

But this intuition and conviction that a good man should lead a good life is not shared only by religious people. On some level we all feel this way. In fact, we become genuinely and sincerely morally indignant when wicked people succeed. It bothers us, not because we are jealous but because we are morally disturbed. It's not right, and evil people should not succeed. We expect them to fail. We expect an evil man to be punished and when this does not happen something of our moral fiber is disturbed. How many times has a schoolchild watched one of his classmates cheat on an examination and because of his cheating end up doing better than he? What does the child feel when the results are announced and he, because he was honest, comes out lower than the child with wandering eyes? He feels wronged. He feels that it is unjust. But this is not due to any belief in God or religious commitment. The child cannot help but feel that something has gone amiss. This shouldn't be happening. The belief, then, in reward and punishment is innate to the human condition. It is automatic and is not predicated on social conditioning.

So the awareness in reward and punishment is not limited to people who read Maimonides. It is deeply rooted in our hearts, minds, and psyches, without which we would not be quite human.

Having shown that the concepts of reward and punishment are universal, we will now proceed to make a few other preliminary remarks. The revolutionary changes that Albert Einstein brought to science in the form of the general and special theories of relativity began with some very simple observations. When someone standing on earth looks at the moon, the moon appears to move while the earth remains stationary. But when someone standing on the moon looks at the earth, the earth appears to move and the moon seems to remain stationary. Einstein asked, which of the two observers is correct? Since there is no way of saying who is correct, we therefore have to accept that concerning the movement of the planets one may only make relative observations. There is no absolute method of determining which of the observers is accurate. Everything depends on a person's point of view. What this is saying, in effect, is that when two equally convincing and equally plausible explanations are offered for a single phenomenon, then you really have no explanation at all.

Applying this principle to the problem of "bad" occurrences, there must certainly be times when from a human perspective something is bad, but to God, an omniscient Being's perspective, the occurrence may be good. For example, there is a true story of a man who was scheduled to take a United Airlines flight from Chicago to Los Angeles. When he arrived at the airport he was told that the flight had been overbooked and that he had been "bumped." He was furious. He had a meeting that evening in Los Angeles, and how could the airline do this to him? He was screaming at the managers, threatening to sue the airline and blow up the whole airport. As he carried on ranting and raving, he was even cursing the day he was born. He felt that this was the worst thing that had ever happened to him.

But fifteen minutes later, he was a changed man. In fact, he was deeply apologetic to those he had offended. Because fifteen minutes later this United Airlines DC10 went down, both literally and in history, as the worst aviation disaster in the history of the United States. One of the four engines fell off and there were no survivors.

So when we try and define whether an event is good or bad, there are two equally acceptable possibilities. At times we see the two possibilities but sometimes we don't. Sometimes God's perspective of events is very different from our own, but unfortunately is also hidden from us.

This issue of perspectives does not only involve events the possibility of whose knowledge is outside the realm of human experience.Undoubtedly, the whole of human experience involves people from different perspectives making different judgments about the same circumstances. Take, for example, the parent–child relationship where each time the parent tries to discipline the child, the parent feels he is doing what's best for the child, and the child feels that his parent is a monster.

The child cannot understand what he did wrong. Why is he being punished? What crime did he commit that he should not be permitted to play with the sharp knife or run across the highway? The very same circumstances that lead parents to feel that they have behaved responsibly as parents, lead children to conclude that they are being deprived, denied, neglected, and underprivileged. But which view is correct? It depends on whom you ask. If you ask the child he will tell you how envious he is of Johnny next door, whose parents allow him to do whatever he wants, while the parent contends that Johnny's parents neglect their children.

When God the regulator of all of the world's events dictates circumstances that will befall us, which to us seem evil and bad, we examine ourselves asking, "What sin have I committed?

What have I done to deserve this?" But at times, God's response is, "What bad thing are you referring to? Why do you complain that you have missed the plane? From where I sit, you shouldn't get on that plane."

Another pivotal thought in determining the nature of the event is the recognition that before we sit in judgment and decide that something evil has happened, we need to collect more information. A famous and often-told hasidic story involved a middle-aged couple who came to the founder of the hasidic movement, Rabbi Yisroel Baal Shem Tov, whose blessings had the power of bringing about miraculous events, to request a blessing for a child. They had been married for many years but remained childless. The Baal Shem Tov changed the subject. When they came back time and again and insisted that the Rebbe bless them, he would always change the subject until, finally, the woman refused to depart until the Rebbe conferred his blessing upon them. The Baal Shem Tov gave them his blessing and a year later they had a baby boy. The boy lived to be two years old and then suddenly died. Grief-stricken, the couple returned to the Baal Shem Tov. "What sin have we committed?" they asked. "What did we do wrong to bring this disaster upon us?" Of course they saw their son's death as something bad. The Baal Shem Tov answered, "After everything you've been through you deserve an explanation, but first I must provide some background information.

"About one hundred years ago," the Baal Shem Tov continued, "there was a terrible occurrence known as the Chemielnitzky uprising, and the raiding Cossacks destroyed entire villages and killed hundreds of thousands of Jews. In one of these villages a Cossack noticed a newborn Jewish baby and, having no children of his own, picked up the child and took him home. When the Polish government finally put down the rebellion and tried to sort through the chaos caused, they heard that in one of the Cossack camps there was a child who was obviously not a Cossack. They returned the child to the Jewish community, where, being an orphan, he was raised as a committed and respectable Jewish individual.

"When this Jew died and his soul came before the heavenly court, it was found that this was a perfectly innocent soul except for a slight blemish that had accumulated on the soul during the two years it had spent among the Cossacks what with all of their violence and vulgarity. In order for the soul to be completely perfect it was decreed in Heaven that the soul needed to be born to a loving Jewish family in a holy environment to relive the first two years of life. Thus, when you came to me years ago asking for a blessing for a child, I refused because I knew that this would be the child that would be born to you and I did not want to be responsible for your grief. But when you gave me no choice and absolutely refused to leave without a blessing, I consented. So, when you ask me what you've done wrong, the answer is nothing. In fact, nothing bad has happened to the child, and nothing bad has happened to you. This was all part of God's plan to have a lofty, special soul cleansed of the turbulence it had experienced."

But what of the parents' legitimate grief? What about the commandment to sit *shiva*, to observe seven days of mourning as prescribed by Jewish law in commemoration of the tragedy that has taken place? Are the parents not allowed to mourn now that they have learned that their tragedy had a beneficial outcome? Of course. The grieving parents *must* mourn. Even Jewish law mandates that they must cry and weep. But feeling grief does not mean necessarily that something bad has happened. Grief means that something sad, something painful has happened. One must be very careful in choosing expressions. The difference between the two phrases is of tremendous significance.

In hasidic thought it is explained that one of the ways that the evil inclination induces man to sin is by confusing man semantically. The evil inclination uses subtle words whose true meaning is overlooked by us until we are duped. Just as when signing a contract, the signee must examine all aspects of the contract to ensure that he is not being swindled, likewise we must proceed very carefully when different thoughts arise in our mind about good and evil.

The earliest example of how someone was fooled by a misuse of terminology, unfortunately with devastating consequences for the rest of humankind, was Eve in the Garden of Eden. The evil inclination, which came in the form of a snake, could not come right out and say, "Eat from the tree of knowledge." What kind of human being would transgress God's express commandment so directly? Rather, as the Torah itself attests, the snake was sly and cunning. The snake came to Eve and said, "Look at that tree, look at the fruit, isn't that a *good* fruit? Isn't that a *good* tree?" He did not tell her to eat from the tree. All he did was emphasize the goodness of its fruit. But Eve's ability to be fooled was the beginning of her sin and that which eventually led her to eat from the tree and bring death to mankind.

Is there such a thing as a *good* tree? Is there a *moral* fruit? A tree can be healthy or it can be diseased. A tree can grow tall or be stunted. A tree can be full of fruit or it can be barren. The fruit itself can be sour or sweet. But what, pray tell me, is a good tree? By the same token, what is a bad tree? Is a bad tree one that slanders and gossips? The terms *good*, *bad*, and *evil* correctly used must remain within the realm of morality. *Good* implies something that is morally good, and *bad* implies immorality. It is a sad commentary on the modern age that we still have only one word—love—to express the most varied kinds of human emotions, and just one word—*bad*—for anything that we find unpleasant. We speak of a bad movie, and a bad check. But the word *bad* applies more properly to the writer of that check.

The problem is that we have so totally misused references to good and bad that they have become largely meaningless. In today's society, *good* denotes simply anything that we like, and *bad* denotes anything that we dislike.

I remember reading a story in the press about a man who had won the state lottery, a total of over five million dollars. At the time he described it as "the best thing that ever happened to me." He certainly saw the winnings as a "good" thing. But one year later one of his two teenage children was dead of a drug overdose. The extra cash provided by the lottery was used by his son to increase a habit he could previously not afford. Now the man was telling the journalist what a curse his winnings had been. Not only was it bad, it was terrible. Had this fortune not disrupted his life, his son would probably be alive.

When he won the money, he said it was a good thing. In other words, "I like it." And at the time it was very pleasant. But he could not know the future of what this money would bring. After his son's death he said, "It's bad," that is, "I don't like it." It once felt good and now it's painful.

The question of whether bad things happen to good people is not inquiring whether painful things happen. Of course painful things do happen. We are also not asking whether *sad* things happen, because we know for certain that they happen all the time. The question is whether bad things, evil things happen. In other words, is this painful experience or sad experience unjust and immoral? Is there something essentially evil in what's happening? Is there something bad about it? This is a very different question from asking about painful experiences, and the difference is not only semantic. In the story of the Baal Shem Tov, this young couple who lost their child are commanded by the Torah to sit seven days in mourning over their son and to take no pleasure from life because they are in mourning. But did something evil happen?

One of the most famous female figures in all the Talmud is Bruriah, the wife of Rabbi Meir. One of the stories related about her concerns the time when, tragically, both of her sons died suddenly as a result of disease. Rabbi Meir was unaware of the deaths and Bruriah searched for a method of telling him the awful news. When he came home she said to him, "Suppose we had a visitor here yesterday and he left his bags and returned today to reclaim them. Would it be proper for me to return them?" Rabbi Meir responded, "What kind of question is that? Of course." So she continued, "God gave us children and yesterday He came and reclaimed them. Could you object? Is there anything immoral or bad about that?" The Talmud ends the story with Rabbi Meir accepting his wife's assessment of the situation, "The Lord has given and the Lord has taken. May the name of the Lord be blessed forever." But even after this explanation by Bruriah and the pronouncement of Rabbi Meir, they still observed a period of mourning, and they grieved over the loss of their two boys and wished that they could be restored to them. Even the justice of the situation did not change the fact that this was a severely painful and sad experience.

15

A MATURE VIEW
OF PUNISHMENT

F rom the discussion thus far it is clear that before we address the question of whether bad things happen to good
people, we must first define accurately what "bad" is.
First, as we have shown, when any event transpires there are
usually two ways of looking at it. There is never only one view.
So which one is correct? We know from our own experience
how, as time progresses and things sort themselves out, we
change our opinions of things that have transpired earlier in our
lives and simultaneously alter our conclusions about them as
well.

Second, to determine whether or not something is evil we
must be sure that we have all the information and evidence
associated with the occurrence. To be sure, there are those
things that appear terribly evil, but do we know what preceded
the event, as in the Baal Shem Tov story above. Sometimes, the
information that is at God's disposal is not at our disposal. If we
were privy to such information, if we were able to look down
the continuum of human generations from beginning to end,
things might be judged differently. To be sure, even in the story
related above concerning the Baal Shem Tov, the death of the
baby was a terrible tragedy that caused untold suffering to his
parents. Still, it could not be construed as an evil occurrence.

In a famous story related in the Book of Exodus, the young
prince Moses smites and kills an Egyptian taskmaster. But before

Moses killed the Egyptian whom he found smiting an Israelite, the Torah relates that Moses first "looked this way and he looked that way and he saw no man." Only then did he kill the Egyptian. Why did Moses look to and fro? Was he a coward? Did he not defend the conviction of his beliefs? If Moses felt it was indeed right to kill the Egyptian for unfairly persecuting this Jew, why did he care whether anyone was looking? Did the great redeemer not have the self-sacrifice necessary to put himself at risk in order to save his fellowman?

The Talmud explains that Moses was not concerned with whether someone would witness the killing and he wasn't looking around for a living person. Rather, "he looked this way and he looked that way" to see if anyone of virtue would emerge from this Egyptian. Moses looked prophetically into this Egyptian's past genealogy to see if there was anyone worthy among his ancestors, and then he looked the other way into the future generations that would be born to this Egyptian and he saw no one of virtue, and so he killed him. By implication we may deduce that had Moses seen among those past and future generations someone just and righteous, that virtue might have been extended to this Egyptian and Moses would not have killed him.

Thus, before we decide whether this Egyptian's death was good or evil, whether it served the cause of justice or chaos, we must obtain additional information. Where does he spring from? Who will rise from him? What did he do in his past life? What will he do in his next life? Information that is not at our disposal is vital for reaching a conclusion.

Third, and possibly most important, do we properly understand the nature of reward and punishment? The intuitive human response to pain and misfortune, whether this is visited upon ourselves or anyone else, is to ask what the person has done to deserve this suffering. We immediately demand justice. We expect God to show cause. "Why is this person suffering? Did he do something terrible to deserve this?" And if we were to investigate and discover, by some clairvoyant means, that indeed this person who is suffering has done wrong and deserves to suffer, has harmed his fellowman, the case would be closed. We would accept this person's suffering as being part of justice. We rationalize to ourselves that certain guilty people deserve to suffer as a result of their destructive ways. We see the need for people to be smitten for some of their deeds.

But this type of thinking is at best childish and superficial and at worst destructive and misleading. Superficial because it is precisely this outlook on life that leads people to serve God out of a fear of punishment, and destructive because it leads people to weigh the gravity of a sin based on the punishment it carries.

To explain, a great many of us refrain from eating on Yom Kippur, driving on *Shabbat*, or eating pork because we fear the consequences. After all, just look in the Torah. It stipulates that for this sin one receives lashes, for another sin one dies an unnatural death brought about through the agency of the Heavens, and for yet another sin one receives capital punishment from an earthly court. So, the average person thinks to themselves that these are severe punishments and who wants to suffer? So we refrain from sinning out of fear. But fear of what? Fear of God, or *yirat shamayim* (fear of Heaven)? No! This cannot in any way be construed as fear of Heaven or of God. Yet, a great many people make the mistake of believing that whenever Judaism encourages man to have fear of Heaven, it means fear of being punished by God. Not only is this impression mistaken, but it is very un-Jewish and unhealthy. This is nothing more than self-preservation and a subtle form of idolatry. The person refrains from sin not because he fears God, but because he fears the consequences to himself.

Anyone who is even vaguely familiar with hasidic philosophy is probably aware that *hasidim* advocate above all else serving God with joy. Not with fear, but joy. *Hasidut* advocates that there be constant singing, dancing, and celebration. *Hasidut* believes it essential that man serve God with a positive attitude and not out of fear of punishment. Why is this so important? Why, as we examined earlier, does the *Mishnah* profess that one should not be like a servant who serves his master for the sake of receiving a reward, but rather like a servant who serves his master without the intent of receiving a reward; "and let the fear of Heaven be upon you."

The reason is that anything else is pure idolatry and self-preservation. Imagine a Jewish individual who dons *tefillin* every morning, studies the Torah daily, keeps a strictly kosher home, observes the sanctity of *Shabbat*—in short leads an exemplary Jewish life, but all with the intention that he not fall prey to disease, or that his business be successful, or that he do well in his university exams. Can this person be said to be serving God at all? Of course not. Rather, he is in business with God. He is a deal-maker. He says to God, "Look, I'll do whatever you say, but just as long as I am the final beneficiary of my service. You must be good to me." This person is literally worshiping himself. God's needs are unimportant to him. Rather, God is the avenue he uses to achieve his own selfish goals.

It is for this reason, too, that Judaism never uses language such as "God is the path to salvation," or "God saves," or "If you reject belief in God, you will never get to Heaven." God is not the road to anything and should not be used as a vehicle to arrive at one's destinations, even if those destinations and ends are noble. God is the ultimate goal and is not a means to any end. One dare not serve the Almighty in order to avoid damnation. This is purely self-preservation. The only motivation of serving God in this scenario is because an individual loves himself and does not wish to suffer.

But the Jewish concept of fear of Heaven, as in the words of the *Mishnah* above, "and let the fear of Heaven be upon you," is fear of being *detached from* God. Fear of Heaven means refraining from sin because the individual loves God so immensely that he never wants to be separated from God or out of favor. Sin creates a barrier that separates man from God and prevents God's countenance from shining through. This is a mature and adult form of divine worship. Any other form is superficial and shallow.

Hasidut illuminates this concept with the following analogy: A father sees his son running around the house barefoot. He tells the child, "Be careful, it's not safe to run around barefoot. You must put your shoes on. If you continue barefoot you may get a splinter and hurt yourself." But the child is not impressed and he continues galavanting around the house barefoot. Sure enough, the day comes when the child gets a splinter in his foot. The wound becomes infected and the infection begins to spread. The child is rushed off to the hospital. Upon examining the wound, the doctor says, "You got here just in the nick of time. I think we can save the leg." He thereupon takes out sharp, cold metal instruments and begins to poke at the very painful area of the foot. He then begins cutting out the infected tissue. The incision hurts the child enormously. He screams in agony. After a short while, the doctor finally gets the splinter out, and treats the infection. The child and his leg are saved.

A few weeks later, after fully recovering, the child is back on his feet and sure enough he's running around the streets barefoot again. Once more, his father says to him, "Don't run around barefoot because you'll get a splinter." But the child knows better and protests that he won't. So his father continues, "If you get a splinter, it will get infected like before." Again his son is unimpressed and tells his father not to worry. Finally, his father says, "If you get a splinter, I'll have to take you to the hospital where the doctor will take out his sharp instruments and cut into the skin on your feet." Upon hearing this the child gets frightened and runs and puts on his shoes. This type of pain is unappealing to him.

Now why is this childish and immature? When the parent tells his son to put on his shoes so that he won't get hurt, his words have no effect on the child. The child is seemingly unconcerned that he will be harmed. But when the father tells his son that even if he does get hurt and even if he endangers his foot, do not fear because there is always a doctor who can heal him, the child suddenly springs to his feet and says, "What! *Heal me?* Okay, I'll put on my shoes." In other words, the child is afraid of the *cure*, not the damage.

This childish attitude is the same as that of an individual who obeys God's commandments out of fear of punishment. When the Torah tells this individual not to commit adultery because it will violate something of the godliness of his soul, the spirituality of his children, the sanctity of his marriage, and of the world at large, this individual responds, "Not to worry. I'll be discreet. None of these things will happen." But when the Torah responds by saying if you do commit adultery God will punish you, the individual suddenly listens. "Oh, in that case, I won't do it." This individual also fears the cure. For God does not just punish people in a vengeful manner. God does not take revenge. God obeys the commandments that He gives to us and He commanded *us* not to take revenge, so He certainly does not take revenge Himself. God is not so petty as to tell man, "If you transgress my laws, if you ignore me, then I will have to hurt you." Einstein maintained that "God doesn't play dice with the Universe." Well, neither does He play games of "tit for tat" either.

Rather, the purpose of godly punishment is cleansing, rectification, and reinstatement. God says that if you destroy some of your holiness and innocence through your own misdeeds, He will come along and correct it. God promises man that in spite of his disobedience and the damage he has done to himself through his transgression, He will still fix it. He will save it. This rectification may have to be a surgical method, as is necessary in saving a limb, and it may be painful, but the purpose of the cleansing is for man to be reinstated. This has always been the Jewish understanding of punishment. What the world refers to as "punishment for sin," Judaism has always called "cleansing of sin," purging of the tarnishing of the soul. Thus, the concept of "hell," or eternal damnation, as in the Christian sense, is unknown in Judaism. God does not punish man for the sake of punishment alone, nor as a form of vengeance or retribution. Rather, God seeks to rid man of the impurity he has absorbed and must therefore cleanse him.

A simple analogy will suffice. A child is running amok outside in the mud. At the end of the day a loving parent takes the son, washes him in very hot water, and takes a strong brush and cleans the dirt off his soiled body. The parent must use very hot water and a scorching brush that in the process may be painful to the child. In fact, the child, unaware of what he has done to deserve this, might think that his father is a barbarian. After all, is there really this great a need to cause him so much pain? But in truth it is a parent who hates his child that forsakes him and leaves him soiled. Sometimes love is shown in ways that hurt. The same applies to children who have misbehaved. A parent must punish the child stringently in order for the child to learn to be better. It was King Solomon, the wisest of all men, who said, "He who withholds disciplining his child, hates his child." Only a parent who has total disregard for his child's welfare will allow the child to go through adolescence without being punished or without teaching him what is right and wrong, sometimes even the hard way.

The same applies to the divine punishment that serves as a means for man to be cleansed of the grime that attaches itself through the committal of sin and transgressing God's will. God who created the world was kind enough to give us an instruction manual that tells us what is good for us and what is harmful. Had he just created us to fend for ourselves, without any instruction of what is good and what is evil, He would have been cruel. One cannot just create people without telling them how to make their lives fulfilling and how to avoid self-destruction. So God gave us a Torah that instructs man what is to his benefit and what is to his detriment. If we choose to ignore his directives, then we are sometimes in need of healing.

Once I bought a computer in New York and took it to Britain. Upon arriving in Oxford I was so excited about getting it up and running that I neglected to read the enclosed manual. I plugged the computer into the wall only to see it blow up in my face. The computer could not take the 240-volt current of Europe. Had I read the manual, I would have known that. As it was, my computer was in need of serious repair and the whole experience could have been avoided.

Once a person has forsaken God's laws for life, he runs the risk of harming his godly character and is in need of rehabilitation. This is what we call punishment seemingly accomplishes. So for someone to refrain from sinning because they hear about the punishment involved is rather frivolous. One should refrain from transgressing God's commandments because it is a sin, not because it is curable. One should avoid the sin because of the damage it causes, not because it can be fixed.

Thus far we have shown the childish folly of adhering to God's code of conduct in order to avoid punishment. Now we will demonstrate how being more impressed with the punishment than the crime leads to a destructive and reckless misconception.

There seems to be a belief that where the Torah specifies a punishment for a given sin, this indicates that the sin is a grave sin, a heavy sin. And where Torah does not prescribe a punishment this seems to indicate that the sin is not very significant. Taking this line of thinking a step further, people believe that the more severe the punishment, the more significant the sin. Thus, from the dawn of time people have assumed the severity of sin as being commensurate with the prescribed punishment.

Unfortunately, the truth of the matter may be the exact opposite. When Torah stipulates a specific punishment or sin, it means to say that if you damage yourself and the world by transgressing this sin there is a method by which it can be rectified. The harm done is salvageable. But then there are certain sins for which there is no punishment because there simply is no means by which to repair the damage done. God says to us that there is no medical or surgical procedure by which to save this particular limb.

But unaware of this, most people avoid transgressing the major commandments specifically because they are the "biggies." For example, most people will avoid eating on Yom Kippur. After all, just look at what the Torah says about someone who doesn't fast on the Jewish calendar's holiest day. They receive excision (*karet*). Likewise, people try and avoid committing adultery because he who commits adultery with a married woman receives the death penalty. So people think, "Aha, this is a big sin. This is one of the heavy ones. I must be careful not to transgress this one." But, marrying a non-Jew carries no penalty in the Torah. So what people think is "Well, in that case it must not be so terrible."

But the truth is exactly the reverse. When a Jew steps totally out of the Jewish community by marrying someone outside his people, the Torah prescribes no punishment because the Torah has no prescription. The Torah seems to have no method of reinstating this individual, because in most cases his children will not grow up, or ever be, Jewish. Tragically, and often through no real fault on their part, these individuals have lost their lines of continuity.

(To be sure, with this statement we do not mean to say that those people who intermarry in today's society are censured from their people, God forbid. For anyone who marries outside of the Jewish faith today does it for no other reason than the fact that they lack the education that would teach them the beauty of Judaism and have them appreciate the vital need for the Jewish people to survive. In most cases, the individual who marries out does nothing wrong other than fall in love.

Those young Jewish individuals who intermarry in contemporary society are not rebelling against their people or their God. They simply were not given the opportunity to get acquainted with their people or their God. Thus, even after intermarriage they carry the full responsibility of being Jewish and everything that this entails. And the world's organized Jewish communities must embrace them and do their utmost to bring them closer to Judaism and their people, rather than shun them and treat them, God forbid, as if they have consciously rejected their people.

They are just as Jewish as anyone else, and it is to the discredit of modern-day Judaism that they have been mistreated in the first place. Rather, when we speak of those who are lost to their people, we refer to those individuals who have studied and been brought up with the concept of the uniqueness of the Jewish people, but hate themselves and hate their Jewishness enough to consciously and willingly distance themselves from their people by marrying out.)

In even the most deteriorating human relationship, we know that as long as there is some communication there is still a possibility for growth, change, and improvement. Many of my students complain to me that the only communication they have with their parents today is a shouting match. The parent finds fault in everything they do and they too find fault in everything their parents have to say. I tell them that still, so long as there is still screaming, there is still a relationship. It may not be an ideal relationship, it may even be ugly. But so long as the two parties still talk, a relationship still exists and the possibility for improvement remains. What is truly sad, however, is that there are parents and children who live on opposite sides of the world and never talk. They have ceased their relationship. Both are so obstinate that they refuse even to communicate. I know of someone who is thirty-seven years old, married with three children, and has not spoken to his father in twenty years. Nor has he allowed his father to see his children. Because when he was young his father forsook his mother for his secretary and destroyed the family. How can these two people ever be reconciled? There is no communication. If someone does something so severe that the other party refuses to communicate with him any longer, this is far worse than shouting matches and expressions of anger.

The Torah is constantly looking for ways to correct our misdeeds. God looks for ways for us to do *teshuvah*, to return to Him and to our communities faithfully. The Torah gives us methods of making amends and undoing the damage we have caused through our actions. The Torah is not a do-it-right-the-first-time or an all-or-nothing doctrine. Rather, the Torah is full of contingencies for us to correct the bad and start anew. Sometimes, correcting the bad will hurt, and that pain will appear as punishment, but we are still connected to our God and our people. But then there are some crimes that are so heinous that the Torah itself has nothing more to say on the subject. No punishment, no reparation is attached to the deed. But far from implying that this sin is less serious, it implies the exact opposite.

16

WHEN LEAVING THIS WORLD IS AN ACT OF KINDNESS

The importance of a commandment not being judged by its penalty applies not only to sin but to *miztvot* as well. For example, the Torah says that it is a *mitzvah* for a man to have children, but not for a woman. Based on this, the average female would be led to feel left out. Her response might be, "If it is only a *mitzvah* for my husband to have children and not for me, then I have no godly participation in the act. And since it his *mitzvah* and there is nothing in it for me, let him get on with it on his own. Why look at me? Obviously it is far more important for a man to have children than a woman, because for him there is a *mitzvah* but not for me."

But this too is superficial thinking and the very opposite is true. For a man to have children is a *mitzvah*. It is something that he is told to do and something for which he will be rewarded. But for a woman to have children is seen in *Hasidut* as being, as it were, more than a *mitzvah*. It is something so holy and significant that it does not need to be said. This is a godly act that supersedes even a *mitzvah* because it goes without even having to be said. While a comprehensive study of the spiritual differences between men and women, and hence the need for men to be commanded to have children, is outside the scope of this argument, suffice it for this example to convey how *mitzvot* that lack the promise of reward are in fact more basic and fundamental than those that do carry a promise of reward.

Returning to our earlier discussion, the fact that death can sometimes be desirable and even beneficial is not a new concept that we must embrace. There are sufficient examples in the Torah of this, and even in our daily lives. While mercy killings and euthanasia are normally prohibited by Jewish law, one is permitted, and at times even encouraged, to pray on behalf of a suffering individual that he be relieved of his misery and expire. And while this does not make death a good thing, it certainly removes it from the realm of bad and evil. An appropriate term might be necessary.

Take, for example, the death of our forefather Abraham at the "young" age of 175. Rashi notes that his son Isaac lived to the ripe old age of 180. So why did Abraham die so young?

Abraham was the man who had strived his entire life to uplift man from his base, idolatrous, and animalistic ways and achieve a proximity with God. But something went wrong. His grandson Esau did not follow his path. The pain of witnessing the evil of Esau would have been too much for Abraham. Commenting on God's promise to Abraham, "But you shall go to your fathers in peace; you shall be buried in a good old age," Rashi explains, "God announced to Abraham that Ishmael would repent in Abraham's days, and that Esau would not go forth to depravity in his days. Therefore, Abraham died five years before his time and on that very day Esau rebelled" (Genesis 15:15).

Thus Rashi explains that as an act of mercy, God plucked the life out of Abraham five years before his time so that he would not have to endure the pain of seeing his own grandson revert to the wickedness from which Abraham had tried to rid the world.

A similar and very famous example is that of the talmudic Rip van Winkle, the famous sage Honi Hamaagal, Honi the Circle-Drawer. He was called the Circle-Drawer because whenever the Jews were in need of rain he would go out into the street and draw a circle and announce to God that he would not move until it began to rain, whereupon it always would. The Talmud relates the following story:

Rabbi Yohanan said: "This righteous man Honi was throughout the whole of his life troubled about the meaning of the verse, 'A song of ascents, when the Lord brought back those that returned to Zion, we were like unto them that dream.' Is it possible for a man to dream continuously for seventy years? One day he was journeying on the road and he saw a man planting a carob tree; he asked him, 'How long does it take (for this tree) to bear fruit?' The man replied: 'Seventy years.' He then further asked him: 'Are you certain that you will live another seventy years?' The man replied: 'I found (ready grown) carob trees in the world; as my forefathers planted these for me so I too plant these for my children.'

"Honi sat down to have a meal and sleep overcame him. As he slept a rocky formation enclosed upon him and hid him from sight and he continued to sleep for seventy years. When he awoke he saw a man gathering the fruit of the carob tree and he asked him, 'Are you the man who planted the tree?' The man replied: 'I am his grandson.' Thereupon he exclaimed: 'It is clear that I slept for seventy years.' He then caught sight of his ass who had given birth to several generations of mules; and he returned home. He there inquired, 'Is the son of Honi the Circle-Drawer still alive?' The people answered him, 'His son is no more, but his grandson is still living.' Thereupon he said to them: 'I am Honi the Circle-Drawer,' but no one would believe him.

"He then repaired to the *Bet Hamidrash* and there he overheard the scholars say, 'The law is as clear to us as in the days of Honi the Circle-Drawer, for whenever he came to the *Bet Hamidrash* he would settle for the scholars any difficulty that they had.' Whereupon he called out, 'I am he.' But the scholars would not believe him nor did they give him the honor due to him. This hurt him greatly and he prayed (for death) and he died. Raba said: 'Hence the saying, Either companionship or death.'" (*Taanit* 23a)

In a similar vein, the Lubavitcher Rebbe explains that this was the argument used by Moses when pleading with God not to destroy the Jewish people after the sin of the spies. The Rebbe points out that superficially Moses' defense of the Jews is ludicrous. God comes to Moses and tells him of His plans to destroy the Jews. "How long will this people despise Me and how long will they not believe in Me, for all the signs which I have wrought among them. I will smite with the pestilence and destroy them and I will make you a greater and mightier nation than they" (Numbers 14:11–12).

One would now expect Moses to say something along the lines of "God! How could you? Do you realize that this is your beloved nation Israel? Do you realize that You are speaking here of killing millions of Your beloved people?" (Numbers 14:11–16).

But Moses says none of that. Incredibly his argument becomes, "But God, if you do that, what will the Egyptians and the other non-Jewish nations say? They will not be very impressed." To be more precise, this is Moses' response as recorded in the Torah: "When the Egyptians . . . and the nations shall hear [of the destruction] they shall say . . . 'Because the Lord was not able to bring this people into the land which He has sworn unto them, He has therefore slaughtered them, *vayish'hatem*, in the wilderness.'" Moses' defense is truly amazing. He ignores mention of any positive reason why the Jews should not be killed but rather focuses on the negative impression this slaughter will leave on the non-Jewish nations.

The Rebbe explains that Moses knew exactly what he was doing. There comes a time when the suffering one will have to endure in order to be cleansed of repeated sin is so great that it is really in the interest of the party concerned that his life be taken away from him rather than suffer such agony. Moses understood that the Jews had reached this stage. Their rebelliousness had reached the point where to be reinstated properly with God they would have to suffer terribly physically and thus God's threat to remove them from this world was actually a blessing. It would save the Jews from the terrible misery that awaited them.

That Moses understood this to be the case is indicated by his use of the word *vayish'hatem* (slaughtered), a term that is normally used only in reference to an animal. The reason for Judaism sanctioning the killing of animals so that they can be eaten is that the animal, when eaten and used by a God-fearing individual, achieves sublimity and is elevated through the subsequent divine worship that this individual undertakes thanks to the added energy gained through the flesh of the animal. The same elevation is achieved when parts of an animal are used in the creation of religious articles, such as parchment for a Torah scroll and leather for *tefillin*. Thus, the term *slaughtered* indicates, not a senseless killing, but an elevation that is undertaken for the sake of the elevation and refinement of the party concerned, albeit at a time amid pain.

Moses therefore did not plead directly for the preservation of Jewish life because he realized that this would be to the Jewish people's disadvantage. Instead, he pointed out the whole exercise would be counterproductive. God sought to punish (or cleanse) the Jews for their noncompliance with His laws amid all the miracles He had wrought on their behalf. But if He were to destroy them now, the only message that the non-Jewish nations, who also have Godly obligations by which they are bound, would extract from this is that it does not pay to serve God since he does not keep His promises. Indeed He took the Jews out of Egypt and had promised to deliver them to Israel but instead He killed them in the desert (*Likkutei Sichot*, vol. 23, *Shlach* 2). Thus we see yet another example in the Bible where physical death can be an act of mercy, although by no means will we allow the issue of suffering to rest at that.

17

"NOTHING EVIL
DESCENDS FROM
ON HIGH"

What emerges from all of the above examples is that indeed there are times when something appears as a punishment but in reality is a blessing and is designed to bring about the best possible results for the party concerned. I do not contend, based on this, that suffering is for our good nor do I maintain that man must bow his head in humble acquiescence while terrible pain is visited on humanity. Rather, by first gaining a deeper appreciation for all the issues involved in the question of suffering, we will be empowered with a far greater ability for offering a definitive response.

Thus, before any comprehensive theodicy can be offered, there must be a proper understanding of punishment. If there is something that we did that needs to be cleansed and corrected, if we need to be put back on the track, and if in order to get back on the track we must experience pain, this certainly cannot be described as bad or evil. On the contrary, it can seemingly be construed as being for our benefit. It can be construed as good.

Imagine the uninitiated coming into an operating theater for the very first time. If a person knows nothing of medical science, what impression will he get from seeing a patient tied down by hand and foot with a bunch of men wearing masks and wielding knives standing over him? Would he think that these hooded men were doing something beneficial for the patient, or would he think that they are a bunch of bandits who are disemboweling a poor prisoner? But after being enlightened that these men went to school for seven years, specialized for three years, and then studied surgery for another four years, just in order to achieve competence at saving life, one's opinion of them changes drastically. They are not bandits, they are angels of mercy.

The great hasidic master Rabbi Levi Yitzhak of Berdichev composed many songs. One of the most popular songs that he composed, which was also one of his personal favorites, was *Adudaleh*. It is a little ditty that he addresses to God. In the first part of the song he says, "Wherever I go You are there, wherever I turn you are there. I go up and it's You, I go down and it's You. I go east it's You, west it's You. Wherever I go it is You, You, You." Then, in the second part of the song he says, "When things are good it is You, and if, God forbid, things are not so good, then it is You. And as long as it is You, it is good." His point is that if it is God who is punishing us, then it is good.

It is times such as these that one must keep in mind and believe fervently that everything descends from God and thus has a purpose and design. The Almighty's purpose in causing the individual to undergo this tormenting experience is for this obstruction and torment to call forth greater powers within the individual so that he may be able to serve God on a higher plane and be cleansed of his ungodly impediments caused by sin.

Superficially, of course, this explanation seems to contradict itself. How can an obstacle to holiness, such as blaming God for the human suffering, constitute an aid in serving God? *Hasidut* therefore explains that even the tests and trials that one endures are designed to uplift the individual, for every time a person's integrity and faithfulness are tested, one must search deep within oneself and call forth the virtue and endurance that one was not even aware he possessed. And it is specifically through utilizing this newfound strength that one is able to continue on a path of serving God properly and righteously. I am not insinuating that the reason for human suffering is that we are being punished for our sins, and as our discussion develops, the main thrust of my argument and my response will become clear. But for the moment we note that at times, human sorrow can cause us to call forth ever greater powers.

The Talmud relates the famous story of Rabbi Shimon bar Yohai, author of the *Zohar* and famed disciple of Rabbi Akiva. A Jewish informant told the Romans of his slanderous remarks against the emperor and the Roman authorities, and a death sentence was passed against him. Rabbi Shimon fled with his son Rabbi Eliezer to a cave near the town of Miron. There they hid for thirteen years, during which they survived on water and carob. In all of that time, having only one change of clothes, he and his son would bury themselves in sand and study Torah together the entire day and night. The acidity of the sand burned deep holes into the body of Rabbi Shimon, which caused him terrible pain. When he emerged from the cave and was met by his colleague, Rabbi Pinhas ben Yair, the latter cried uncontrollably because of the deplorable physical state in which he found Rabbi Shimon. His tears entered the cavities in Rabbi Shimon's body and caused even more pain. Rabbi Shimon told him to stop crying. He explained to Rabbi Pinhas that as a result of these very trying experiences he had grown immeasurably in piety, learning, and holiness. "It is not terrible that you see me this way. It would have been terrible had you not seen me this way." Indeed the Talmud relates that whereas before going into the cave, Rabbi Pinhas was the superior of Rabbi Shimon in scholarship, after emerging from the cave Rabbi Shimon was able to offer twenty-four answers to each question posed by Rabbi Pinhas (*Shabbat* 33b).

Suffering causes man to search the very recesses of his soul and tap into unlimited storehouses of energy and spirit. What emerges is a human being so driven that he can even conquer suffering and use it to his advantage.

In her celebrated book, *Hasidic Tales of the Holocaust*, Yaffa Eliach tells the story of how Rabbi Israel Spira, the Bluzhover Rebbe, was sawing wood, as part of a slave-labor contingent of the notorious Janowska Road Camp. One morning, on Hoshana Rabbah, the forest was filled with terrible, heartrending cries. Rabbi Israel was informed by a fellow inmate that a children's "*Aktion*" was taking place. The piercing cries were those of the mothers of the infants and little children who were being torn from their mothers' breasts, to be slaughtered like cattle in a nearby clearing. As the procession of weeping, distraught mothers and children came closer to Rabbi Spira's labor contingent, one woman, desperately clutching her infant child to her breast, cried out, "Jews, have mercy! Give me a knife."

Rabbi Spira, believing she wished to commit suicide, tried to dissuade the woman from taking her own life. A Nazi officer approached, and, when the woman persisted in her request for a knife, extended to her a penknife he was carrying in his pocket, thinking, perhaps, that he would now enjoy some sport at the expense of this entirely distraught Jewess.

But this was not to be. Clutching the knife in her hand the woman placed her infant on the ground, and quickly circumcised her baby son. In a clear, emotion-charged voice, she recited the *milah* benediction: "Blessed art Thou, O Lord, our God King of the universe, who has sanctified us with His commandments, and has commanded us concerning circumcision."

Where in the history of humanity have we ever heard tales of such power and dignity? They seemingly can only transpire when man is called upon to exhibit the infinite part of God that is within him by overcoming the most impossible situations. The level of committment in this tale above can only be called forth during the most trying circumstances.

Therefore, while we will challenge this premise in the coming chapters, for the meantime we note that for many individuals the very recognition that beyond the shadow of any doubt God is the master and regulator of the world and controls everything that we experience can sometimes lighten the burden of the individual who must endure great pain. Even one who endures great suffering, be it suffering inflicted by man or through natural causes, must be constantly aware that there is nothing which transpires in our world outside of God's control. Since God embodies "the ultimate goodness and kindness," then everything that God does is for the good. It is impossible that God should bring about an evil occurrence without something rewarding and worthwhile waiting at the end of the tunnel.

The Talmud maintains that, "nothing evil descends from heaven." Unfortunately, however, pain and suffering do not allow us to be objective, and they render us incapable of transcending our physical limitations and keeping in mind the issues cited above. When a man undergoes terrible suffering and wishes to damn his Creator, he must at least try, to the best of his ability, to put things into perspective. And while later, as our discussion develops, I will contend that this theology of protest is the only proper Jewish response to the problem of suffering, the underlying premise behind this protest, what allows us to call out to God in the face of terrible evil and be confident that indeed He is listening is the knowledge that what He truly desires is always for our best, that God wishes for us to lead good happy lives, and therefore we must call out to Him when things go tragically wrong.

We must therefore ask ourselves, first, do we have all the necessary information to conclude that this is a bad event? There are many instances in which it appears to a human being that he is suffering, but in the final analysis he finds out how this experience has benefited him greatly. It is only that the person lacks information about his present predicament that could truly tell him that what he is presently undergoing is not suffering but indeed a blessing.

Second, even if the individual concludes that what he is undergoing is indeed suffering and punishment, he must keep in mind that this suffering that is coming upon him, God forbid, is not only a form of justice and divine retribution to recompense him for his misdeeds, but may in reality produce some beneficial results. The explanation is not only that God is just and therefore punishes man according to what he deserves. Rather, even while punishing man God still assures us that His love for us remains undiminished. The question we must ask, however, is how this is so.

But it is for this reason that the Talmud says, "Just as one must recite a blessing for the good, one must also recite a blessing for misfortune" (*Berakhot* chap. 9, *Mishnah* 5). Just as an individual understands that when something good comes his way he must thank God who is the controller of the world, out of complete joy, for the good that God has bequeathed him, likewise one must also thank God for those things that appear bad. For if one will objectively and rationally examine all the factors

involved, he will conclude that he cannot be wholly sure that
the occurrence is completely bad or evil.

Hasidut even maintains that the reason why a person cannot see the goodness hidden deep within suffering, is that it is
the kind of goodness that is so high, so lofty, and so elevated,
that it cannot reveal itself to man's limited comprehension. It
is a much higher form of good than revealed goodness and cannot be apprehended by man's constrained cognitive faculties.
As Rabbi Shneur Zalman writes in *Tanya*:

> In the Gemara it is explained that one should accept misfortune
> with joy, like the joy of a visible and obvious benefit, "For this is
> also for the good," except that it is not apparent and visible to
> mortal eyes, because it stems from the "hidden world," which is
> higher than the "revealed world," the latter emanating from the
> letters *vav* and *hai* of the Tetragrammaton, whereas the "hidden
> world" represents the letters *yud* and *hai*. [Thus the misfortunes
> are blessings in disguise, originating in the "hidden worlds."]
> Hence the meaning of the verse "Happy is the man who You, O
> God, chasten" (Psalm 94:12). Therefore, the Rabbis, of blessed
> memory, commented (*Yoma* 23a) that it is to those who rejoice
> in their afflictions that the verse refers: "But they that love Him
> shall be as the sun going forth in its might" (Judges 5:31).
> . . . Therefore the man who accepts affliction with joy merits
> to see the "Sun going forth in its might" . . . meaning that then
> the "hidden world" will be revealed and will shine and will send
> forth light in a great and intense revelation to those who have
> taken refuge in Him in this world and have taken shelter under
> his "shadow"–the shadow of wisdom. . . ." (*Tanya*, chap. 26)

Rabbi Shneur Zalman is out to emphasize that when an individual accepts in his mind that within suffering goodness is to
be found, and blesses God even for the suffering, the reward
the individual receives is that this very lofty and infinitely high
goodness reveals itself to man in his physical life to the point
where he can comprehend it and see it. Thus, the recognition
that one's suffering is a tool for God to bestow upon him goodness, which entails one calling forth great and lofty devotion
from the depths of his soul, lifts a person out of his constraints
to the point where the goodness inherent in suffering need no

longer be hidden. The individual has elevated himself to the point where he can comprehend it. By ascending the ladder and achieving spiritual heights, the individual is afforded an opportunity to glimpse the truth that lies behind the veil. Before when he saw everything in a very superficial way and was only partially devoted to God, this form of goodness transcended his grasp. Now that he has undergone the suffering and revealed within himself greater spiritual powers, he is no longer as limited and is able to digest the goodness God has waiting for him.

The Baal Shem Tov found expression for this esoteric concept of suffering being hidden goodness in the word *tzarah* itself. *Tzarah*, which means "trouble" or "suffering," contains the exact same letters as the word *tzohar*, meaning "radiance and illumination." The Baal Shem Tov explains this phenomenon to mean that an individual must find within suffering both radiance and illumination. He explained that from hurt and pain one is able to achieve a very lofty level of revealed goodness, which brightens up one's life. This ability to extract light from pain and to see a light at the end of the tunnel comes from the recognition that *tzarah* and *tzohar*, both human problems and their eventual resolution for a higher good, are from God. They are, in fact, one and the same. God's intention is that through calling forth greater strength a person will be capable of servng as a recipient of that goodness in an unconcealed manner. Thus it is absolutely essential that one constantly recognize and accept fully that God is the supreme Master of the entire world, that nothing can exist outside His unity, and that ultimately all things that God wishes for man are for his benefit.

Therefore, a virtuous person, a person who wishes to grow spiritually, emotionally, and mentally, treats pain and misfortune as tragic and sad, but not bad. The mature individual is the one who can distinguish between questions of morality and questions of subjective pain.

In reality, however, even if we are to expound the belief, as we have already at length, that suffering, although painful, is not intrinsically evil or bad, this still offers little solace or comfort to those who ache and anguish. Surely, Judaism, as a religion that has always accommodated the needs of humanity amid the obligations imposed by the Creator, can postulate a *human* response to suffering that is both sensitive and emphasizes above all else that people deserve good lives in which they experience far more joy than heartache. It is this that we are about to explore.

18

CHALLENGING GOD ON
HIS OWN TERMS

I can imagine that at this point many a reader is saying to himself that this argument might be acceptable and logical from a Jewish theological perspective. But in the real world it simply does not work and does not comfort. Are there not places like Auschwitz that can definitely be described as being not just painful, but intrinsically evil, and seem to have no redeeming factor whatsoever? How about Mengele's experiments; are they also for the good?

How do we respond to questions of this type? After all of the above, what is the definitive Jewish response to suffering? While it may indeed be true that we mortals are ignorant of the ultimate purposes of the world's events, including the reasons for tragedy and pain, and are largely oblivious to the cosmic reasons for creation, nevertheless there are those events that are unmistakably manifestations of gross and unforgivable evil. What is the Jewish response to this kind of pain?

Indeed, there are a number of modern Jewish theologians who argue that the Holocaust was a unique event without precedent in the history of human evil. They point out that other great evils have been committed in the course of war, or for self-interest. But the Nazi program of genocide actually hindered the German war effort. Troop trains were diverted from the Russian front in order to transport Jews to Auschwitz. There have been other persecutions of Jews and non-Jews killed because of their faith. But the Jews of the concentration camps were killed not because of their faith but because of the faith of their great-grandparents, whether the victims themselves held the same faith or another faith or no faith. There have been other murders but never before an attempt to implicate the victims themselves in the murders, as when the Germans set up Jewish councils in the ghettos, and the system of Kapos, to facilitate the gassing of the Jews.

The Nazis issued work permits in the camps to separate useless from useful Jews: the former to be killed immediately, the latter to be killed eventually but led to think that they would be spared. But customarily when they issued permits to an able-bodied man, they issued not one, but two: one for himself, the other to be given at his own discretion to his able-bodied mother, father, wife, or one child. The Nazis forced their victims into making the choice. In the words of one of the important theologians making this point, "I search the whole history of human depravity for comparisons. In vain. The Holocaust was unique. It was not just evil, it was evil for evil's sake" (Emil Fackenheim, *To Mend the World*).

To answer questions of this magnitude, I will now qualify everything that I have said thus far. Everything stated above applies in only one circumstance and one circumstance only: when suffering is visited upon *oneself*. But none of the above thoughts and techniques to explain suffering apply or pertain to a situation where we witness *someone else's* suffering and pain.

To explain: When misfortune comes *our* way we are obligated to rethink our deeds and find the justice in God's ways. We know ourselves. We know that we are not perfect. And we know that at times God must come along and rectify our deeds and rectify the confused godliness within ourselves that has been damaged. We must also give God the benefit of the doubt that what is happening may indeed not be suffering at all, but has positive and beneficial consequences that may only be seen at some future time. But, when something painful or sad happens to someone else, there can be only one response: to object. The authentic Jewish response to witnessing suffering of another human being is not to reconcile God with evil and postulate theodicies. Nor is it to assume that the person suffering is guilty and getting his just reward. Nor is it even to vindicate God and find reasons why God would allow such a terrible thing to happen. Rather, the only Jewish response is to scream, "Wait a minute! As far as I know this person is guiltless, so this couldn't possibly be a punishment. If it were a punishment then it would be good. But as far as I know, this person is righteous. I know that I am not. But to my knowledge this person who is suffering is totally innocent. Therefore, his suffering is not a punishment. So as far as I know there is no ground, no reason for him to be suffering. This is not a corrective measure. So this person deserves better and therefore I object! I demand that he be given a good and decent life!"

When a Jew sees another human being hurt his responsibility is to challenge God and ask Him how He can allow a good person to suffer. Humans are not supposed to accept the suffering of other people and assume that they deserve it. Human beings are *commanded by God* to alleviate suffering. If there is any possible way for us to stop suffering, then we must stop it—immediately.

And here we arrive at a uniquely Jewish response to suffering. From a truly Jewish perspective, there are two responses to witnessing another person suffering: one in relation to the person suffering, and the other in relation to God.

In relation to the person suffering, the only possible response is to do something about it. Stop the suffering. Don't sit and provide the person with reasons as to why he may be suffering, or why amid his suffering, he should still believe in God. Do something positive to alleviate his pain.

But the challenge that must be posed to God upon witnessing another's suffering is to ask God, "How could you?" Any other response that tries to reconcile either why this person is bad and deserves to suffer, or why God is good and this really isn't suffering at all, is immoral. To the person who poses theodicies that posit either of the above we ask, "Who are you? Did you create the world to understand what is and what isn't suffering? Are you the supreme judge of the universe that you are able to rule on the other person's guilt and hence his being deserving of punishment? And what's more, who are you to dignify death and suffering with an explanation? How great is your arrogance that you can rationalize something that has no tangible meaning? This person does not deserve to suffer, so stop giving meaning to those things that have no meaning."

Once I heard a man ask Elie Wiesel why the Holocaust had happened. Wiesel gave him a perplexed look as if he did not understand the question. The man repeated it. Wiesel assured him that he had heard the question the first time but couldn't understand why he had asked it in the first place. "Do you really want an answer?" he asked him. "Will it help in any way? Let's say I do provide you with an answer, will you then sleep easier tonight?" What he was saying is this: Now that you know the reason why five million Jewish adults and one million children were slaughtered will you say to yourself, "Oh! Well that's a relief. I finally know. Now I can get this whole Holocaust riddle out of my head. It's been solved."

But will the answer bring six million Jews back to life? Will it undo all the horror and monstrosities that Mengele perpetrated against Jewish twins? Will it end the pain of millions of children who saw their mothers and fathers alive for the last time aboard a cattle train? Who is so immoral that he can posit an answer to such perversions of justice? What we Jews want in the wake of the Holocaust should not be a divine explanation. Rather, we want all of those who suffered and perished to be restored.

There is an unfortunate trend growing in Orthodox Jewish circles in which many calamities, but especially the Holocaust, are interpreted as a punishment for the Jewish people's sins. This is not a new trend. Variations on this line of thought were offered immediately after the Holocaust by the Satmer Rebbe and subsequently by Rabbi Menachem Immanuel Hartom. The former said that the Holocaust was a punishment for Zionism and the will to create a Jewish national state without a messianic redeemer, while the latter said that the Holocaust was a punishment for the *lack* of Zionism, and the phenomenon of Jews becoming too smug in Germany and forgetting that they are in exile in Gentile lands. Whether or not these two lines of thinking cancel each other out is irrelevant. Of late, this mode of thought has experienced a renaissance. One of Israel's leading *yeshivah* heads gave a public lecture before the Gulf War in 1991 saying that if the Jews in the modern state of Israel don't start keeping *Shabbat*, then they run the risk of God visiting the same kind of destruction on them as that visited on the Jews of Europe during the Second World War.

Since such time, I have heard a number of Orthodox rabbis in Britain give similar speeches. It seems that many rabbis affiliated with his *yeshivah* have taken his speech as a personal license for them to propagate this repulsive message.

I will not bore the reader will all of the details of their nauseating theories, but it goes something like this: The Jews in Germany were enmeshed in assimilation and intermarriage. They considered themselves first Germans and only then, if at all, Jews. They abandoned God and His covenant. So from their cherished homeland, Germany, God had them reminded that they were Jewish in the form of horrible edicts, persecutions, and finally extermination. The Jews were punished in the worst way imaginable, but they were to blame. By discarding their Judaism they invoked the divine wrath as outlined in the portions of the Torah known as the *Tokhahah*, sections dealing with punishment.

There are many ways to refute such a theory, but I do not care to waste my time. I will, however make three short comments that are pertinent to our entire discussion.

First, from an empirical perspective the explanation is ridiculous because it ignores the true facts of who it was who suffered most and died in the Holocaust. To be sure, the Jews of Germany suffered under Hitler's regime. But fully 80 percent of all German Jews escaped extermination. They emigrated out of Germany before the extermination program began. But among those who suffered and lost their lives in the millions were the observant Jewish communities of Poland and the Soviet Union. The estimated losses for the strictly Orthodox and pious *hasidim* were well over one million. And what of the over one million innocent children who died? Factually, the Holocaust as punishment for the assimilation of German Jewry theory is rubbish.

Second, from a religious perspective it is interesting to ask who these individuals think they are helping when they propagate these thoughts. Do they believe that they are doing God a favor? Can anyone really believe that God wants to be known in such terms? Was it not God who, when asked by Moses, "Show me Your Glory, Your essence," responded, "I am full of mercy, compassion, benevolence, and long-suffering when it comes to man's iniquities"? Where in the history of apocalyptic literature is the Supreme Being characterized at His very core, His very essence, as being sensitive to the suffering of man? Is it the same God that these individuals are talking about? Furthermore, is it their opinion that what God truly desires of them is to defend Him at humankind's expense? Are these people God's defense attorneys? Are they really so arrogant or naive as to believe that what God desires of them is to condemn man while promoting Him? And what of the biblical commandment "Thou shalt love thy neighbor as thyself," whose minimal requirement, according to Hillel, translates as "That which you hate, do not do unto others." In this context it means "Just as you hate to be judged, do not judge others. Who are you to proclaim that six million victims, whom you never even met, were deserving of the fate that they received?"

Finally, from a Jewish and moral perspective, what magnitude of arrogance does it take for one human being to claim to know how guilty someone else, or even an entire generation, is? Or to know the reasons God has in bringing misfortune upon mankind? How sanctimonious and self-righteous must one be to point a finger at half the world's Jewish population and claim that they were deserving of death? What mighty opinion of oneself must one have in order to condemn God's children, His people Israel, the apple of His eye?

Here I will take the liberty to quote extensively from a public response delivered by the Lubavitcher Rebbe to the people who publicly made these assertions. It is my preference to quote the Rebbe's own words due to their deeply moving content and the eloquent emphasis they put on the need for love between all Jews, and all humans.

The following excerpts are from the Rebbe's address on the Tenth of *Tevet* and *Shabbat Parshat Vayehi* 5751:

> "God loves every Jew more than parents love an only child born to them in their old age."

This teaching of the Baal Shem Tov applies to every member of our people without distinction. Even a Jew's failure to observe the Torah and its commandments cannot detract from this love, for it is rooted in the very essence of his being and that of God, as it were. The essence of every Jew is his soul, which is "an actual part of God from above"(*Tanya*, chap. 2). This defines his fundamental personality.

A person's failure to manifest this dimension in his actual conduct does not affect this essential connection. A Jew always remains a Jew. Thus Maimonides rules that "every" Jew, even one who protests the contrary, "wants to be part of the Jewish people and desires to fulfill all the '*mitzvot*' and separate himself from sin, and it is only his Evil Inclination which forces him [to do otherwise]" (*Mishneh Torah, Hilkhot Geirushin* 2:20).

There is a yet more fundamental flaw in criticizing the conduct of one's fellow man. No person has the right to sit in judgment over his colleagues. Maimonides writes (*Mishneh Torah, Hilkhot Teshuvah* 3:2): "The reckoning [of sins and merits] is not calculated on the basis of the mere number of merits and sins, but on the basis of their magnitude as well. Some solitary merits can outweigh many sin. The weighing of sins and merits against sins."

Can any mortal presume to be capable of assessing a colleague's ultimate spiritual worth "according to the wisdom of the All-Knowing God"? This is particularly true in the present generation. In our days, a Jew whose performance of the commandments of the Torah is imperfect must be judged leniently, according to the principle of *tinok shenishba*. [In its original context, this phrase describes an individual who, for no fault of his own, was deprived of a childhood environment conducive to Torah observance (*Mishneh Torah, Hilkhot Mamrim* 3:3).] If, then, though pressured by tensions of time and place, a person does fulfill any *mitzvah*—and, of course, every Jew has numerous *mitzvot* to his credit—how dearly must it be cherished in the Heavenly Court?

Looking at all our fellow Jews with a favorable eye is in place especially now, for our generation is "a firebrand saved from the blaze"(Zechariah 3:2), the smouldering remnant preserved from the horrors of the Holocaust. After so many of our people have perished, we must try to appreciate—and in this manner, help reveal—the positive that "every" Jew possesses.

This potential is enhanced by the luminous legacy bequeathed to us by the martyrs of the previous generation. Our Sages (*Pesa-*

him 50a) teach that the very fact that a person dies *"al Kiddush Hashem"* (in sanctification of God's Name), elevates him to such a level that "no creature can stand in his presence." Thus, every man and woman who died in the Holocaust is a holy martyr.

Accordingly, to say that those very people were deserving of what transpired, that it was a punishment for their sins, heaven forbid, is unthinkable. We cannot "explain" the Holocaust, for we are limited by the earthbound perspective of mortal understanding. As God says, in a prophecy of Isaiah, "For My thoughts are not your thoughts" (*Yeshayahu* 55:8). *No scales of judgment could ever condemn a people to such horrors.* The Torah promises that "[God] will avenge the blood of His servants" (*Devarim* 32:43), indicating that the death of these martyrs is against His will. On the contrary, God is "the Master of mercy." It is blasphemous to picture Him as a cruel King who punishes His people for their disobedience and then waits until it mounts again to the point at which it is fitting to punish them again.

The very opposite is true. As our Sages say (*Bereishit Rabbah* 68:4), "What does God do since creation?—He arranges marriages," that is, He is involved in bringing joy and happiness to mankind, establishing families, "eternal structures" which produce ongoing joy in future generations.

We must seek to emulate this conduct and try to spread happiness among Jews, reaching out to all our brothers, regardless of their level of observance. In this manner, hopefully, "one will be able to draw them close to the Torah and the service of God, and even if one fails [in this goal], one has not forfeited the merit of loving one's neighbor." (*Tanya*, chap. 32).

This is the direction in which we should focus our efforts, for, as our Sages taught (*Shabbat* 31a), "The totality of the Torah is"— not to criticize, to chastise, nor to threaten with Divine retribution, but rather—"to love your neighbor as yourself" (*Vayikra* 19:18). Furthermore, as mentioned above, brotherly efforts in reaching out to our fellow Jews are meeting with ever-increasing success, and thousands are awakening to *teshuvah*, to repentance, and discovering their Jewish roots.

Our Sages explain that, at the time of the ultimate Redemption, God will ignore the sins of the Jews and redeem them in His mercy.

Indeed, the Rebbe makes a compelling argument. How could people be so immoral as to justify someone else's suffering? If it was a case such as the Egyptians where God afflicts them with ten plagues and specifies in the Torah that this was punishment for their imprisonment of the Israelites, that would be fine for them to elaborate on the reason for Egyptian suffering. God, the Master of the Universe, revealed to us the reason for their suffering. There is no room for speculation. But has God revealed to these Rabbis and theologians the reason for the torture and wholesale slaughter of six million Jews?

A *New York Times* report stated that Dr. Mengele was accused in absentia of the following crimes: selection of prisoners for immediate gassing; the throwing of live children into fires; conducting medical experiments on living prisoners by injecting their eyes, spines, and brains with camphor and other chemicals; shooting children in order to perform autopsies on them; exposing healthy prisoners to yellow fever and extreme X-ray radiation for study; sterilizing and castrating prisoners; draining the blood of children for study; and cutting off body parts of female prisoners for tissue cultures.

These clerics and theologians who maintain that the Holocaust was a divine punishment claim that Jews whom they never met and who for all they know were far more righteous than themselves, and who finally bear the title "*kadosh*" (holy), because they died because of their Jewishness, were nevertheless so sinful that they deserved all of these grotesque horrors. Is this the kind of response God desires from man upon witnessing such injustice?

Definitely not. This type of grotesque arrogance has no place in the humility that God requires the man of faith to exhibit. The unquestionable Jewish response to other people's suffering is what we shall continue to present in the upcoming chapters.

19

IN THE TRADITION
OF ABRAHAM:
THE OBLIGATION
TO AFFIRM LIFE

I n one of my first weeks at the helm of the Chabad House in
Oxford and the Oxford University L'Chaim Society, I was
having the traditional *Shabbat* dinner with a group of students from the university when the subject of the Holocaust
came up. I stated my position on the subject, much to the amaze-
ment and disappointment of some of the Orthodox students
sitting at the table. I said that I cannot understand, nor will I
accept, why God allowed the murder of six million Jews. I
vociferously object, and I encouraged them as students to
object, to the catastrophe that had been visited on our people.
I said that any attempt to justify the Holocaust from a Jewish
perspective was grossly immoral.

A heated debate ensued. In the midst of the discussion, three
Orthodox students got up to leave. Clearly indignant, they asked
me how I could question God's judgment and His ways? How
could I refuse to accept God's deeds? They said they could not
tolerate blasphemy in any form, let alone from an Orthodox
rabbi. I halted their words and responded.

"Blasphemy?" I asked. "If questioning God in response to
other people's calamities and misfortunes constitutes blas-

phemy, then Abraham, Moses, the prophet Jeremiah, and the ministering angels in heaven were all blasphemers as well!" They sat down again. I began to explain.

Where do we get the idea of objecting, of challenging God's justice, when confronted by other people's suffering? What makes this the authentic Jewish response to tragedy? It began with the first Jew—Abraham.

The Greeks embraced the concept of tragedy, whereby man is victim of some unseen power that foredooms him to disaster; as Sophocles says, "Awful is the mysterious power of fate. Pray not at all, since there is no release for mortals from pre-destined calamity." The Jews have always appealed against catastrophe and calamity, asking God how He could conceal His kindness and vent His wrath?

The Book of Genesis relates very clearly how God came to Abraham before He destroyed the cities of Sodom and Gemorrah. God said, "Shall I hide from Abraham what I am going to do? Abraham is about to become a great and mighty nation, and through him all of the nations of the world will be blessed."

So God discloses to Abraham His intention to destroy Sodom and all of its inhabitants. "The outcry against Sodom is so great, and their sin is so very grave." Not only have they sinned but their immoral lifestyle poses a threat to all of the surrounding cities. Hence, they must suffer and be obliterated, lest they serve to influence the outlying areas in their immoral ways.

Now, how does Abraham react? The most upright and moral human being on earth, the man who abandoned idolatry and introduced to the world the concept of monotheism has just been told that on a hill not far from where he dwells is an evil inhabitance. This evil inhabitance threatens to undermine everything Abraham has accomplished in terms of elevating the world, promoting monotheism, and bringing people closer to God. This city is a bad influence on his child (and future children). It is just plain evil. Its inhabitants are corrupt and base. So God is going to put an end to this cancer. Does Abraham see this as a victory for himself? Does he say, "Blessed be God who is destroying the wicked. O God please vanquish, punish, and annihilate those who oppose Your ways"?

No. He has the audacity to argue with God. He asks *"How*

could you, how could you? Far be it from You to do such a thing, to slay the righteous with the wicked, so that the righteous fare as the wicked. Far be it from Thee! Shall the whole world's Judge not act justly?" And so he stood and sparred with God, pleading with Him to spare the city's inhabitants.

The question on this episode is this: There are those people who do not believe that when the city is destroyed, God is behind it. Thus, they call it a bad thing. Maybe it's random, maybe it's a product of some evil force at work, but it is still evil. But Abraham certainly knew that God was behind the destruction of Sodom. God Himself told Abraham, "I am going to do it. It is not a freak accident, I am doing it. I've thought it over. I have my reasons and I am going to destroy the city." But in spite of this Abraham asks, "How could You?"

Now, where was Abraham's faith? In truth, he did not even require faith in this particular circumstance. God spoke to him directly and told him that He was going to punish Sodom. Shouldn't Abraham have thought that God is just and knows what He is doing? Wouldn't this have been a greater virtue than to challenge God? And how could the Torah, in telling us about the prototype for the Jewish people, the ideal Jew, how he served God and how we must learn from his examples, disclose to us that Abraham did not trust God's judgment?

What is even more puzzling is that later in the Torah when God comes to Abraham and tells him, "Abraham . . . Take your son, the only one you love—Isaac—and go away to the Moriah area. Bring him as a burnt offering on one of the mountains that I will designate to you," here Abraham offers no resistance whatsoever. God has just told him that he must put his own son, a young innocent man, to death, and how does Abraham react? "And Abraham got up early in the morning and saddled his donkey" (Genesis 22:2-3). Not only does he execute the command, but he does so enthusiastically. He gets up early! He performs God's request with zest and humility. But what happened to justice? Why not object to the command to end the life of your only son? Abraham can object to the destruction of Sodom but not to that of his own son?

What we can extract from this episode is: God is in control of everything, and just as the Berditchever says, as long as it is

You, O God, who is in control of what is happening, then the event must be good. But all of this only applies if some misfortune is befalling oneself. Thus, when God tells Abraham that he has a tragedy coming his way in the form of the death of his son, Abraham submits and accepts it. But if it is happening to someone else our reaction must be that although we believe that God is good, and although we know that God is causing this misfortune and that God certainly has his reasons, nevertheless we are commanded by God to pursue justice. And justice cannot be pursued on a level of faith.

God commands man in the most emphatic of terms, "Justice, Justice shall you pursue" (Deuteronomy 16:18). In order to have justice, one must have proof. Thus, for a human being, who is not all-knowing, to accept that something dreadful is happening in Sodom and not have this bother him because he has faith in God, is an insufficient and flawed response. As far as faith, his faith is perfect, but where is his pursuit of justice? God may have his reasons and thus for God it is just to afflict Sodom. But where is this person's justice? Where is his evidence that the people of Sodom are deserving of this punishment and that what is happening is just and good?

God's commandment to man is to establish justice, and always to promote life, not to trust that God is just. The question of God's justice is a non sequitur. Of course He is just. But this is not the issue. Are we just? is the real question. Where is our concern for another human being? God created us with a mind and a heart and told us to pursue justice until we actually achieve justice. God did not instruct us to believe that He is just. When it comes to issues of life and death God wishes for us to affirm life and challenge those who would deny it. God is the Judge of the earth. He requires no helpers. But He does expect to concern Himself only with an affirmation of life.

Thus, immediately at the beginning of our history, it was established that everything that transpires is by a divine plan. God is behind it. There are no two Gods. We are not Greeks who believe in good gods and bad ones. Neither are we Christians who believe that there are evil forces, such as Satan, who are outside of God's jurisdiction. We believe that God is fully in control. But even as we retain the faith that God knows what

He is doing, we object to what we cannot see or prove to be moral.

Here, in effect, we come across the idea of dual roles or purposes. There are times when equally valid and appropriate roles actually conflict without invalidating each other. Rather, each party has a different role to play. For instance, in the parent-child relationship, it is the duty of the child to remain a child, and it is the duty of the parent to discipline the child and try to get him to behave better. So the parent runs around correcting the child, getting angry at him for making a mess, and writing on the walls. But if the child were to stop behaving as a child, if he were to suddenly just sit around doing nothing and acting like an adult, the parent would become terrbily worried. She would take him to the doctor and ask him what is wrong with her child. And what parent would be happy with a child who behaves like an adult at the age of seven? So although her role of disciplining the child and his role of running amok and being naughty conflict, both are not only acceptable but proper.

In effect God says to us, "I am the Creator of the universe and I have a job to do. I give life and I take life. I give health and I deny health. I am the Master of the world and there will be times when I will be taking someone else's life. I may take somebody's happiness or their health. And when I do any of these things, I want you and your consenting and loyal opinions of me to stay out of it. I don't need your help. Don't doubt that I am doing it, and don't doubt that I know what I'm doing and that what I'm doing is just. But stay out of these deliberations. They are my domain.

"On the other hand when I give life," God says, "when I distribute health and happiness, here I invite you to join Me. Assist Me in bestowing goodness." This is the correct definition of good and evil. A bad thing is anything we do in which God forbade our participation. God said that He is in control of death, we dare not assist Him. On the other hand, a good thing is anything we do in which God enjoins us to participate. So doing a *mitzvah* like giving charity and enhancing another's life is good. But stealing and detracting from someone else's livelihood or causing our fellow human sorrow, grief, or pathos is a sin.

Moses is told by God on the occasion of the Jews building a

golden calf in the desert, "I have observed this people, and they are a stubborn, unbending group. Now, do not try to stop Me when I unleash My wrath against them to destroy them. I will make you into a great nation." Does Moses comply? God Himself has told Him that the Jews deserve destruction, and He has even told Moses to refrain from defending them and objecting to God's intention. But what does Moses do? And here I must get personal. Every year when this portion of the Bible is read, I get goose bumps, for the ensuing words of Moses constitute the single most eloquent defense of human life recorded in the Bible. Moses stands his ground. He is not prepared to let the Jews die without a fight. He stands tall and argues with his Creator. His mission is to save the Jews, and at this he will not fail. "Moses began to plead before God his Lord. He said, 'O God, why unleash Your wrath against Your people, whom you brought out of Egypt with great power and a show of force . . . withdraw your display of anger, and refrain from doing evil to Your people.'" Subsequently Moses uses even stronger tactics to elicit a pardon from God on behalf of the Jewish people. "Moses went back to God, and he said, 'The people have committed a terrible sin by making a golden idol. Now, if you would, please forgive their sin. If not, then blot me out from the book [the Torah; Rashi on Exodus 32:32] which you have written.'" Where in the history of divine literature do we ever have a human who asks the Almighty to be purged from His own book because he wishes to be disassociated from a God who is not forgiving and loving?

What kind of audacity does it take on the part of a mortal being to blackmail God? How could Moses object to God's judgment when God comes to him and warns him, "Do not try and stop me" from destroying the Jews? How could Moses rebel against God?

The answer to this critical question is in the directive itself. The Talmud (*Berakhot* 32) notes that God tells Moses "Do not try and stop me [alternative translation: Leave me alone]" before Moses even opened his mouth in defense of the Jewish people. In the words of Rashi, "We have not yet heard that Moses prayed for them yet He says, 'Let me alone.' However, here He opened a door for Moses and informed him that the matter depended upon him, that if he will pray for them, He will not exterminate them." In other words, what God was saying to Moses was this: My responsibility is to punish and cleanse those who are deserving. But you Moses, why are you just sitting there listening to all of this? Why haven't you opened your mouth to protest my planned destruction of the Jewish people? As a human being you have an entirely different responsibility than Me. You must affirm life, not your acceptance of my judgment. The Jews need an advocate. Plead for them.

The idea of responding to suffering in the form of protest and challenging God's judgment is found again in the Talmud in relation to Moses. Commenting on Moses' request of God, "I beseech You to show me your glory," the Talmud explains that what Moses was asking was "Why are there righteous people who suffer?" Likewise at the destruction of the first Temple, the prophet Jeremiah asks God, "Why do the wicked prosper?" (*Berakhot* 7a). Even among the ministering angels there is a tradition of challeging God in the face of human suffering. One of the most famous examples of this is to be found in our Yom Kippur prayer books in the story of the Ten Saintly Martyrs who were put to death by the Roman emperor. After the horrific murder of Rabbi Yishmoel the High Priest, in which the skin of his face was flayed off, we read, "The heavenly angels cried out in bitter grief: Is this the Torah and such its reward! O You who enwraps Yourself with light as with a garment, the foe blasphemes Your great and awesome Name, scorns and desecrates the words of the Torah."

Therefore, a person may not hold a gun and think to himself, "Since God is the master of the universe and nothing transpires outside His will, therefore if my intended victim dies after I pull the trigger, it will be God's will. So there is nothing wrong with me shooting at him." This kind of thinking is wrong. But it is wrong not because one might kill a person who was *not* meant to die, but rather because one might kill a person who *is* meant to die—and that is a sin. Death is one of those areas that are totally in God's domain. It is His affair and not ours. Our business is life.

Can one imagine a patient being brought before a religious, God-fearing doctor and the doctor refusing to treat him on the grounds of "Let God decide. First, if God wants this person to be sick, then who am I to question God's judgment or reverse His will. Obviously, this person must be a sinner and is receiving his just reward. Second, if God wishes the patient to die, then at the end of the day all of my efforts will be in vain. And if He does not wish him to die, then my efforts are not even needed. Therefore I refuse to treat him." This doctor is not only a lunatic, but is grossly immoral and acts in contradiction to God's will. If someone is sick and there is a possibility of healing him, we are commanded by God to *run* to heal him, not to engage in theological polemic. And if one is to ask "Who are we to interfere with God's plan?" in this half of God's plan we are not only invited, but obligated, to interfere. We must offer a cure. The duty and obligation for doctors to heal is a godly obligation, not just a concession. And our responsibility as humans is not to focus on the success of our efforts. Even if it appears that a patient has little or no hope of living, we must still endeavor to save them, for God never told us to be successful at saving lives, but rather *to concern ourselves* with the saving of life.

Interestingly, the Torah instructs man, "Do not stand by when your friend's blood is being shed" (Leviticus 19:16). But the literal translation is "Do not stand in his blood," as if the blood had already been shed. What this is telling us is that it is very possible that one may come across a person whose blood has already been shed, a person who is destined to die for some divine cosmic reason. His blood is already shed, theoretically. Yet even then we have a commandment of not standing in his blood. We cannot be passive and allow him to die even when his death is preordained. One must object to this individual's death even though one is a believer and accepts that no one dies before their time. One must object as did our forefather Abraham. Indeed God may of course know what He is doing, but until we see an intelligible reason for why this individual is dying, one must try to prevent it from happening. One must attempt to heal, pray, and plead on his behalf.

Challenging God for the pain He causes human beings is not a contradiction to faith. Rather, it enforces the belief that everything emanates from and is dependent on God. It is much like the obligation to pray whose central premise, according to Maimonides, is that man acknowledge his total dependence on God. Maimonides maintains that the obligation to pray to God arises every time man is in need of physical sustenance. In this way man comes to recognize that it is God that controls His world, and it is to Him that man must pay homage. In the same way, challenging and asking God to rescind the suffering caused to humans acknowledges that all things come from God, the good and the bad, and it is to Him and to Him only that supplications must be offered.

The story is told that in the early years of the Baal Shem Tov, the great master would devote almost all of his time to traveling around the Russian countryside asking unlearned Jewish peasants how they were doing. They would respond, *"Barukh Hashem*–However we are, we thank God." Eliciting this response from the simple Jewish countryfolk was the Baal Shem Tov's purpose from the beginning. He would travel all over Russia just to get a simple Jew to say *Barukh Hashem*. And why all the effort? "Because," the Baal Shem Tov explained, "God has no greater pleasure than hearing the heartfelt, sincere, and straightforward proclamation of faith on the part of a simple, yet devout and pious Jew." The statement of *Barukh Hashem*– the acknowledgment on the part of the individual that for good or for bad, it is God who controls the world–these are the things that God wishes to hear most.

In effect, when we do challenge God and demand that He rescind His decrees, we are not introducing any new concepts of justice and forcing God to conform to our standards of morality and fairness. Rather, what we are saying to Him is this: It was You who told us about the obligation to "love your fellow as yourself." And it was You who taught us to be sensitive even to animal suffering as in the commandment that before one removes the eggs from a nest, one must first send away the mother bird so as not to grieve her. And it was You who taught us always to feel the pain of an orphan and a widow, as well as make a convert feel at home. And it was You who taught us not to stand idly by the sick but to engage in medical practice so as to heal them. And it was You who obligated us to always be responsive in large quantity to the poor and destitute. *Should You, then, not do the same!*

Was it not You who described Yourself, at Your very essence as being, "merciful and kind, slow to anger, with tremendous resources of love and truth. He remembers deeds of love for thousands of generations, forgiving sin, rebellion, and error." Was it not You who described Yourself as the one who listens to the poor workman who has given away his only cloak as a security for a loan? Should you then not listen to our pleas for this poor soul who languishes in pain and misery? In other words, we are obliging God to keep to the standards and practices that He instituted as special and sacred.

What was Abraham's attitude to God after the city of Sodom had been destroyed? He had begged, pleaded, and bargained on their behalf. Was Abraham's faith shaken by what had happened? Certainly not. His response was *"Barukh dayan emet"* (Blessed is the true judge). This response, which has traditionally been recited by Jews upon hearing evil tidings, acknowledges that ultimately it is only God who knows what is right and what is wrong.

But if this was Abraham's response after the event, why did he not spare himself the effort of arguing in the first place? Instead of challenging God's justice and then, after the event, affirming his belief in divine justice, why not just say *Barukh dayan emet* when he first heard of God's plans to punish the guilty and forget about the whole affair? If indeed Abraham had that much faith in God's goodness, then why did he save it for the end?

It has to do with obligations, as we mentioned earlier. The Jew challenges God's intention because this is what God requires of him. God wants us to affirm life. And so long as there is any possibility of enhancing life and alleviating suffering we are obligated to do whatever is in our ability to achieve those ends. If there is a possibility that this person can be saved, that this person can be healed, that this person can be cured, that this situation can be salvaged, then we must save whatever can be saved. But after the fact, once we see that nothing more can be done, we must accept God's ultimate judgment, fairness, and wisdom and recite *Barukh dayan emet.* Once things are over and done with, we are no longer obligated, we no longer have the *mitzvah*, to try and stop what is happening because it is already done. One cannot salvage, one cannot cure, the victim is already dead. The *mitzvah* is no longer available to us. Here it is time to leave things in God's hands and affirm His justice and how everything He does is somehow for the best. Because death, destruction—anything that is outside the realm of life—is none of our business. It is God's domain. It is now time, not to challenge the Almighty, but to attempt to find comfort in Him.

So Abraham tries to do whatever he can to save Sodom. He begs God, "Let my Lord not become angry and I will speak once more," and then once again, and again. He gallantly takes to court the Supreme Master of the Universe and tells him that the destruction of Sodom is not just. But once he has done everything within his ability, once Abraham has exercised his full capacity for defense and the affirmation of light, "Abraham then returned home." Once he had discharged his obligation, Abraham returned home with the full confidence that he had done everything within his ability and now it was time to put one's trust in God that whatever would happen would be just and fair. Abraham now looked for solace in the One, true, and loving God who desires what is best for the earth's inhabitants.

We find King David reacting the same way when his first son with Bat Sheva lay deathly ill. David had fasted, wept, pleaded, and prayed to God on behalf of the child. But the moment the child died, it all changed.

> When David saw the servants whispering, he said to them, "Is the child dead?" And they said, "He is dead." And David rose and washed and changed his clothing and asked that food be set before him, and he ate. The servants said to him, "What is this that you are doing? You fasted and wept for the child when he was alive, and now that he is dead, you get up and eat?" And David said, "While the child was yet alive, I fasted and wept, for I said, 'Who knows whether the Lord will be gracious to me and the child will live?' But now that he is dead, why should I fast? Can I bring him back? I shall go to him; but he will not return to me." (2 Samuel 12:19-23)

20

DEATH:
THE FINAL CHALLENGE

I have always been startled by those who seek to dignify death and suffering with explanations and rationalizations. Unfortunately, all too often those who do so tend to be members of the clergy. The rabbi or priest is under the impression that his main responsibility to his community in the face of tragedy or pain is to provide comfort by offering cosmic whys and wherefores. "We cannot understand the ways of God, but we must still believe that everything that God does is for our best." "You will be strengthened by this experience, you will emerge a better person." Remarks of this nature sound all too familiar for anyone who has paid a pastoral visit in the wake of a family disaster. But is religion really that insensitive? Does religion lend dignity to suffering by explaining the positive consequences that may arise from misfortune, or maintain that man, in his destitute lowliness, has no right to complain against or even question God as to why he suffers? Are those who seek to dignify suffering with explanations really so confident that they are correct in doing so? Are they sure that there in fact is a reason for suffering? Or is it possible that suffering is no more than an aberration that must be rooted out by man to the best of his ability? And is it possible that every time we do dignify suffering with explanations, we serve only to dissuade ourselves from our true mission? Instead of seeing suffering as an aberration that must be abolished, should we lend it credibility by accommodating its presence, perhaps even its necessity, in the larger scheme of creation?

There is a story that Theodor Herzl, the father of modern-day secular Zionism, approached the Kaiser, the leader of the Austro-Hungarian Empire, who granted him a private audience at the turn of the century. He told the Kaiser his idea of building a Jewish national homeland in Palestine. The Kaiser started laughing and said, "In order for that to happen, you would need three world empires to fall." The first was the Ottoman Empire, which controlled Palestine prior to World War I; the second was the German Empire, which guaranteed Palestine for the Lutheran Church; the third was Czarist Russia, which guaranteed Jerusalem for the Eastern Orthodox Church. But seventeen years later all of those empires had disintegrated. These Jews held the belief that they could somehow reconstitute themselves as an independent entity.

As I write this chapter, a great leader of the Jewish people, Rabbi Menachem Schneerson, the Lubavitcher Rebbe, is in a New York hospital fighting for his life. The Jewish people have always refused to accept seemingly inevitable situations, choosing instead to forge their own destiny against the highest odds. I found it astonishing, therefore, that so many leading Jewish publications, including anglo-Jewry's principal newspaper, *The Jewish Chronicle*, should print a series of articles on their front pages making the extraordinary, scandalous statements that the health of the Lubavitcher Rebbe is worsening and that "the family of Lubavitch" was counseling its members to cope in a post-Rebbe world. Not only are these claims inaccurate but the tone of the articles is in direct opposition to the traditions of Judaism.

As we have stated elsewhere, whereas Christianity advocates acquiescence and faith above all else, and the word *Islam* literally translates as "submission to the will of God," *Yisrael* means "he who wrestles with God." In the same way that Abraham pleaded with God for the lives of the inhabitants of Sodom and Gomorrah, and in the same way that Moses refused to accept that the Israelites should be obliterated for their building of the Golden Calf, as religious Jews we follow their example by challenging fate and praying for the Rebbe's recovery.

The Rebbe's loving followers, Lubavitcher *hasidim* the world over, have been extensively criticized by friends and foes alike for speaking confidently of his recovery, rather than making preparations for his succession. They contend that the Lubavitch movement is living in a dreamworld, and that by neglecting the world of reality their movement will suffer from lack of preparation for what is inescapable. Thus, a movement that has carried the flame and hope in a messianic awakening, in a perfect world free from death and suffering, is being criticized for not making peace with death, for not humbly submitting to its inevitability, like all realists throughout time. But how can we account for the tremendous phenomenon of human progress and achievement if not for the belief that mankind, against all probability, could make their world better? When President John F. Kennedy spoke in 1961 of landing a man on the moon before the end of the decade, he was laughed at in an age when even commercial airline flights were still in their infancy. But a team of dedicated scientists and researchers, believing that nothing was impossible, set forth to translate that dream into reality. And they succeeded. Should we as *hasidim* be no less dedicated? Is eternal life really an impossibility, and is death the one facet of life to which we must all eventually bow our heads in humble submission?

Surely a much better reaction to the Rebbe's ill health would be for the Jewish people to collectively beseech the Creator for the recovery of a man who has almost single-handedly sparked global Jewish revival, bringing untold millions of Jews to a greater degree of observance and giving them pride in their identity and traditions. Rather than indulging in speculation about the Rebbe's succession, should we not appreciate a remarkable leader every moment that he is in our midst? This is what the members of Lubavitch are doing. We do not sit idly pontificating as to who might be next in line, having passively accepted that this special and irreplaceable man will die. I say irreplaceable because we relate to the Rebbe not as an office or an institution, such as the presidency of the United States, but as an *individual*. And no person is ever replaceable. Rather, in keeping with the pillars of our faith, we continue to affirm life, confronting destiny and thundering against the heavens.

In the movie *Shadowlands*, which is close to my heart, having watched it being filmed just three blocks from my house over a period of six months, we see the celebrated Oxford author C. S. Lewis first embracing a position whereby suffering is necessary in order to discern between that and true happiness. His dying wife, played by the Jewish actress Debra Winger, tells him that the happiness they experience together now, the fact that she is alive and they are married, is directly dependent on the impending tragedy of her death. He accepts this position so long as she is alive. But as soon as she dies, the once submissive Lewis, who was a lifelong apologist for Christianity and was filled with prayers to the heavens prior to his wife's demise, is angry and can no longer be comforted by religious platitudes. When his friend, a doctor of divinity at Magdalen College, tells him that now is the real trial of faith, and that surely God allowed his wife to die for a purpose—"How dare we question God, and who are we, with our limited intelligence and understanding, to claim that we understand the divine"—the heretofore accepting Lewis shouts and orders the minister to be silent. He swings his cudgel at the thought that God could somehow desire someone's death, especially a good person who has caused no harm to anyone.

I sympathize entirely with this response, not because the aggrieved Lewis was understandably pained at the time and was thus incapable of quiet submission to the will of God at that moment, but rather because his wife should have remained alive. There was no reason whatsoever for her death. Suffering and death have no rightful place in our world, not according to the Bible, nor in Jewish thought. Who is the cleric, then, who is so sanctimonious, so insensitive, and so arrogant as to dismiss the death of someone else's relative in the belief that it carried with it a cosmic reason when the Creator himself says there is none (as we are shortly to explore)? In the aforementioned scene, it is the aggrieved Lewis who epitomizes the proper theological response to the question of suffering. The cleric displays nothing but self-assured arrogance. He fails in his calling as a cleric to inspire a collective humanity to work together toward destroying and uprooting suffering from our midst for all eternity.

To be sure, Judaism has always had a different approach to suffering than most other world religions, and I am probably being very unfair to the aforementioned cleric since his words and approach are in keeping with his tradition. Christianity advocates and emphasizes that faith and obedience are the central tenets of the Christian faith. Man has no right to challenge God and must upon experiencing terrible suffering bend his head in humble resignation. It has always been the Jewish tradition to wrestle and grapple with God, rather than to bend one's head in capitulation. The Jew has never made peace with suffering. As the bearer of a two thousand–year-old belief in the coming of a perfect messianic age, the Jew knows at the core of his being that suffering must and will be defeated. He refuses to accord death any latitude in his thought or life. Rather, he cries out to God to keep his promise to abolish death from the earth, and to restore to life those who have already died. It was God who promised that "death shall be defeated." It behooves every human being to dedicate every moment of our lives to a two-pronged effort to abolish all forms of affliction, rather than sink our precious time and energy into trying to fathom the reason for suffering. First, we must endeavor our utmost and exhaust every available opportunity to find a cure for suffering. We must give time, resources, and money to charity. We must give time to our fellow man. We must dedicate ourselves to medical and scientific research. We must institute better safety procedures to protect humans from misfortune. We must do everything humanly possible to find a cure for disease, and to create peace between nations who are at war. In the words of the Mishnah, we must "be like the students of Aaron. We must love peace and pursue peace" (*Ethics of Our Fathers*, chap. 1). Second, for those things that transcend a human capacity to fix—diseases that cannot be cured, wars that cannot be stopped, accidents that cannot be prevented—we must cry out to our Creator and demand that He bring an end to this suffering and give us what we all deserve—prosperous, joyous, and happy lives. Lives that are good not just in the spiritual sense but also in the physical sense.

It was specifically the less Orthodox, and in many cases completely nonobservant, Jews, who constituted the pioneering Zionists who built the State of Israel, the correct response to the terrible tragedy of the Holocaust. While many more observant and traditional Jews grappled with the problem of how to explain the suffering of the Holocaust within a traditional framework, a multitude of less observant Jews, many of whom were atheists, rejected any theological justification or self-blame and set themselves to work even harder toward the creation of a Jewish state. Although they were not religious, the exposure that they had to three thousand years of Jewish thought rubbed off on them in a magnificent way. They understood almost intuitively that the only authentic Jewish response to suffering was not to attempt to understand it, but to wage war against it. They did not sit and pontificate as to why God had allowed so many innocent millions to die, but rather built a state that would ensure Jewish lives. They fortified an army that would defend the Jewish masses against anti-Semitism and aggression. I applaud their efforts, and we are all deeply indebted to all of those brave and heroic Israeli soldiers who have defended and continue to defend our people so gallantly over the past half-century.

Similarly, I would contend that it is specifically the doctor who sits late at night in search of a cure for AIDS who has done more to advance the Jewish response to suffering than the rabbi who tells us either to submit to the inevitability of death, or even worse, that AIDS is a divine punishment for sexual immorality and promiscuity. I once heard a lecture in Australia delivered by one of the ablest rabbinical speakers in the world. The lecture took place in the mid-1980s, and the questions afterward turned to the AIDS epidemic. When asked by one of the listeners if the rabbi felt AIDS to be a divine curse against a sexually active generation, he stunned me with his response: "Who says it has to be a curse? In my opinion it is a blessing." While some of the members of the audience applauded, a whole stream of people immediately walked out. He thoroughly alienated many members of his audience. This story is especially tragic because the average person uninitiated in Jewish thought or law will automatically assume that this is an authoritative Jewish view on the subject and the way in which Orthodox Judaism deals with human suffering. But his words contradict everything that Judaism stands for in the form of a good, loving, long-suffering God who asks His creatures to emulate His mercy and compassion.

My enthusiasm for this position is no less diminished by the vanity of many of the doctors involved in the search for the cure for AIDS and cancer. I can personally attest to the fact that some of Oxford's leading researchers, who are at the forefront in finding a cure for AIDS, might be doing so more out of a desire to win a Nobel Prize than to serve the cause of humanity. Yet even these scientists are more in tune with the biblical response to suffering than many observant Jews who do not cry out for a messianic age and have reconciled themselves to the fact that there will always be lethal diseases, and that there will always be people who have to die, in both early and advanced age.

In this respect, I am in sharp disagreement with those who seek to explain the suffering of the Rebbe in terms of a cosmic necessity for the longed-for Messiah to suffer, or to be written off by the Jewish people prior to his revelation. Chabad houses around the world have recently received faxes sent from one to the other that quote, among others, the explanation given by the great German rabbi Samson Raphael Hirsch to the story of Jacob on his deathbed blessing his sons, as recorded in the last few chapters of the Book of Genesis. Rabbi Hirsch explains that only when the actual coffin of the Messiah is being built and his death is imminent will he then rise and redeem himself. There have been other quotations circulated by Chabad thinkers and emissaries, such as that by Nachmanides, that suggest something very similar.

But leaving aside the question of whether or not the Lubavitcher Rebbe is the hoped-for Messiah, and certainly he possesses many of the qualifications to be proclaimed as such, how dare we dignify the Rebbe's suffering with explanations? Who are we to say that the misery and misfortune that has been visited upon the Rebbe of late, what with horrific seizures, strokes, and (temporary) blindness, has any higher purpose? To be sure, if it turns out that the Rebbe is the Messiah, we will overlook all of this ephemeral pain. But is God not infinitely powerful and wise? Can He not usher in the messianic era in a manner that will not necessitate shocking unpleasantness first being endured by the righteous of the generation?

I believe that we have done the Rebbe a great injustice by explaining away his suffering, and especially by describing it as a piece in a larger messianic puzzle. Worse still, we of all people, Lubavitcher *hasidim*, have not remained loyal to the overall Jewish, and specifically hasidic, tradition of never making peace with suffering, and never accepting theological explanations that will justify another human's pain. How dare we as the followers of a man who has selflessly dedicated his every waking moment to the benefit of humanity in general, and the Jewish people in particular, who has always done his utmost not only to commiserate with the pain of others, but to remove that pain through incessant prayer, pleading, and blessing, suddenly renounce the precedent he has set by explaining his suffering as being part of a higher, cosmic plan? Are we really so sure that even if the Messiah does come in the midst of the Rebbe's suffering, all his pain will have been worth it? I have always been at odds, for example, with the people who intimate that the Holocaust was worth the travail because the State of Israel followed. Balderdash! No outcome is ever worth that kind of price. And every human life is infinitely precious and can never be weighed against a positive outcome. We must demand from God that the Rebbe's suffering stop. No explanations, no theology, and no peace. Just an end to the Rebbe's agony and pain.

I saw the aforementioned film *Shadowlands* with two close friends, one a Mormon, the other a Christian, both devout in their religious observance. As we drove home from the film my Mormon friend said C. S. Lewis's response to the cleric was blasphemous. "God has a reason as to why we suffer. It is always and must always be to our benefit, since God loves us. Human beings just have to understand their limitations." My Christian friend was slightly less submissive. His response was that it appeared as though Lewis's wife was completely innocent and that she didn't deserve this horrible and tragic end. However, who are we to know the full truth of the actions of her life and whether or not she deserved to suffer? While suffering is not good, still, God is always just and everything that man gets he deserves, both good and bad.

I took up the cudgel with both of them. "What are you guys talking about?" I asked them. "Do you really think that God needs you to defend Him? Are we so arrogant as to believe that we know for sure that this woman was guilty, and deserved to suffer? What of our human obligations, incumbent upon us from God Himself, to affirm and promote life and always try to prevent death? If this woman was suffering before you and you were a doctor, you would be under a religious obligation to save her. Why not take up her defense in the face of the Almighty as well? God does not need our defense; human beings do. God is not vulnerable, neither can He suffer the way that humans do. He is eternal. But humans are defenseless; they ache and they die. They need our support and our love."

This difference of approach to the problem of suffering finds its roots in the Bible, in the earliest parting of the ways between Judaism and Christianity. When God created Adam He placed him in the Garden of Eden and instructed him that he was permitted to eat from all the trees of the garden, with the exception of one. "And the Lord God commanded the man saying, Of every tree of the garden you may eat; But of the tree of the knowledge of good and evil, you shall not eat from it; for on the day that you eat from it you shall surely die" (Genesis 2:16–17).

There is a simple problem with the above verse. Adam later does eat from the tree of knowledge, but he does not die. In fact, he lives on for close to another thousand years, and only then does he die. How to account for this discrepancy? The Jews and the Christians deal very differently with the problem.

According to traditional Christianity, what God meant with the words "You shall surely die" is that Adam would die a spiritual death, not a physical one. Thus, as soon as man committed his first, "original" sin, he was spiritually dead, he was damned. The damnation of man even necessitated the son of God coming down to earth and dying on a cross for the purpose of saving man and granting him salvation. Those who believe in Christ believe that he is able to undo the sin and fall of man and to restore their souls once again to eternal life. But the body was always meant to die. In Christianity, there is a recognition of a body-soul dualism whereby people are viewed not as integrated beings but as possessors of an eternal soul and an ephemeral body that is designed to fill the needs of the soul. It is only the soul that is immortal and that can once again be restored in heaven through an affirmation of belief in Christ.

The Jewish interpretation is radically different. Why didn't Adam die when he ate from the tree? Because God never said that he would die *immediately*. He said he would die in due course. And although the verse we have just quoted says "on the day that you eat from it," this does not mean that on the very same day you will die, but rather that at the moment of eating, death shall be decreed on you. You shall no longer be immortal, as was originally intended. Stated in other words, *man was never meant to die*. Having been created in the image of God and with the purpose of serving his Creator, he was meant to serve his Father in Heaven for as long as God Himself would be in existence. He was meant to be eternal. As long as Adam remained attached to his Source, as long as he followed the Will of his Creator, he was eternal just like his Creator. Anything that is attached to the Source of life is likewise imbued with life. Through his sin, however, Adam brought death and destruction into the world, and now he would die. He might live to 120, but then he would succumb to death just as surely as every apple when detached from a tree succumbs to rot and decay. Thus, the sin of Adam that served to obstruct his direct relationship with God made him ready prey for the elements.

A fetus in the womb of its mother is animated by her very life, and everything she eats and drinks directly nourishes her child. But if the umbilical cord, which serves as the fetus's lifeline, is damaged, a healthy child will never emerge. The same was true of Adam. His umbilical cord with the source of all life had been ruptured; he would not be eternal.

The implications of this rabbinical exegesis on this crucial passage of Genesis are both mighty and profound. What this means is that there was never meant to be any place for death in our world. Neither was there ever any plan for suffering or pain. The Garden of Eden, which was previously this earth, was perfect. The sin in the garden brought about gross imperfection.

But what this also connotes is that there is no meaning to suffering whatsoever. It had no place in God's original plan and was not present in the original world that was inhabited by Adam and Eve. No human was ever predestined to suffer, die, or ache. Neither will any form of misery be present in the perfect messianic age that has been promised for three millennia by the Almighty through his prophets and wise men. Only now, in this interim period between life in Eden and life in the perfect world to come are we ravaged by cancers, AIDS, car crashes, hatred, war, and genocide. And the only purpose for man in this interim period is to declare war on the world's imperfections by drowning them in myriad acts of loving-kindness, a plethora of love, and an ongoing battle on what seems to be the fate that God has in store for man. Whereas the stars and constellations tell us that man must die, we respond that we will live. We will wrestle with the heavens and draw our swords against the angel of death. And notwithstanding how many unfortunate casualties we take in the interim, in the words of Winston Churchill, "We shall never surrender." We shall employ every means—medical research, charity and philanthropy, kind words, and millions of prayers—until such time as God recognizes our deep disenchantment with the world and finally reinvolves Himself visibly with history and removes from us those tragic occurrences that are still out of our control. Neither will we accept that those who have already perished shall never rise again. We shall firmly assert our conviction that we will be rejoined with them in an era of peace and joy.

One of the most powerful modern works of literature on the subject of suffering is Elie Wiesel's *The Town Beyond the Wall.* This challenge to the Divine is perhaps best contained in the character of Varady, who preaches a sermon to the town:

He emphasized the strength of man, who could bring the Messiah to obedience. He claimed that liberation from Time would be accomplished at the signal of man, and not of his Creator . . . "each of you, the men and women who hear me, have God in his power, for each of you is capable of achieving a thing of which God is incapable! [Man] will conquer heaven, earth,

sickness, and death if he will only raze the walls that imprison
the Will! And I who speak to you announce my decision to deny
death, to repel it, to ridicule it! He who stands before you will
never die!"

According to the Sages, Michael, the guardian angel of Israel,
performs the role of a high priest in heaven, who every day
offers up a sacrifice consisting of the souls of the righteous. In
Wiesel's story, it is Michael who protests the sacrifice of the
innocents that it is his tragic role to behold. Conventionally, we
think of God and man being vastly unequal in their dialogue,
God being omnipotent and the human protester merely His
creature. But in Wiesel's *The Town Beyond the Wall*, we find a
significant inversion of this relationship. The Orthodox Jewish
thinker Norman Lamm describes it as "a keen awareness not
only of man's power but also of his self-consciousness as an
autonomous agent. . . . It is not rational or even mystical explanations that Wiesel is seeking but rather human approaches and,
even more, a confrontation with the God who permits suffering" (*Faith and Doubt*, pp. 320, 316).

This dynamism in our relationship with God because of the
existence of suffering is also extended to our relationships with
others. One of Wiesel's main characters in *The Town Beyond
the Wall*, Pedro, says, "The dialogue—or . . . duel . . . between
man and his God doesn't end in nothingness. Man may not have
the last word, but he has the last cry. That moment marks the
birth of art . . . and friendship is an art" (p. 103). In other words,
the meaning of suffering is discovered when we protest against
it to God, and the most effective way of dealing with suffering
is to extend ourselves to other humans in friendship, which is
an art in the same way that Wiesel's book is art. This is made
even clearer a few pages later: "To say, 'I suffer, therefore I am'
is to become the enemy of man. What you must say is, 'I suffer,
therefore you are.' Camus wrote somewhere that to protest
against a universe of unhappiness, you had to create happiness.
That's an arrow pointing the way; it leads to another human
being. And not via absurdity" (p. 127).

This theme of challenging the divine and of death as an aberration is further reflected in the writings of the leading hasidic

thinker, Rabbi Adin Steinsaltz. In his collection of essays *The Strife of the Spirit*, he clarifies a concise philosophical overview of death:

> The Jewish approach to death is that it is a problem to be solved by and for the living. . . . The basic attitude of Judaism to death, which, it is said, was ushered in with Adam's expulsion from the Garden of Eden, is that it is not a natural, inevitable phenomenon. Death is life diseased, distorted, perverted, diverted from the flow of holiness, which is identified with life. So side by side with a stoic submission to death, there is a stubborn battle against it on the physical and cosmic level. The world's worst defect is seen to be death, whose representative is Satan. The remedy is faith in the resurrection. Ultimately, "death and evil"—and the one is tantamount to the other—are dismissed as ephemeral. They are not part of the true essence of the world, and, as the late Rabbi Kook emphasized in his writings, man should not accept the premise that death will always emerge the victor. . . . In the combat of life against death, of being against nonbeing, Judaism manifests disbelief in the persistence of death, and maintains that it is a temporary obstacle that can and will be overcome. Our sages, prophesying a world in which there will be no more death, wrote: "We are getting closer to a world in which we shall be able to vanquish death, in which we shall be above and beyond death." (pp. 193–195)

Death, then, is the absence of life, in the same way that Judaism views evil as the absence of goodness. It is a state that is empty and must be filled with something positive.

Who indeed is to say that man must die, and who would effortlessly surrender in the endless battle against death? In the true story of the critically acclaimed film *Lorenzo's Oil*, Susan Sarandon and Nick Nolte play the parents of a child who is terminally ill with adrenoleukodystrophy (ALD), a terrible brain disorder from which no child had ever recovered. They are told by professors of medicine that their child will unquestionably be dead within twenty-four months. The Catholic clergy urge them to accept the boy's fate, for such is the will of God, and they have no right to question why. But they reject the words of both and embark on a two-year search for a cure to their son's illness. They simply do not accept that their son *has* to die. And lo and behold, miracle of miracles, they found a cure, and not just for their own son. Although neither had any medical training whatsoever, they went to libraries and educated themselves on the body's immune system in order to find a cure. They refused to surrender to death and the spectacular fruit of their effort was "Lorenzo's Oil," the cure that has saved the lives of tens of thousands of children suffering from ALD throughout the world.

We should learn from the example of people like these and fight for the Rebbe's life and the lives of so many others rather than sinking into fatalistic apathy or entertaining damaging and ultimately irrelevant speculations as to the future. This is the only authentic Jewish response to the problem of suffering: to join with God as junior partners in creation and to correct the world's ills and to right its wrongs. Man is a creature in the image of God. It is to God's credit and glory that He empowers man with the ability to play the role of the Creator by filling in the little gaps and holes left in creation. Never should we succumb to fate in silent acquiescence. "I shall not die, for I shall live and by doing so sing the praises of the Almighty" (Psalm 118). We must raise our hands toward the heavens and declare with fortitude and conviction: "Glorious Creator, he who stands before You shall never die, but shall live eternally as an angel of mercy to proclaim Your grace and serve the needs of Your people. I shall be your administering angel."

The only meaning for suffering is a call to arms on the part of mankind to eradicate and destroy it. We should never make peace with suffering, never dignify it with anything short of outright contempt and hostility. We must act like the human body's immune system. Whenever it witnesses even the tiniest germ, bacteria, fungus, or infection, it immediately declares war on the alien presence that threatens the overall health of the body. The immune system, which was created by God, aside from its obvious function, was also designed to teach us a lesson. It is not the purpose of the body's immune system to understand why the body suffers and why it has been affected by illness. Nor is its purpose to sit around pondering the cosmic whys of existence. When a germ enters the body, the immune system does not send a signal to the brain to try and explain why this terrible tragedy, this potential for illness, has occurred. Rather, the immune system sees a germ as an invader that has no place in the body and immediately sets out to destroy it. The germ has no meaning and requires no explanation. It simply must be got rid of. The same applies to the human view of suffering. Let us dedicate our existence completely and wholeheartedly to being sensitive and caring human beings and let us set our goal as the total eradication of every form of pain from the earth.

21

THE REQUEST FOR A
LESS-PAINFUL MEANS

Our explanation is as yet incomplete. Everything we have explained thus far in terms of the Jewish response to suffering still lacks the most important component in order to make it plausible and coherent. Let us now take everything we have said thus far a step further.

The Talmud declares that forty days before a child is born there is an angel in Heaven, whose task it is to make announcements, who announces that the child about to be born will be either rich or poor, strong or weak, whom he will marry, and many other important factors that will govern his earthly sojourn. So wealth and poverty levels in a person's life are actually predetermined, even before the person is born.

Based on this information, why is it that when we, as a community, a Jewish community, which believes in the truth of the Talmud, witness hunger and poverty, we exert our utmost effort to alleviate it? Why do we take up a collection on behalf of the poor? Even better, why is it that we pray to God on the poor's behalf, as well as on our own behalf, that He make us wealthy, or at least able to make ends meet? Why not put our complete faith in God and assume that He knows what He is doing? Since God does nothing but for man's good, then we are probably better off poor. And in any event, everything is predetermined, so that our efforts are for naught.

We answered this question in the previous chapter. If one is content being poor and wishes to remain so, that is fine. The *Mishnah* says, "Who is rich? He who is content with his lot." So, by all means if one is noble enough to thank God for what he has, this is very laudatory. But when we witness someone else's poverty, we cannot say that this too is God's will—that God knows what He is doing and that God is just. Because just as it may indeed be God's will that this person be poor, it is also God's will that we do our utmost to alleviate people's suffering and wish the best of all things for all of mankind. So, when we witness someone else's poverty or hunger, our response should never be to consider God's reason for doing so, but rather to find means by which to feed him and pray on his behalf. Through this we fulfill our own obligations in the matter. And even if many things are predetermined, still, this does not absolve us from our obligation to pray and do everything we can for the welfare of others.

But here is where things become difficult. If we believe that everything that God does is for the good, and through God's actions man can achieve great redemptive virtue, then how is it that we can come along and remove this virtue by changing or praying for a change in circumstance? A person is about to gain some fantastic, wonderful merit by being poor and we come along and take that merit away from them. How dare we do that? If it's *good* for a person to be sick, how dare we heal him? He'll only have to be sick again later, and furthermore, if it's necessary for the person to be sick, and to his advantage, even if we don't immediately see that advantage, then we must leave him to be sick. Clearly, when someone loses a relative, God forbid, and has a genuine need to mourn, it is a disservice to try and persuade them to laugh. Notwithstanding the fact that laughter and happiness is far better than misery and tears, at this juncture in time this person *needs* to mourn. It is for their benefit. It is a legitimate requirement, and we cannot deny the person this necessity, notwithstanding how noble our intentions might be. Likewise, in the divine scheme of things there may be a legitimate need for a person to be poor, and we are taught to believe that it is for their benefit. So how can we pray to God, challenge Him and protest that He alter this person's condition?

The truth of the matter is that when we pray to God and demand to change things that He ordained, what we are really saying is this: Those things that You, O God, do for us that hurt and are painful, we really believe them to be acts of kindness. Kindness that we cannot fathom because it is a higher kindness, a more divine kindness that our limited understanding cannot comprehend, just like the parent who smacks a child when he runs out into the street. And what we are asking of you, Master of the universe, through our prayers and protest is not that You stop being kind, or be less kind. What we're asking is that in Your infinite wisdom, in your infinite power, can You please find a way to give us the same benefits in a more pleasant and less painful form? Is it not possible for us to experience the same growth, the same advantages, and the same maturity that we need and that we indeed acquire if we go through the pain, through a less hurtful medium? After all, You are unlimited. Nothing constrains or hinders You from doing whatever You wish. So can't you bring about a painless method by which we could receive the same benefit?

People hate going to the dentist, because it hurts. When the dentist gives you a shot in the mouth to numb the tooth he is about to drill, you shout "ouch" and ask him why he did that. But what are you asking? Was it not you who called up and made the appointment? Was it not you who even offered him payment in exchange for his services? Rather, what we are saying to the dentist is that we understand that everything he is doing, including giving us the novocaine shot, is for our benefit. We believe that sincerely. If not, we would not be sitting in his dental chair at that moment. But, can't you numb my tooth in a less painful way? Hasn't dental research reached the point whereby a nerve can be numbed without having to stick a needle in it? Can't you accomplish the same task, for my benefit, in a way in which it will not hurt?

This is what we are asking of God. The dental profession has its limitations and we do not expect them to have the means by which to remove a cavity without having to drill through the tooth and create pain. But God is omnipotent. He has no limitations. So why can't He give us a less painful pill when He goes about enhancing our lives? So this theology of protest against suffering that we are advocating is not at all a challenge to God's justice or providence. Rather it is an affirmation of His infinite power and a request that He utilize some awesome strength in bringing about the good ends He has for man through a similarly good, and painless, means.

What would be a less painful way? It would be less painful if we could just *see* what was happening. If we could just understand why these events were necessary, we could swallow things a lot easier.

Take, for example, a man who is married but is discontent. He has complaints about his wife, and she has complaints about him. Both are unhappy. He walks around as if his life is over and there is nothing he can do about it. He is unable to concentrate on his business, or anything else. He feels utterly ruined and that his life is a miserable mess. Now suppose that suddenly God comes to him and says, "I have a request. I have this woman that I created and for whom I am responsible. Naturally, I need someone to marry this person. But, I must tell you that her personality is just a bit eccentric. Could you do Me this one favor? Would you marry her for Me? This will be your entire mission in life. I will give you life, health, and everything else. All I ask is that you make this one person happy. She is not the easiest person in the world to make happy, and she can be quite demanding. But this is very important to Me. Please make this person happy."

If God would indeed appear to this individual and make this request, he would do it enthusiastically. He wouldn't see this as a burden at all, and certainly not as a tragedy. He would not be calling his marriage the lousiest thing that ever happened to him and he would be making a much grander effort to ensure that his marriage works and that his wife is happy. In other words, if we could only see the reason for the pain, if we could only understand how there is a beneficial, cosmic purpose for the hardships, then we would not view them as pain at all, but rather as a pleasure. It is only due to the fact that this husband feels that since in any case he chose his wife without any heavenly guidance and for no higher cosmic reason and that he could have done much better, there is no reason for his suffering and basically he ruined his own life through his choice.

This need for information is the general rule lying beneath almost all pain and disputes in human relationships. The average wife, for instance, is willing to do anything for her husband and vice versa. The only reason she may sometimes refuse, and which may lead to a major marital dispute, is that she sometimes cannot relate to the request. She doesn't understand why her husband needs this thing so badly, so she objects. If he could explain it to her, the friction would disappear. Of course, the truth is that this can be quite a cheap excuse and we must learn to respond to those parts of our spouse that we cannot comprehend, but as an example it makes its point.

When we plead and object that God alleviate our suffering and change the present deplorable circumstances, we are not implying that God is doing something wrong, neither are we denying his providence, and neither are we failing to trust His judgment. All we are saying is that we believe that it is good, but we cannot see it. We ask God to either change the circumstances to the point that even in a revealed sense, this thing will be seen to be good, or at least, if we must continue in the present circumstance, to disclose to us how this even is benefiting us. The Jewish tradition has always been that upon blessing someone we bless them not just with goodness, but with *revealed* goodness. We know that God is infinite and we know that there are many ways of achieving the same end. So please God, bring about your objectives in a way in which we are aware of their beneficial outcome. To us humans, it is not only the ends that are important but the means as well, just as important as it is to You.

In the Talmud there is a statement to be found that a person should accept the bad things that happen as gracefully as he accepts the good things. There was a student who tried desperately to understand what this meant. He came to the *Maggid* of Mezritch, Rabbi Dovber, the successor of the Baal Shem Tov, and asked him to please explain what this meant. How could one enjoy bad things? It didn't sound very Jewish. The *Maggid* told him, "I cannot answer you but one of my great disciples, Reb Zusha, who lives far away in the village of Anapoli, has the answer. Go to him." Perplexed at the brilliant *Maggid*'s inability to explain a talmudic passage, the man nevertheless heeded the *Maggid*'s advice and traveled the long distance to Anapoli. He was certain that if the great *Maggid* did not know the answer to this difficulty but Reb Zusha did, then the latter must be an even greater authority than the former. In the village the student asked where he could find the celebrated and holy Reb Zusha, but no one knew what he was talking about. They had heard of a poor Jew named Zusha who lived in a little shack on the edge of the town and taught children. The man came to this Zusha's house and asked to be admitted. In the house he found utter poverty and hunger. A large family with barely anything to eat. In the place of furniture there were a few tree stumps, and the children all wore torn and patched clothing. Clearly this Zusha led a difficult life.

"Are you Reb Zusha of Anapoli?"

"Well, some call me that."

"Reb Dovber of Mezritch sent me to you."

Reb Zusha's face lit up. Filled with joy and enthusiasm he sprang to his feet, put on his *gartel*, and asked, "Please tell me, what did the Rebbe say?"

"The Rebbe told me that you can provide me with an answer to my question. How can we accept bad things in the same way in which we accept good things, as the Talmud instructs us?"

Reb Zusha was puzzled. "The Rebbe sent you to me for an answer to your question? But I don't understand. How could I know how to accept bad things happily when nothing bad has ever happened to me?"

The student then understood the answer and why the *Maggid* had sent him to Reb Zusha.

There is no explanation for how one is expected to accept bad things. Bad things are evil and we are not meant to have anything to do with evil. One should not accept bad things. What the Talmud means with its statement is not that one should like bad things. This is not a Jewish approach. What the Talmud means to say is that one should see beyond, behind, beneath the surface of those things that appear bad and realize that they are just as good as the good things in life, and perhaps even better. The only difference between the two is that whereas we like the good things because they are pleasant and overtly beneficial, we hate the bad things because they are overtly harmful. But we transcend its overt layer and try and understand.

But even amid this need we still pray to the Almighty that He bring about the same goodness in a way that will be more acceptable and more pleasurable to us. He has this ability and we request that He bring it forth. It is simply not good enough to advocate that suffering is really good. Even if we believe this, it still does nothing to fully placate God, because it merely begs the question of His omnipotence. If He is God, then He is fully capable of saving man the agony of having to receive a good thing in such a painful way.

A practical application of the mistakes people make in understanding where human control ends and human obligation begins is the following. Rabbi Manis Friedman relates how in a conversation about raising children a woman said to him, "You know, if I hadn't had my abortion, my child would now be five years old." So he called her aside and said to her,

> Wait a minute. Your child would not be five years old. If this *neshamah* was destined to live five years, then it would be here today. If the *neshamah* is not here today, then it wouldn't be here even if you hadn't decided on the abortion. It's true that the decision to have the abortion was not a very good one and it's true that you may have made a mistake when you decided to abort. For this you have to search your soul and ask why your thinking was so wrong? How could you have had such little compassion? Why were you not in favor of life? Those are all good questions. But that's your problem because you made a questionable decision and you had the freedom of choice to make that decision. But don't ever believe for a moment that the life and death of another human being lies in your hands. That's arrogant and it's wrong. This *neshamah* that was conceived but not born is a *neshamah* no less than yours and just as you have a destiny that you are going to live out, it had its destiny and there's no way that you could interfere with that destiny. The fact that you made a poor choice should cause you to search your soul, search your heart, and discover where this idea came from. But don't ever take credit for life and death. That's not in your hands.

Another story concerns a true happening in which a young student was walking home from his *yeshivah* in Brooklyn on a

Friday night, and a juvenile delinquent jumped out from the bushes holding a gun and demanded all of the student's money. But it was Friday night and the student was walking home from *shul* and had no money. So he brushed the mugger off and refused to take him seriously. The mugger said to him, "Give me the money or I'll shoot!" The student still refused and the mugger pulled the trigger. They were only standing three feet apart and he shot him point blank in the face. The *yeshivah* student just stared at the mugger as if nothing had happened. The mugger became so frightened with this "demon" who refused to die that he got terrifically spooked and ran away. Until he arrived home the student did not even realize that he had been shot in the chin and was bleeding. What had happened was that the bullet had entered his chin and lodged against the jaw bone but had not penetrated the bone. Because it was a leather-tipped bullet, it flattened but did not go any farther.

The story may be rather dramatic, but it depicts two people living out their destinies. This juvenile delinquent had freedom of choice to be good or bad. He decided to be bad. So bad that he was even prepared to kill a human being. So he made all the necessary preparations. He stole money and bought a gun. He loaded the gun and hid behind a tree until a passerby could become his victim. Sure enough, he found his victim, threatened him, and then pulled the trigger. But is that enough to make one a murderer? Did his victim die? Life and death are not in our hands and if this student was destined to live a long and healthy life, no bullet in the world could alter that.

Likewise, when the woman above says how her child would now be five years old, this is totally inaccurate. Does she really believe that based upon her decision a child died? Is that all life is about? The child did not die because of her choice. God does not create a life to have it extinguished senselessly. A murderer is senseless, not the death. Rather, the woman must rethink her action, but not because she took a life. She couldn't even if she wanted to. Rather, she must repent for her *decision*.

The underlying premise is this: God has many methods by which to bring about His will. If He wants to end someone's life, He can send a lightning bolt, disease, or locomotive. He doesn't need human help. So when we are punished for murder, it is not because we murdered someone. As stated above, that is outside our ability. Rather, we are punished for making the wrong choice. And if a person asks, "But wait. God intended for this person to die anyway. So why am I being punished? While it is true that I pulled the trigger, it was God's will that he died. Otherwise, he could not have died." The answer is that God has many ways of bringing about this death without human assistance. So why did you choose to do something you were expressly warned against?

Maimonides takes the same approach to this problem in his *Mishneh Torah* (*Laws of Repentance* 6:5). In a discussion of man's freedom of choice he points out that in the Torah God expressly tells Abraham at the historic incident of the covenant- between-the-parts that the Jewish people will be enslaved (Genesis 15:13) in a foreign land. Maimonides then asks how is it that God could punish the Egyptians for enslaving the Jews when it was preordained by God that it be so? Likewise, he asks, God tells Moses that after his death the Jewish people will worship idols and forsake His covenant. How then could God hold the Jews responsible for their actions when they were preordained and foreseen well before the event?

Maimonides then answers that when God said that this people will become idol worshipers, he did not single out individuals. God said generally that they, the Jewish people, will do so. But who told this particular individual to be part of the sinners? God merely stipulated that there would be a multitude of people who would engage in idol worship. But why are *you* being punished? Because who asked you to be part of this multitude? God's saying that there will be idolaters in the Jewish people, writes Maimonides, "is no different to Him saying that there will be both righteous people and wicked people within the nation. But this of course does not constitute an excuse for the wicked one to say that it has already been decreed that he be wicked and thus he had no choice in the matter."

The same applies to the Egyptians. It is true that God had ordained for the Egyptian people as a whole to enslave the Jews. But who asked this particular Egyptian to become the instrument of the oppression? There are many Egyptians and God has many agents to fulfill his bidding. So no Egyptian should walk around thinking, "Look, God wants the Israelites made slaves. Therefore, I must pick up the whip and smite this Israelite man." This is not the case. God has his agencies and He expressly told man to stay out of His business, which includes all forms of pain, suffering, and punishment inflicted on another human being. Thus, this Egyptian is being punished for being a part of something he was never invited to participate in. He has entered a domain that is exclusively God's.

The same applies to all of our choices in life. We must recognize that human jurisdiction and death never mix. But human responsibility and life go hand in hand.

Therefore, even when pain comes our way and is caused by another person, it should be put into perspective. When people abuse us, criticize us, or hurt us, to a certain degree we must make a conscious effort to extract something positive from this experience for the reasons mentioned above. If it were true that it is only a *human* hurting us, someone has made the awful choice of being cruel to another human being and it is *he* who is causing the pain, then we could just fight back and hurt him in return. But because the power to harm another individual and alter someone's fate is not in human hands, this pain is being caused by God and is there to help us grow and rise above it or remind us of something important. It is true that the person causing the pain is making a terrible mistake for choosing to act as the agent that God does not need, but it is not that person who brings about the pain.

So our first reaction should not be to return insult for insult or to immediately take revenge. We should not even say something like, "I'm going to be nice to you in spite of the way you behaved toward me." Even this latter half of the statement is forbidden by Jewish law. We must try and transcend the hurt because whatever pain we experience, that pain is *our life*. It is part of what we are. Do not make the mistake of crediting it to someone else. It is not someone else who makes us suffer. It is our life and we must learn to handle it and utilize it to grow and become stronger from it. Since you're using it, since you're accepting it in those good graces, why should you be angry at the person who brought it to you? To be sure this does not mean that we should be passive in the face of cruelty. We must stand up and defend ourselves and stop an aggressor. What it does mean, however, is that simultaneous with our displeasure and animosity toward the person causing the pain, who honestly deserves to be put down, we must also recognize that this pain is there to somehow benefit us. We must ponder our hurt and attempt to emerge stronger and wiser than we were before. We must try and find God's finger in everything that transpires. The world and everything that happens is in need of redemption. The world looks forward to the dawn of the messianic era.

22

DOES CHALLENGING GOD MAKE ONE A HERETIC?

The views expressed in this book are accumulated from years of lecturing and writing on the subject of suffering, as well as from a personal preoccupation with the subject from my earliest youth. My parents were not blessed with a successful marriage, and well before the inevitable divorce was finalized I wondered to myself about the gross imperfections of the world. Why did human living seem so flawed and why did people seem so imperfect? Why did mankind itself seem so defective, and why couldn't people overcome their differences simply and easily? What was it inside us that caused us to stand up for vainglorious sentiments of pride and obstinacy in place of love and companionship? Is there really anyone among us who can explain why a husband and wife would rather argue about the color of furniture than fall into each other's arms and be comforted from all the other, far more serious, worries of life? Throughout all these deliberations, I maintained the belief that the greatness and glory of man, the single most sublime accolade we could accord him, was that he was a fighter; that he would never submit to the inevitability of circumstance. I believed that even a child who witnessed parents arguing could still lead what he believed he and every human being deserved: a good and happy life. I became convinced at an early age that notwithstanding the imperfections of life, we could still all be happy, or at the very least if we could

not, then we would go down fighting. We would never succumb to predestined doom. Although witnessing parents' quar-
rels, one might still lead a storybook exiₒtence with one's future
spouse, notwithstanding what the statistics say, or that empirical evidence might counter one's ambiₒions.

It came as a total surprise to me, then, when I began to meet
people who strongly disagreed with me. They felt that my position of arguing against the inevitability of death, as well as the
uselessness and meaninglessness of suffering, was naive at best,
and constituted grave heresy at worst. I was particularly sur-
prised to hear this position being advocated most vehemently
among the more religious quarters of Jewish life. I tend to lecture far more to nonobservant Jewish communities than to
Orthodox ones. But virtually every lecture I have delivered to
audiences on this subject has met with the following response:
those who are largely ignorant of Jewish thought and tradition
find my words refreshing, relieving, and inspiring. Less-obser-
vant and nonobservant Jews embrace this message. They feel
the Jewish response to suffering affords them the opportunity
to remain fully human and voice their grievances to a benevolent Creator who is always prepared to listen and soothe, rather than rebuke and tell them how evil they are and how their
very actions precipitated the pain they now feel.

But commensurate with an increasing level of observance
there appears to be an increasing level of discomfort among
those who hear my views on this subject. Hence, I have endeav-
ored throughout this book to emphasize that my ideas are in
no way personal and are in accordance with biblical and traditional Jewish example and thought. It is an ancient staple of
Judaism, and the precedent set by its giants, to challenge God,
especially in the area of human suffering. We have already seen
that this was how Abraham acted upon hearing how Sodom and
Gomorrah would be destroyed because of their sin and iniqui-
ty, and that Moses protested time and again when the Almighty
threatened to devour the Jewish nation for its sins.

Thus, the responses I encountered came as a considerable
surprise to me when I delivered my first major lecture on the
subject of suffering. I was speaking to a group of fifty Jewish
employees and vice-presidents of a bank in New York. The more

religious participants were aghast: "How can you challenge God? Who are you to question His justice? Are you implying that God doesn't know what He is doing?" But even amid these questions, the response was polite and rather mute, since I was officially invited by the bank to lecture, and as Mr. Edmond Safra, the chairman of the bank, is a friend of our society and a financial supporter in Oxford, many of them had no choice but to be nice. But they were vexed nonetheless.

Two months later I gave a lecture at the Manchester Jewish Cultural Centre in Manchester, England, to an audience of three hundred, one-third of which was devoutly Orthodox. I was somewhat proud of myself when the first questioner rose and preceded his question by stating that this was the most comforting lecture he had ever heard on the subject of God and suffering. But subsequent questioners rose to heap scorn and ridicule on everything I had said. It was not long before people were openly calling me a heretic and phrases such as "blasphemous," "sacrilegious," "profane," and "deeply offensive to the sensitivities of all Orthodox Jews" were being bandied about. I left the city under a cloud and hoped that the incident would pass. After all, those comments had come from the 100 observant people in the audience, people who were vastly different from the community to which I administered in Oxford.

There was to be no calm after the initial storm. Instead, a new tempest arose in the North of England where I had delivered the lecture. First, the sound engineer for the evening who had promised me a copy of the tape told my secretary that it would not be forthcoming since he was going to burn the tape due to its heretical content. Then, the letters began. I was visiting my family in Miami when I received a phone call from Lubavitch headquarters in London telling me to return to England at once, as a terrible uproar had exploded over my lecture in Manchester that was deeply damaging to my reputation. They wanted me to respond.

I was faxed three letters that had appeared in the Manchester *Jewish Telegraph*. One claimed that if Lubavitch wanted to retain its credibility among Orthodox Jews it would have to do something about me, and another accused me of disregarding authentic Jewish values. The third claimed that my views were opposite to those of the Torah and warned that people must not be brainwashed by me.

Whenever suffering is visited on humanity, especially when those who suffer are visibly righteous people, a terrible contradiction is posed. How can this be? There can only be two possibilities: either the person deserved the suffering, and therefore God is just and metes out to all according to their actions, or the person did not deserve to suffer, in which case God is cruel and unjust, or powerless to prevent the suffering, or simply indifferent, looking on as an unaffected spectator as humans succumb to the elements of fate and chance. To sum up, either man or God is responsible for human suffering, but one of the two has got to give. They simply cannot coexist. Even if God has not directly caused the suffering, He still may be held accountable for not intervening to save man. And although His intervention would deny man his freedom of choice, this is not a proper objection because, as we have explained earlier, a murderer, for example, is not punished for taking a life, but rather for the bad choice that he made. Every human being is utterly incapable of taking the life of another. A human is simply not empowered to play the role of the Creator. A person can exercise his freedom of choice by aiming a gun at another person and pulling the trigger, but who says that God cannot intervene and insure that the trajectory of the bullet does not reach its target? And who says that even if a person is shot, the injury cannot be only minimal?

In short, man can certainly exercise his freedom of choice to do evil, without evil actually occurring. God can certainly intervene without man losing his freedom to choose to live like an angel or an animal. So who is responsible for the terrible pain of life and the tragedies that befall humans—God or man?

The underlying premise of each of the hostile letters mentioned above is a steadfast determination to defend God at all costs, and simultaneously, or automatically, indict man for his own torment and misery. But is this authentic Judaism? Is it even necessary? Unfortunately, sometimes people think they are defending God when really they are just covering up their own insecurity—not willing to accept new ideas that might threaten their cosy beliefs. Most people would rather accept platitudes as answers than continue to struggle with the questions.

I believe that the primary purpose of man as dictated by the Creator is always to serve the purposes of his fellow human. And I believe, as Rabbi Israel Baal Shem Tov, the founder of the hasidic movement, passionately affirmed, that love for God is shown first and foremost through one's love and devotion to one's fellowman. What God principally desires of us is not to defend Him, but to care and love our fellowman. Indeed, the laws that regulate man's treatment of his fellowman accounts for a colossal portion of our Torah and Jewish living. Rabbi Akiva, one of the greatest Jewish sages, affirmed that the divine imperative to "love your neighbor as yourself" (Leviticus 19:18) is "a general principle of the Torah." Similarly, the great sage Hillel, when asked to encapsulate the entire Torah, told a potential convert, "That which you hate, never do unto others. This is the entire Torah, the rest being commentary on this one principle" (Talmud, *Shabbat*, 30a).

One can only wonder at the degree of arrogance necessary to promote the belief that God is in need of our defense. The mind can only startle at those who are only too eager to condemn man in favor of the all-powerful Creator, as if they believed that He is pleased at one human being selling out his fellow for the benefit of the Creator.

There are many things that children do that will anger their parents. But one of the worst is a child expressing not unity, but rather selfishness and factionalism against his or her siblings. If my child breaks something in the house, I may not be amused. But I am far angrier if he blames it on a sibling. In the same vein, what the Almighty desires most from a collective humanity is unity. We are His children, and He wishes to see us come together as brothers and sisters, the same wish that any parent would have.

Once while on holiday with my family, we took the children for ice cream. My second-oldest daughter pulled her sister's hair, and I told her that I would not be taking her inside the store unless she said she was sorry. True to her obstinate character, she stubbornly refused. "Good," I told her, "then you'll stay in the car," whereupon her oldest sister, the innocent victim, suddenly began to cry that her younger sister didn't mean it and that she would not go in the ice cream store without her. It was one of my proudest moments as a father.

If one could somehow encapsulate the vast contribution made to Jewish life and thought by the Baal Shem Tov and Hasidism over the past three hundred years, it would be that *Hasidut* taught man that in his effort to achieve proximity with God, he must learn to put his fellowman first, at times even before God, and certainly in those areas where God does not require man's protection. In other words, by challenging God in the face of human suffering, by asserting an individual's righteousness and affirming that he did not deserve this fate, we do not degrade God, but glorify Him to the highest heights. We demonstrate that His beautiful teachings in the Torah of love, compassion, and togetherness have actually had an effect upon us. Time and again in the Bible the Lord bids us to defend the cause of the oppressed, to show special sensitivity to widows and orphans. Does this then only apply to giving them something to eat, but never to defending them against a perilous fate, even at the expense of indicting the Creator? Do we show compassion to the millions of widows and orphans that survived the Holocaust by telling them that their husbands and fathers died because of their sins? Is this the kind of compassion of which the Torah spoke?

By defending man, even at the expense of the Creator, we show God that we have learned something from our constant exposure to His teachings. The same is true of parenting. When people see the love and bonds forged between two brothers, it reflects gloriously on their parents. It shows that they have had a good upbringing. It demonstrates that indeed they are brothers and that they share the same parents, that they are one. When two human beings cannot get along, when friction and hatred exist between them, they simultaneously and perhaps inadvertently demonstrate that they did not emanate from the same Creator. Ultimately, they deny the unity of God. Those who condemn man and explain why he deserved to suffer, far from doing any justice to the reputation and standing of their Creator, do Him an injustice by fragmenting the human race, thereby fragmenting the Creator of the human race.

We have shown that it was the Almighty Himself who prodded Moses to step in and save the Jewish nation from His wrath after the sin of the Golden Calf. Similarly, Maimonides, in his celebrated "Epistle on Martyrdom" sharply rebukes, in the strongest possible language, another rabbi's condemnation of Jews who were living in Spain during the terrible Islamic Almuhad persecutions, many of whom pondered conversion to Islam rather than face death by the sword. Maimonides goes to great lengths in his rebuttal to show that God Himself had rebuffed and even punished those who had said negative things about His nation Israel. Maimonides discusses how Moses, Elijah, Isaiah, and even the ministering angels of heaven were severely chastised by the Almighty when they came to Him with reports that the Jews were sinful and had broken God's covenant, even though all the empirical evidence supported their claims. So great was God's anger at Isaiah, for example, after having said, "I sit here in the midst of a nation who have defiled and profaned their lips [with prayers to idols]" (Isaiah 1:6-7), that the Almighty sent a seraph of heaven with a pan of coals to put into the mouth of the prophet. But if Isaiah's allegations were true, then why was he punished? If Moses was correct in accusing the Jews of "abandoning the path of God, assimilating into Egyptian culture, and forsaking the covenant of Abraham through neglecting to circumcise their children," why was he so sharply rebuked by the Almighty for his accurate report? The reason is that even if the reports were accurate, even if the statements were true, those offering them all entered a domain that was none of their business. God is the only Judge of the earth, not man. The purpose of a human being is always to stand up and defend and protect his fellowman, never to damn or condemn him. Man will always be held accountable for entering into realms that are not his. God gives and takes life, humans protect and defend life.

"Even then," writes Maimonides, "was Isaiah not fully forgiven, his complete atonement coming only when he was killed by [the king] Menashe. . . . If this was the punishment meted out to the giants of the world, Moses, Elijah, Isaiah, and the ministering angels, how much more so when a man of far less worth has the gall to open his mouth against the Congregation of Israel, its sages and their students, priests and levites, and label them 'Sinners, wicked, gentiles, and unfit for court testimony, heretics' . . . how great will be the punishment not of them, but of the man who speaks these words."

Perhaps our greatest form of protest, then, must be reserved for those misguided, conceited individuals who are so sanctimonious as to assert that other people suffer because of their sins. If they wish to say this of themselves, they are welcome to. But never of another human being.

If there is one thing that we humans must learn in the face of suffering, until such time as the world will be perfected, it is that we must approach and deal with one another with uncompromising love, a love that is not predicated on any self-interest. Until such time as we, together with our Creator, abolish every form of pain from the earth, we must band together and comfort each other. Never can we watch someone else's pain, even that of an animal, in silence, and never dare we rationalize and explain away his pain, especially by asserting something as repulsive as the possibility that he deserved it. If there is one thing we must gain from the experience of suffering it is always to be on the side of man, and not on that of God, for this is the will of the Creator. Our role is to promote life, not justice.

23

RISING ABOVE FATE
AND CREATING OUR
OWN DESTINY

O ne of the most moving and dramatic events in the entire Torah is the story where Joseph, as viceroy to the
king in Egypt, reveals himself to his brothers who
earlier had sold him into slavery. I remember once in synagogue
listening to the man reading the Torah when he suddenly broke
into tears as he read Joseph's confession to his brothers. It is a
truly heart-wrenching episode. "Joseph could not hold his emotions. Since all his attendants were present he cried out, 'Have
everyone leave my presence.' Thus, no one else was with him
when Joseph revealed himself to his brothers. He began to weep
with such loud sobs that the Egyptians could hear it. . . . Joseph
said to his brothers, 'I am Joseph! Is my father still alive?' His
brothers were so startled, they could not respond. 'Please come
close to me,' said Joseph to his brothers. When they came closer, he said, 'I am Joseph your brother! You sold me to Egypt.
Now don't worry or feel guilty because you sold me. Look! God
has sent me ahead of you to save lives! . . . God has sent me
ahead of you to ensure that you survive in the land and to keep
you alive through such extraordinary means.'"

The extreme beauty and eloquence of the story lies in the fact
that Joseph effectively says to his brothers, "You sold me into
slavery because you wanted to hurt me. You had bad intentions.
But it was not a bad thing. I am here for a reason, and the reason is obvious. I am now the viceroy of Egypt. I saved Egypt

from a disaster by advising the king on how to deal with the famine. Now there is food for everyone to eat, because I happened to be here in Egypt at the right time. Had you not sold me down to Egypt, millions of people might have died, not to mention the fact you and your families also need a place to reside during the famine and I can provide for you. But this does not mean that all of you don't have to repent. You have your problems because you made bad decisions. You intended bad. *But don't expect me to be angry at you, because from my point of view nothing bad happened. Elokim Hashavah Lotoyvah,* God had it all planned out for the good."

So it is humanly possible to remain kind to a person who is not kind to you, to remain generous to a person who is not generous to you, to remain respectful to a person who is not respectful to you and so on. All this is possible because if one accepts pain as forming a part of one's life then one may grow from it. To be sure, this indeed is making peace with the imperfections of society. Nevertheless, until such time as God perfects the world in the messianic era, we must do our best to rise above pain and suffering. One learns to exercise one's faith and trust in divine providence. And what about the other person who hurt you? He has significant faults that he must deal with. But the pain he caused me is my problem that I must utilize.

Thus Judaism speaks of three ways to handle suffering, which in actuality are three levels of maturity. The first level is that when something tragic befalls someone, he cannot continue. He becomes stuck and feels that all is lost. For all practical purposes this individual has come across an insurmountable obstacle in his life that forces him to stop growing and feel paralyzed. In short, he is crushed. This reaction leads to devastation. Needless to say, it is neither constructive nor mature.

A second and far more constructive reaction is when a person thinks to himself, "I am a dignified human being. I am strong, capable, and able to overcome this setback. I will not permit it to interfere with my life. I will fight it, I will resist it and I will win." And with that kind of resolve most of the time the tragedy is conquered. The problem with this reaction is its residual effect. The individual may overcome the pain, but he will probably emerge a bitter and angry person. It's mature but it's not positive. It is still viewing the event as an impediment in one's life. True, the impediment caused the person to be strong and fight, but nevertheless the individual feels victimized. Why did this calamity have to come his way? After such an experience, the person usually emerges unwhole and chipped. They only win by shutting off part of themselves. You hear them making statements like, "What can you do? Life is not fair and what happened to me was not fair. But that's the way it is and you have to live with it. You can't take it sitting down and you can't give in easily. But ultimately you have to move on and accept the injustice of life." This is a more workable solution than the former one, but it has significant disadvantages. It is also by far the most prevalent, with people constantly citing the imperfections of the world and human life but getting on with it nonetheless.

There is a third possibility. Something tragic, God forbid, happens in your life but it's not an interference, it's your life. Your life is made up of hills and valleys, but that's *your* life. Therefore, when you come to the hill, that's your life, and when you come to the valley, that's your life, too. You react to both exactly the same way because you have only one response to your life—you like it, you desire it, and refuse to exchange it for anything else. You are mature enough to recognize that the grass is not greener on the other side of the fence. You think to yourself that if this is my pain then this is my destiny. I refuse to become bitter over this experience. Neither will I shut a part of myself off as a result of it. Rather, I will grow from it. I will fight it, I will not circumvent or ignore it. I will overcome it by developing it, by incorporating this event into the enthusiasm for life that I have because I cannot accept it as an interference, but as continued growth.

So I have no reason to be angry, I have no reason to be bitter, I have no reason to be overly aggressive, and I certainly have no excuse for putting the blame on someone else because nothing is getting in my way. And the pain, that's not getting in my way, that *is* my way. It's my pain and if it's mine then I tolerate it, even though it is unpleasant and it hurts. Because it makes me become more me. The same is true of my wife, my children, my family, my community, my people. Even if the Jewish people suffer, they are my people and I want them, even though there are hills and there are valleys in Jewish history. There are Jews who are easy to love and there are Jews who are difficult to love. But all of them are my people. I don't desire to be a part of another group. I want them. And the same applies to my children, my wife; if it's mine then I see no faults. If it's mine then I cannot resist, I must have it, it's exactly what I need. It's perfect for me because it's mine. I love my wife because she is my wife. For me there is no other.

Notwithstanding how radical this concept may sound, there is much truth to it. No person would ever agree to exchange their child for another, regardless of whether the child offered in the exchange is more perfect and more accomplished than your own child. Even if, God forbid, your child is handicapped, you still cannot even imagine wanting to exchange him for someone else's child. And the reason: Because it is *your* child. It is a part of you. It is inconceivable to live life without the child. Part of you would be missing.

The same is true of our joy and our pain. We must understand and accept them in the same terms. They make up what we are and who we are. To destroy them and refuse to grow from them is to destroy a part of ourselves. To embrace them and develop from them is to become whole and at peace with what we are. Our lives incorporate both mountains and valleys. We are human and there is a certain beauty to that. And surprisingly enough, it is specifically the pain and the hurt that make us more and more human.

There was an article in *Time* magazine about the transformation in President Bush since the time that his heart began to fibrillate as he was jogging at Camp David. "The result has been a subtle but unmistakable change in Bush's outlook. In both public and private he has become more candid and confiding, less guarded and much funnier. His patrician reserve has cracked a bit and the emotions he has long held in check are suddenly visible. . . . Old friends say that Bush has become more thoughtful than usual and . . . is exhibiting a new human dimension. . . . For Bush, who tends his public persona meticulously, this is a startling departure" (*Time*, June 17, 1991). That people become more sensitive as a result of pain is a fact that we are all aware of. But that they cannot even disguise that added humanness, even if they want to, is truly incredible. There is a visible change in the man who comes face to face with his own mortality—a dimension of caring, compassion, and openness that cannot be suppressed. He comes to realize that he is indeed fallible, vulnerable, and human, and he wishes to share his life with others. As part of his awareness of his own mortality, he recognizes his dependence on other humans and his need for their love.

In the final analysis, just how realistic is all of this? Actually, it is very realistic indeed.

The proof is that in a moment of crisis we actually find ourselves rising to that level. We have the capability of dealing with everything which rises against us and emerging from it better and more mature individuals. We have all been there before. We have all seen the world from that perspective. In those moments of crises, we find that we become really good. We become noble and see the world exactly the way we're describing it now. Our ambivalence about this attitude arises from dealing with the problem of suffering on a day-to-day basis. But when we think of the people whom we respect and admire, when we think of those we hold in awe, we know that the reason we admire and envy them so much is that they have exactly this kind of attitude. They are larger than life. They suffer, yet they emerge not only whole but wiser than what they were before the event.

Just today, as I write this chapter, I read in *Time International*, in an article examining the ethics of conceiving a child in order to serve as donor for an older sibling who is gravely ill, a story about parents who had a daughter born with "Fanconi's anemia." Unless Natalie received a new immune system from transplanted stem cells, the units from which all blood cells derive, she faced a short life of severe anemia and possible retardation.

Her parents didn't waste time searching for bone-marrow donors outside the family. Instead, the mother got pregnant. When that fetus miscarried, the mother waited a month and then got pregnant again. The couple gained a healthy baby but she was an unsuitable donor. Within twelve weeks the mother was again pregnant, this time with a daughter whose tissue proved compatible. Doctors collected the blood from the baby's umbilical chord, and the blood was transplanted into her sister. To those who say it is wrong to produce one life to rescue another, the mother responds, "Who are they to judge? Now, my oldest daughter is healthy as are her sisters."

The ability to take a tragedy and create a beautiful warm family from it, to create children, to do something positive in order to deal with a potential catastrophe, to take valleys and make them into hills, is a uniquely human ability. It is man at his finest. It is man at his noblest. It is man at his most godly. It is the unquenchable desire to overcome and never to be denied. And it comes from making a bitter experience sweet. The greatness of man is his unwillingness to subject himself to fate; rather he creates his own destiny. Every time an awful experience is thrown at him, man not only hurdles it, but turns it to his advantage. When Abraham was childless, God promised him that he would have a son. His response was, "I am an astrologer. I have seen in the stars that I am to remain childless." But God responded to him, "Don't be so submissive. *Ein mazal leyisrael*, the Jewish people are not governed by constellations or fate. Fight your prescribed destiny. Never give in." Abraham heeded that advice, and not only did he later have his son Isaac, but he fathered a glorious nation (*Genesis Rabbah*).

Now if we can appreciate and find this virtue in someone else, then we can achieve it for ourselves as well. We can do it and God expects us to do it. God wants us to look past what seems to be a fault on His part and realize that He really means well and this too will be for the good. God asks us to use our wisdom and foresight to fathom His wisdom and foresight. Likewise, we ask Him to treat us the same way. We want God to look past what seem to be our faults and see our inherent goodness. We say to God, "Sure we sin, we make mistakes. We rebel from time to time but surely it can't be taken too seriously? We will eventually apologize, we will eventually make up for it, we will all eventually do *teshuvah*. In the end all will be for the good." And we ask God to look past the surface. Do not dwell on the sin but look at what will come of it. We do not look at the tragedies in the world and reject God and claim that He is, God forbid, cruel or a sadist. We do not say immediately that God is doing something bad. We say that there is something more to it and we'll soon see the greater good that comes from it.

And what we learn from this is that God treats us the same way. Although we sin, He sees how in the final analysis the sin will lead to us doing *teshuvah*, repenting, and thus constructing an even stronger and more sincere bond with Him. We ask God to see how the sin is not as bad as it appears and thus, measure for measure, He looks at our sin and says, "All they need is a little more time. They'll make amends and all will be fine."

24

LEARNING FROM
THE HOLOCAUST

We were all born into a world greatly preoccupied with the effects of prejudice and malice. Many of us can recall our parents forewarning us of the hatred and animosity that we would inevitably find in the *real* world. Their intention was not to frighten us, so much as prepare us for what we were sure to encounter. And the single most used event by the older generation as the greatest example of man's indecency to his fellow man and the perennial hatred for the Jewish people was, of course, the Holocaust.

I, for one, do not disagree with these teachings of the harsh realization of man's nature, the cruelty of life, and the primary use of the Holocaust as an example. Yet, in an effort to caution us for the future, as well as remind us of the past, we have collectively failed to yield any positive reflection as to what constructive lessons, if any, can be derived from the Holocaust and passed on to our children. If we do not do so, then we have committed a crime against those who perished as its victims. If there be nothing that we as their survivors learn from their martyrdom, if we can gain no enthusiasm or commitment as a result of their ultimate sacrifices, then, dare I say it, they have died in vain.

My purpose in the next few lines is by no means to justify the Holocaust or to offer opinions as to why it was divinely ordained, for that in itself is a crime. The truth is that we don't know. It would be cruel, even blasphemous, for any individual to try to rationalize the reason for the Holocaust. None of us is even capable of thinking in such big terms. I can't imagine how anything would ever justify the death of six million Jews or even one guiltless human being, for that matter. It would be immoral for any of us to think that we have the answer and to be content with that answer. Any explanation about the Holocaust serves to dignify it. Any rationalization of the Holocaust serves to make peace with the fact that it occurred. But this we must never do. We must never, ever, come to terms with the Holocaust. We must thunder and rail at the heavens and shout, "Why? How could such a travesty have happened? How could a God of love and mercy have allowed such atrocities?" Whenever the Lubavitcher Rebbe speaks publicly of the torment of the Jewish people, of the daily murders of Israeli soldiers, and the long wait for redemption, he clenches his fists together and pounds the table and cries out, "How long? *Ad mosai*? How long will this continue?" This is the only legitimate response to suffering and something that we must all emulate—to thunder at the heavens and to seek goodness. God owes this to us and we will not be shortchanged.

An answer to the Holocaust means that one can understand and accept the death of six million Jews. But to come to terms with the slaughter of so many innocent people is a barbaric thing to do, certainly not a Jewish one. That's what makes a Nazi a Nazi. We are not Nazis. We are Jews and therefore we cannot find an explanation for the death of six million Jews, because it is anathema to Judaism.

No explanations will suffice, because any explanation is limited. It is human. But what happened in the Holocaust is well beyond anything human. If the loss of even one soul is beyond human comprehension, then six million defies imagination. It is true that God owes us an explanation, but as of yet He has not given us that explanation. And we cannot make up our own answers. We cannot say why. Therefore, we cry out!

Nevertheless, something must be said about it, something that pertains not to the question of why it happened, but to the question of *what* happened.

My intention here is to point out some useful lessons as to the unconquerable spirit of man in general, and the inherent qualities of the Jewish people in particular, which can be learned from the Holocaust and which have heretofore largely been overlooked.

We, the Jewish people, have suffered martyrdom ever since our birth as a nation. In fact, our very beginning was in servitude and bondage. This is a time that spans well over three thousand years. We have suffered atrocities and horrors the likes of which are only described in fiction books and are believed to be impossible. We have suffered death at the sword by the Crusaders for being infidels, burning at the stake by the Inquisition for being heretics, and wholesale liquidation by the pogroms for being "Christ-killers." We have endured all this inhuman affliction to the point where martyrdom has become a complacency to the Jew and a possibility he must forever live with. Joan of Arc, had she been a Jewess, could never have achieved the fame that she did. Not unless millions like her were to become famous as well. Among the Jews, hers was just another tale.

Yet an important difference exists between these annihilations of past history and the Holocaust. In all of the aforementioned instances, the Jew was given a choice as to whether he would die. He was told either to renounce his faith and deny his Judaism, or die by the sword. In the words of Rabbi Jacob Immanuel Schochet, to "kiss the cross or kiss the sword." Accept Mohammed and Allah, or accept death. Faced with this challenge, the Jew never hesitated to die for the inherent faith he possessed for the God of his forefathers. It had become a part of himself, and as such he could never depart from it. Death, in retrospect, was an easy alternative.

But in the Holocaust, for virtually the first time in our long and woesome history, the Jews were not given any choice. We were merely ordered to die. The Nazis did not distinguish between the Jewish believer and agnostic. Regardless of the Jew's personal allegiance and convictions, all were Jewish rodents who had to be exterminated. There was no escape. No alternative to death was offered.

In other words, the Holocaust was the first time Jews died simply because *they were Jews*. It was not the Jewish nation under attack. There were other means to destroy the nation, such as compelling the Jews to assimilate, the process that many European Jews had already begun. Rather the Jewish *people* were under fire. The Nazis wanted to obliterate the word *Jew* from the face of the earth. Jews were not murdered because they worshiped in a manner different to their countrymen, but because of their very name: Jew. The Jew as an entity was being attacked.

Even the analogies that are made between the Holocaust and the proposed slaughter of the Jews by the wicked Haman in the Book of Esther are invalid. Even Haman complained to the King Ahachveirosh that he desired to murder the Jews because they were different. He complained, "There exists a nation who are dispersed throughout all the nations of the earth, and their religious practices are different from that of all other peoples." Thus even Haman would seemingly have let the Jews be if they had adopted the practices of their fellow citizens. Of course, Haman's original antagonism to the Jews was generated by Mordechai's refusal to bow to him, due in turn to the fact that Haman wore an idol. Truly, then, there are absolutely no comparisons that can be made between all the previous persecutions and killings and the Holocaust.

Given this situation, one would naturally expect the victims of the Holocaust to choose the last remaining alternative left to them: To damn and curse their Judaism. Hitler is telling you that you are a Jew. So much are you a Jew that you are being murdered for it. There is nothing you can do to stop it. You will die only because you carry that description—Jew. Don't you hate your Judaism? Don't you hate being a Jew? After all, it is your Jewishness, and nothing else, that is causing you all this suffering. You cannot even renounce it in order to be spared! So, at least damn your Judaism! This, the opportunity to go to the grave regretting that they were Jewish, was the only option left those who died at the hands of the Nazis. They were not given the opportunity to deny their Judaism, only to curse themselves for being Jewish and wish they had never been born that way. This was to be expected.

Yet, in all the thousands of histories that have emerged concerning the Holocaust, such a statement has never been recorded. To be sure, many different accounts of the Holocaust exist. Some historians relate the great unity and brotherhood that existed between the inmates of the concentration camps, even under the shadow of death. Some historians relate how although the Jews in the camps were starving, nevertheless, whenever one inmate would somehow acquire a morsel of bread, he would share it with his fellows. Other historians relate quite the contrary. They report how the Jews in the camps, torn by the ravishes of hunger, did anything to feed themselves. And when one would make the mistake of revealing a piece of bread that he had concealed, in the blink of an eye it would be ripped from his hands. So there are definitely diversity and discrepancies in the historical account of the Holocaust.

Yet, in this matter they all concur. No historians record that the Jews went to the gas chambers damning or renouncing their Jewishness. Although this was the only avenue left to them, they never followed this path. They were Jewish enough to die, and at the same time, Jewish enough to live proudly as Jews, even for the last few moments of their tragic lives. They went to the gas chambers and furnaces with a profound love for their congenital faith, even though it had brought them such hell and agony.

These, then, were the greatest and proudest Jewish martyrs of all time! Their love for God and *yiddishkeit* is unparalleled in the annals of Jewish history, already rich in spilt blood. We stand in awe and dread when confronted with their memory, wondering if we might have died as proud as they. And when they shall reawaken with the coming of the Messiah and assume their rightful places at the forefront of the Jewish people, let us only hope that there will be a place for us to hide. For who can face them?

The only way we, standing in their shadow and having assumed their mantle, can prove ourselves worthy is by undertaking the firmest commitment to fortify and continue our Judaism. The modern-day challenges are significantly different from those of the Holocaust and we must build up Jewish education as a bulwark against any intruder that might attempt to weaken our resolve. Our continuity with Jewish heritage is a living testimonial to their pride and courage. If we are lost there shall be none to remember them or continue their fiery and invincible Jewish spirit.

This need is especially acute in light of the fact that so many survivors of the Holocaust (and a significant number of nonsurvivors as well), understandably ironically, maintain that in light of the great tragedy visited by God on the Jewish people, we should not worship or even believe in Him. Judaism, and the struggle for its survival throughout the generations, has largely become meaningless or valueless to them based on their experiences.

Having, thank God, never witnessed such horrors, I am in no position to judge those individuals who feel estranged from their God and their roots. What is, I believe, incumbent upon all of us to bear in mind is that Hitler's primary objective in the Holocaust was the obliteration of the Jewish people. If then, as a result of the Holocaust we are to lose our faith and forsake God and our heritage, we are, in the words of a contemporary Jewish theologian, awarding him a posthumous victory, Heaven forbid. Hitler was determined to terminate the Jewish nation. If it were up to him we would be nothing more than an object of fascination in some history book. In the Czech city of Prague, Hitler was already building his "Museum of the Extinct Jewish Race." Thank God, he did not succeed. Yet, if as a result of Hitler's monstrosities we, the Jews, forsake tradition and forget God, then we shall be finishing his work for him. And while we may not be actual accomplices in his evil, our apathy and anger will have caused a callous response to the urgent needs of today's surviving generations. No Jew dares be Hitler's accomplice, and it is inconceivable that any Jew would actively support his program. It behooves us then not to become passive accomplices either.

Therefore, if anything, we must strengthen our resolve to adhere to the Torah and uphold our Judaism. This is the only way that we can assure Hitler's defeat. His monstrous actions should inspire us to keep the Jewish nation in existence. Pouring fire and brimstone on his name and memory will not dig him deeper into the grave. Only a concerted effort to restore

Judaism to its invincible plateau will quash Hitler and all the beasts who have survived him.

The reader should not be misled to believe that my words are merely an argument for the 614th-commandment response to the Holocaust proposed by Emil Fackenheim, who argues that the Holocaust has added a 614th command to Jewish life. After Auschwitz we are commanded to carry on being Jewish, for if we do not, then we complete Hitler's work. We become accomplices in the disappearance of Jews from the world. This, he argues, has changed the nature of the Jewish world. Before the Holocaust there were religious Jews and secular Jews. Now, even the most secular of Jews is a religious Jew, because in merely choosing to be Jewish at all he is obeying the 614th commandment. Putting it another way, precisely because Hitler made it a crime simply to exist as a Jew, simply existing as a Jew becomes an act of religious defiance against the force of evil.

As several critics have pointed out, his argument is crucially flawed. There is no 614th commandment. The Holocaust did not make Jewish survival a *mitzvah* unless it was already a *mitzvah*. In the Holocaust, for example, gypsies too were singled out, but that did not make it a command to be a gypsy. We can imagine a hypothetical Hitler who decreed a final solution against homosexuals, but that would not of itself sanctify homosexuality. Jewish survival has religious significance after the Holocaust only because it had significance *before* the Holocaust.

Above all Fackenheim has erred in building a Jewish theology on the very foundations of the Holocaust. There is no way of building Jewish existence on a command to spite Hitler. That is giving too much to Hitler and too little to God. The people Israel did not survive Egypt to spite Pharaoh, nor did it survive Purim so as not to hand Haman a posthumous victory.

My purpose is not to say that the Holocaust gives new meaning to Jewish life. On the contrary. We are Jews today despite the Holocaust, not because of the Holocaust. The Holocaust has not changed the meaning of Jewish life, and that is the miracle. Thus, we should not build a 614th commandment on the ruins of Auschwitz. But neither should we use Auschwitz to justify our apathy about the future of the Jewish people. It is inconceivable that the same people that mourn the loss of millions of their brethren at the death camps should use those same death camps as a right of passage to abandon Judaism, or to justify apathy about others forsaking Judaism.

If someone says that because of Hitler and the Holocaust he will not send his children to a Jewish school, will not take them to *shul*, and will essentially lose himself and all his descendants in the melting pot of society, then the very same tears that mourn the loved ones who did not emerge from the Holocaust also serve as the passport for further tragedy. Amid our terrible grief and unsurpassed losses, we must get a grip on our thinking and ensure that at the very least it is consistent.

Furthermore, as stated briefly above, even those individuals who claim to have lost their faith in God as a result of their experiences in concentration camps have never really abandoned their faith. The very statement presents a paradox. Faith must bear a believer. Belief is something that defies human cognitive faculties and thus cannot be refuted. On the contrary, that which one understands and accepts as a result of comprehension, is not faith at all. In such a case, the person does not believe, rather he *knows*. Knowledge and belief are inversely proportional. If someone knows something, then it is impossible for that same person to believe in that same thing, simultaneously. Knowledge results from intellect; faith transcends intellect.

These individuals, therefore, including Holocaust survivors, since they admit to having once believed in God, in reality still believe, for it cannot be lost owing to some catastrophic event. One cannot say, "Before the Holocaust, I believed in God, yet now that I have witnessed the destruction that God has wrought, I no longer believe!" The statement is a contradiction in terms. If one believes, and belief, as just noted, does not result from observable fact, but is brought about by faith, then no occurrence in the world can contradict one's faith. Atheism results from a denial to believe and accept, and not from intellectual study and proof. There is no atheist that has proven that God does not exist.

Rather, the proper description for the present religious outlook of these individuals is that they are angry with God. Before the Holocaust they perceived God as being a benevolent and merciful Ruler, and now their perception of Him has changed. God to them now is a rash and harsh Ruler. Owing to this fact, they do not to want to have anything to do with Him. Consequently, they disaffiliate themselves from Him by saying that there is no God, yet all the time believing that He exists, just as He always has, and always will. So it is not their *belief* in God that has changed, but rather their attitude toward Him and their desire to preserve a relationship with Him.

Reverting to our previous discussion, there are those who object to equating the abandonment of Jewish heritage with the designs of Hitler. To be sure, as far as maliciousness and evil are concerned, there is no comparison whatsoever. The average individual who rejects his Jewish heritage, for whatever reason, does not do so with any intent to harm Judaism. Rather, he simply wants to lead his own life. This is certainly true. But what is also true is that the long-term consequences of this person's attitude and the designs of Hitler are the same. Both approaches will yield a severely weakened Jewish nation.

Imagine for a moment that Hitler did not murder six million Jews in the gruesome manner of the Holocaust. Let us say Hitler, with his great power for oration, actually talked six million Jews into jumping into the ocean and drowning themselves. Or better, let us imagine that Hitler was a great sorcerer, and with his wizardry uttered a single magical formula that caused six million Jews to disappear from the face of the earth. Now things are not as gory as before. No more horrible films of death camps, firing squads, gas chambers, crematoriums, gallows, starvation, disease, and torture. No more photos of live skeletons searching aimlessly for a morsel of bread, or children's bodies lying in an endless heap of human carnage and corroded flesh. No more Mengeles and human guinea pigs.

The challenge I present to the reader is this: Will we still sit and cry? If six million Jews were to disappear by way of some more humane means, will we still lament and mourn? Will our hearts still be torn with unmendable sorrow? Will our very lives still be dedicated to the preservation of their ineffable memory? Will our conscience be stricken with unforgivable anger? Will we still call it a Holocaust? Notwithstanding the fact that the Jews either chose on their own or departed this world without pain and suffering, will we still mourn the genocide of six million Jews? Will we still rend our garments and cry out against the greatest single inferno in Jewish history?

I would like to believe that this is a rhetorical question and the answer is "Undoubtedly, absolutely, yes!" It is not only the manner in which six million Jews were killed that we bewail, but the mere fact that they were killed, that they are no more. The fact that there are six million Jews who were removed, however humanely or inhumanely, from this world is an atrocity commensurate with no other in the history of the world. The fact that the Nazis murdered them in the most sadistic way, and the fact that we know that these people not only died but also suffered, adds terribly to our grief. But it is not the means of death that makes the Holocaust a cataclysm without compare. It is the fact that six million Jews died in the space of approximately five years. Slaughter on this scale defies any human comprehension and we find ourselves talking of six million without even vaguely comprehending the magnitude of the number.

But we cannot allow it to ever happen again. And what this means is that we must not only combat the Saddam Husseins of our era, who have promised to repeat the gassing, or the Louis Farrakhans, but we must also ensure that they don't disappear of their own accord or through some far more humane and acceptable means. If we will not educate our children formally in proper Jewish schools, and if we will similarly not educate them privately at home with the observance of the *mitzvot*, and if we impart to them nothing of the richness of three thousand years of Jewish living, then, the mind shudders to think, a further million might be lost, obliterated through the ravages of assimilation. The products of this lack of education will assimilate beyond recognition. They will be completely lost in the melting pot of society without the proper identity and stamina that could guarantee their survival.

And although it can be argued that the situation may be mended sometime in the future through Jews returning to their source, returning to religious observance and so on, this still does nothing to alleviate the pain of the untold millions or even one, who will be lost. We should not concern ourselves with the question of whether Judaism has the potential to replenish its numbers. We must concern ourselves with individuals. A collective approach to the survival of the Jewish people is vital, but it should never overshadow the fact that this mass is made up of people. People for whom we must care, whom we must preserve.

Yet another argument for the need to fortify and reinforce our dedication to tradition and Jewish pride specifically because of the Holocaust can be made by examining why the Holocaust was a watershed in Jewish history. Is it merely that the most Jews died then in the shortest space of time ever? Such an outlook is fallacious and overlooks the fact that automated methods of death did not exist in earlier persecutions. For example, the terrible Chemielnicki massacres in Poland and the Ukraine of 1648–1649 reportedly claimed the lives of over 350,000 Jews. This figure constitutes a terrifyingly high number of Jews who had to be killed by hand. The poor Ukrainians did not have the luxury of mechanical death devices, such as gas chambers. They were given the singularly unpleasant task of having to murder each and every innocent victim by the sword, or similar method. The same applies to the tens of thousands of Jews who died in the Spanish inquisition. Their inquisitors had to physically burn or torture to death each convicted heretic, a most inefficient means for death.

Thus, if the Holocaust is to be distinguished as unique, it cannot be said to be by virtue of the unspeakably high numbers who perished. Nor can we say that the Holocaust necessarily contained greater horrors than previous persecutions. First, who indeed can measure the intensity of human suffering? Second, amid the unparalleled evils of the Nazi doctors and their human experiments, the likes of which may indeed never have had a precedent, the tortures of the Spanish inquisition might have been just as bad. One shudders just to read of their "Spanish boots," filled as they were with open blades, knuckle screws, and the like. The same applies to the Chemielnicki massacres. In his eyewitness account of the terrors of the Ukrainian pogroms of that period, Rabbi Nathan Hanover, in his landmark historical work, *The Abyss of Despair*, depicts with terrifyingly graphic reality the horrors that the Jews endured.

Similarly, the Talmud itself depicts the gruesome events of the destruction of the Second Temple and the city of Betar later in the Bar Kochva revolt.

How then, indeed, is the Holocaust unique? I believe the answer lies not in the *event* of the Holocaust but in its *aftermath* and in the Jewish reaction to its occurrence. In every previous disaster, and there have been all too many throughout our woesome history, the Jews have looked to their God and their religion for solace and comfort. They might have been badly burned, but they felt that as long as their God was watching over them, even if significant numbers fell, they were still part of a special, chosen, and eternal people. Immediately following the destruction of the First Temple, we witness the Almighty exclaiming through the medium of His prophet Isaiah, "Be comforted, be comforted my people" (Isaiah 40:1). It was God who sought to comfort His people and, paradoxically, instead of blaming Him or holding Him responsible for the tragedies that had passed, they looked to Him for solace.

But the Holocaust was the watershed in this process. The main distinguishing characteristic of the Holocaust was that for the first time the Jews found no comfort. They felt utterly bereft of everything. They grieved and continue to grieve without respite. But why is this? Why could they find no comfort?

A father who loses a child experiences pain beyond imagining, but he nevertheless finds some degree of comfort in his wife and in his remaining children. He grows more attached to his other children precisely because of this tragic loss. Although he has experienced a terrible degree of misfortune, it is not total. He has something to fall back on. And it is those things on which he can fall back that serve to comfort him.

But what if all his children die at once, for example, in an airplane crash? On whom can he fall back now? Where will he derive his source of comfort? There is nothing. Everything has been lost.

This is what happened in the Holocaust. During and after previous disasters, the Jews found comfort in each other. They were a people, and although they suffered terribly and large numbers were lost, whole communities absorbed other communities. It was specifically the concept of peoplehood that kept them together, because wherever they wandered, they found someone to take them in. Thus, they did not despair of their God either, because the same God who admittedly might have allowed this terrible tragedy to take place was also gra- cious enough to have dispersed the Jews throughout the world, so that they might always support one another. Thus, even in the concept of diaspora and dispersion they found a hidden blessing. The Jews found a silver lining in every cloud and be- lieved that it had been placed there by their ultimate and only protector, the God of their forefathers Abraham, Isaac, and Jacob. Thus, God was seen not only as the problem, but also as the solution. In the words of the Talmud, "the Almighty always readies a cure prior to the injury."

But all this changed with the Holocaust. Everyone was up- rooted and millions upon millions were lost. There simply was nothing left. What was there to fall back on? Who was left to comfort the Jews and of what could they possibly be proud? All was destroyed. And it was for this reason that they largely gave up. Neither their God, nor their religion, nor their people could comfort them, for all was in tatters and the Jews remained a pitiful vestige of their former selves.

But now we are finally witnessing the cure, the remedy to this most awful situation. When the Jewish world began to re- built itself, when the State of Israel was founded, the Jews had something in which to be comforted. They had each other, and they had a strong and revitalized nation once again. And what this means is that the stronger the Jewish nation, the stronger our religion, and the stronger our God, the greater our sense of comfort will be. None of us can bring back the millions of in- nocent people who died at the hands of the Nazis. But what we can do is firmly commit ourselves to our roots and ensure that our people are always strong and there to depend on and defend one another. No other solution will do. And if, God for- bid, millions are lost through assimilation and intermarriage, it makes the comfort that should rightfully follow the Holocaust all the more difficult to achieve, and all the less intense. Those who have witnessed the ravages of the Holocaust firsthand, and we who have learned of it through the chronicle of history, will only achieve any real degree of comfort through a completely revitalized and strengthened world Jewish community. Thus it is imperative that we educate our children with a strong sense of Jewish pride, history, and values, thereby ensuring that the Jewish nation will live again. And while we cannot yet bring back those who were lost, we can use their memory to spur us toward a fighting effort to ensure that this ancient people shall never die.

Finally, what may be the single most important lesson we may learn from the Holocaust is that culture and society alone cannot civilize man and guarantee that he will act within the norms of acceptable human, decent behavior. Germany at the time of World War II was the most culturally and technologically advanced country in the world! Theirs were the greatest musicians, architects, scientists, professors, statesmen, and look what it all led to—mass murder and sadism. The cultural supremacy that Germany enjoyed prior to the war years ended not with any utopia, but with Buchenwald and Belsen. Germany went from the highest pinnacle of human achievement to the subhuman depths of beasts and brutes, a country in which power and might prevailed over ethics and morality.

We have learned the hard way that there can be no goodness, there can be no humanity without godly commandments. What happened in Germany proved one thing—that studying music, art, literature, architecture, and philosophy does not necessarily make one more human. It makes one more skilled. Before the world wars, everything was in Germany. In those days if one wished to study art, one went to Germany. If one wished to study philosophy, one went to Germany. Physics, again Germany. It was the most enlightened country on earth and we mistakenly believed that this made them superior people. We have allowed ourselves to believe that being more educated in the arts makes someone more human and less petty. It would have been unthinkable before the war that Germany would abuse human rights. We thought they couldn't possibly steal from each other, they're thinking philosophy. They're not going to hurt anybody, they're studying art. And yet they were the monsters of the world, with their art, with their poetry, and with their philosophy.

How could such a "cultured" nation have wrought such savagery? Because Germany felt that the pinnacle of humanity lay in just that—man's ability to create his own culture and, with his own innate talents, overcome his environment. Germany believed in the supremacy of man. That man, by virtue of his intellect and ability, could overcome any obstacle without outside assistance, or for that matter, interference. They were responsible to no one, not even their innate human conscience. It goes without saying that a deity who prescribes rules of conduct and behavior had no place in the German system.

But this ideology also meant the right for one man who had so-called greater intellect and greater ability than his fellow, to overpower, conquer, and even cut off his fellow. To the victor goes the spoils. The victor, by virtue of superior strength and cunning, had the right to possess the territory. By replacing God with strictly human ability, Germany introduced a new kind of morality—one dictated by authority and achievement, domination and mastery. There would be no mercy for the underachievers; on the contrary, they were to be eliminated as a menace to the race. In the human "race" for power and perseverance, the noble and strong would succeed and continue; the weak and lame would succumb and perish.

Human logic dictates that murder is wrong and will lead to the eventual breakdown of society, anarchism, and mobocracy. The Germans who were rational people understood this quite well. Man, they decreed, was not allowed to be killed and Germany laid down a punishment for murder similar to almost every other civilized and democratic country in the world. Murder in cold blood was outlawed, just as it is in any decent society. But there was one important proviso in the German scheme. It was they who determined who is classified as human and who is not, who is protected by these manmade laws and who not. The Jew, as a lower and inferior "race," was not included and thus was not only unprotected by law, but marked as a target for extermination. Thus, the superior races could continue and flourish without the hindrances of the subhuman species. This is the criteria for the Nazi code of ethics, a result of the Nazi substitution of God with culture and technology.

On the other hand, a society that follows a divine code of ethics can never descend to such horrors. This society will always be bound by an unalterable code of conduct. If God says,

"Do not murder!" then one cannot murder regardless of whom it is he wishes to kill. One cannot redefine "man" and exclude those individuals he wishes to liquidate. The individual who subjugates himself to God's law understands that these are divine commandments that cannot be altered or tampered with. Mortal man cannot manipulate or mend a God-given command. If it is God's command, then only He can determine the parameters of the command and the various clauses that dictate to whom the law applies. In its most basic sense, a divine commandment is an expression of God's will. As such, man cannot voice any opinions concerning the manner in which the divine command should be fulfilled. Mortal man is certainly no authority on God's infinite will.

It is for this reason that Jewish history can boast a high degree of morality and scrupulous ethics throughout the centuries. The Jews have not perpetrated any Crusades, Inquisitions, or holocausts. But this is not due to any great moral fiber that is part of the Jewish people. Rather, it is due to the fact that the Jews have always accepted upon themselves the will of their Master in Heaven. So how could they murder? If God says, "Do not murder!" one may not murder! Not in the name of one's religion, not in the name of humanity, and so forth. It is only our strict adherence to divine commands that has kept us human and sympathetic throughout the generations. God's laws are immutable, and the Jews have always respected them as such.

Thus from the Holocaust we learn a very sorrowful lesson as to the limitations of man. Science, culture, and technology do not have all the answers and cannot guarantee that man will remain fully human. Being more educated means having more information at one's disposal. But it has nothing to do with whether or not a person will be a good person. This lesson is extremely pertinent to our age when science seems to be replacing all the religious answers for all the unexplained phenomena in the world. In the past few decades the universal trend of thought has become that science is the logical alternative to religion.

It is only of late that the world at large is beginning to perceive that science does not have all the answers and that it is a poor replacement for the morality of religion. This is quite understandable. Science was never meant to govern the properties of the world, but rather to explain them. Science was developed to help insure the mental growth of man and cultivate his ability to master the world around him, but at the same time, with no guarantee for where that mastery would lead him and his descendants.

Recently, large and influential Arabic countries, such as Iran and Saudi Arabia, who only a few years ago had undergone a technological revolution and were being rapidly propelled into the modern age, trading in Islamic religious truths for scientific ones, have now returned to their religions with a vengeance. Religious fundamentalism and fanaticism thrive in these countries that were only a few years ago pouring tens of million of dollars into a technological revolution. What they got instead was religious revolution with the people rejecting en masse the Western values being offered them in replacement for their spiritual truths. This fundamentalism is the product of that scientific exchange for religious values. These countries and their inhabitants learned the hard way, through unyielding religious leaders, upheaval, and violence, that science is no replacement for religious belief. We now see a trend among the Arabic nations to despise the West, the symbol and forerunner of technological advance. To them the countries of the West, especially the United States, the world leader in science and technology, have become Satan incarnate.

Moreover, this realization that science cannot replace religion is slowly becoming a universally accepted trend. The world is discovering, through an increase in rape, murder, and other violent crime, that by replacing God with scientific theory, one is effectively removing justice from the world. Without a supreme Judge, man will stop at nothing in the abuse of his fellow-man. Consequently there is a general move toward religion to provide answers and a governing pattern for the peoples of the world.

As Jews, let us hope that we too will not have to embrace our traditions because of negative impulsion. Rather, let us return to our religion out of love and sincerity, not desolation and despair.

We conclude then, with the words of the martyred victims of the Holocaust who, even in their darkest hour on the brink of death, never lost hope and utilized the final breath in their nostrils to utter the words: "I believe with a complete faith in the coming of the Messiah. And even though he may tarry, nevertheless, I await him daily that he will come."

We hope and pray that speedily in our days our righteous redeemer, the promised messianic king, will come and take us out of this long and bitter exile and return us to the land of Israel. Then shall we dance and rejoice with all the holy martyrs in unprecedented jubilation—please God, NOW!

Epilogue

DAWN OF THE
MESSIANIC ERA AND THE
END OF ALL PAIN

Throughout this book I have made the case that the proper response to suffering is twofold: First, a steadfast commitment to removing from our midst every trace of human suffering and pain that lies within our reach, to declare war on every form of heartache and misery until they are utterly abolished; and second, protesting to God the suffering that lies beyond our power, such as diseases for which there is as yet no cure, natural disasters, and car accidents.

The question may be asked, Why rely on God at all? Has He responded to our protests? Do we see the active hand of God operating in our world, relieving the suffering of the innocent and answering the prayers of the dying?

When my book *The Wolf Shall Lie with the Lamb: the Messiah in Hasidic Thought*, was published, I delivered a broad overview of the subject on the occasion of its official launch. I debated secular versus Jewish messianism with Danah Zohar, the world-renowned author of *The Quantum Self*. I wanted the audience to consider whether a perfect world can be achieved by human efforts alone or whether, as I believe, God's assistance is necessary before all wrongs can be eradicated; that we must indeed call out to our Creator and object to injustice in the belief, nay, the knowledge, that He *will* intervene and deliver us from oppression.

Zohar's book is a brilliant synthesis of quantum physics and human consciousness that constructs an entire worldview based on what Zohar refers to as the "new physics." She argues that the insights of modern physics can illuminate our understanding of everyday life. Drawing on the strange and fascinating workings of the subatomic realm, she constructs a new model of human consciousness, and addresses such questions as whether modern physics can explain how our consciousness can continue beyond death, and whether there is a subatomic wellspring from which our creativity, our empathy with others, and our feelings of unity with the inanimate world originate.

Zohar's book is the first of a trilogy. In the second book, *The Quantum Society*, Zohar argues for a new societal perspective that can be culled from the new physics. Because the overtones of the book are blatantly secular, and yet messianic, I asked her to debate with me the subject of Jewish messianism versus the alternative visions of secular messianisms that have been promoted, with increasing frequency, over the past two centuries.

Zohar and her husband, Ian Marshall, a renowned psychotherapist, are regulars at classes on hasidism and Jewish mysticism we provide here in Oxford, and which are taught primarily by myself and Dr. Tali Loewenthal, the author of *Communicating the Infinite*. As a result of these classes, Zohar admits to having many of her ideas deeply influenced by Chabad hasidic thought, although she has always complained to me that the one great setback within hasidism is its parochialism. She claims her approach is far more universal. To her, Judaism suffers from its distinctiveness, and could offer the world more if it were to promote a universal religion, embracing all peoples, all cultures, and all tongues.

I do not think this charge is true. I see inherent universalism within Jewish messianism, and I wanted to debate the subject of whether or not humanity can usher in a utopian age without divine assistance. Zohar was adamant that messianism cannot be representative of just one group or even just one messianic figure, but should be more collective so that humankind as a whole represents the messianic redeemer. This is largely what her book *The Quantum Society* is about. The question of why divert such vast quantities of energy into so illusive and intangible a goal must be given serious thought and addressed.

There is a tale of a man who brings some material to a tailor and asks him to make a pair of trousers. When he comes back a week later, they are not ready. Two weeks later, they are still not ready. Finally, after six weeks, the trousers are ready. The man tries them on. They fit perfectly. Nonetheless, when it comes time to pay, he can't resist a jibe at the tailor. "You know," he says, "it took God only six days to make the world. And it took you six weeks to make one pair of trousers." "Ah!" the tailor says. "But look at this pair of trousers, and look at the world."

This joke ostensibly describes a fact that is almost universally acknowledged to be true: the world is deeply flawed. Even the greatest optimist cannot help but notice the prevalence of injustice, disease, suffering, and deep unhappiness in the world. The disparity between God's perfection and the imperfection of the world He created inspires much of the humor about God. Indeed, while the Bible itself may contain little humor, it does have plenty of complaints. "Awake, why do you sleep, O Lord?" the Psalmist cries out (Psalms 44:23-25), in protest at God's seeming indifference to the Jews' suffering and oppression. The Talmud records the bitter reaction to God's silence during the Roman destruction of Jerusalem. "Who is like You among the dumb?" (*Gittin* 56b). The question, "God, why do You permit the righteous to suffer and the wicked to prosper?" seems to lie at the root of almost all the biblical and rabbinic complaints. The complaining spirit that runs through many anti-God jokes and witticisms is, in part, rooted in the Bible and other Jewish holy writings.

No Jewish text has ever answered the question of suffering satisfactorily, although the prophets repeatedly insist that because God is good, justice will one day triumph. Contemporary Jews, most of whom lack the prophets' religious faith, do not usually find this response consoling. Countering the comforting cliche that good people have at least one advantage over the wicked, that they sleep better at night, Woody Allen notes with his usual urbanity: "But the wicked seem to enjoy their waking hours more."

If indeed we long ago accepted the inherent design flaws within Creation, how can we still simultaneously hope for the future? Human beings seem to be obsessed with perfecting the world, as if we somehow know, contrary to all the evidence, that it is indeed possible. Why have we not reconciled ourselves to the fact that there will always be war, famine, tyrannical regimes, and mass murder? Has this book merely been an exercise in futility? Have I written utter fantasy about the abrogation of suffering and the defeat of death? We must ask ourselves, Do we really believe any of this?

In the final analysis, the only response to suffering is to cry out for the messianic era, in the firm belief that pain and heartache have no place in our world and no person deserves to suffer. Indeed, the Almighty promised that one day he would return the world to its primordial state of perfection. As explained earlier, when Adam sinned in the Garden of Eden, he brought imperfection and death into our world. But God promised that if the inhabitants of the world would do their utmost, expend every effort, to rid the world of its ills, to drown the evils of this world in a tide of good deeds, to care for one another, and do acts of lovingkindness, then the world will have attained a critical mass at which point the Almighty Himself would step in to add the finishing touches and free the world of those terrible tragedies that lay outside the ability of man to correct. He would finally send the Messiah to lead the peoples of the world and His nation Israel into a messianic era. This can be the only authentic response to suffering, simply because no rationalization and no explanation that God could offer us, through His prophets or otherwise, could ever equal what we truly desire and need: an end to all suffering and sadness.

Is there really anyone so bold as to assert that parents who lose a child to leukemia are more interested in hearing why their child died than in having the child back? Are there any words, spoken even by the most eloquent of poets, that would equal the magnificence of human life, or that would compensate for the loss of that life?

I pour scorn on those clerics who sit with bereaved mothers and tell them that God loved their child and therefore took him up to heaven. Will this bring their child back? Will it allow the mother to once again nurse her child at her breast? Will it allow her to gently rock him to sleep? Will it compensate for the bedtime lullabies that she can now never again sing, for there is no one to listen? She wants someone to hold, someone to hug, not theodicies, however deep and inspiring. She wants her child back, and she will never get over his loss, even if the Almighty Himself appeared to her and explained His reasons. Words are simply a poor substitute for life. And this is the way it should be. If words could replace life, if anything could stand in place of our loved ones, then what indeed makes them special and unique?

At the conclusion of a lecture I delivered on suffering, a woman in her fifties came over to speak with me. "Rabbi," she said, "I hope that I will not hurt you if I tell you that I am utterly uncomforted by your talk on this subject. You see, three years ago, my eldest daughter, a mother of three who was only twenty-seven years old, was speaking to me on the phone, when suddenly the phone went dead. I called back, but it was busy. Finally, I went around to the house to see what had happened. My daughter was dead on the floor; she had died, while on the phone, of a sudden aneurism. I have not slept one night peacefully since. I cannot understand how this could have happened. She was such a devoted mother and wife, whose entire life was dedicated to acts of kindness. I came here seeking solace, and have found none."

I thanked the woman for her honesty, and then responded, "Is there really anything I could have said, indeed that should, bring you comfort? If I could stand before you and deliver a lecture as to why you lost your beloved daughter, and if you could walk away feeling happy or comforted thereafter, then how special would she have been? If she could be substituted with words and explanations, if your feelings of grief for her could be traded in for mere rationalizations, then how much would you be missing her? On the contrary, you will always hurt because you're always supposed to hurt. This way you will never be satisfied with religious explanations, and will instead call out to the Creator to be kind and restore her to you. You will also call out to the Master of the Universe that, at the very least, and until such time as the Messiah comes and you and your daughter are reunited, that He never allow this to happen to any mother ever again. If you could get over your grief, then the next time one of your friends, God forbid, loses a daughter, your response might be, 'Look, I know it hurts, but I got over it, so you can get over it too. Just pull yourself together again.' But because you can't ever get over the pain, the next time someone hurts, you will sit beside them, and cry out together with them, 'God, when will all this stop? When will You finally bring an end to suffering? I implore You, I demand of You, end this all immediately. And bring our children back to us again."

Indeed, notwithstanding the seeming fantasy of this pronouncement, I maintain with great conviction that these words are completely realistic, and their acceptance by mainstream society, and their deep penetration of Western ideas, can easily be attested to, as I shall now demonstrate.

Here at Oxford I have found that young and idealistic students are usually completely unwilling to accept the injustices of society. The students not only preach utopia, but devote a significant proportion of their time and energy to organizations and efforts that actively seek to rid the world of cruelty. Some students volunteer for The National Society for the Prevention of Cruelty to Children, Rhodes Scholars Against Apartheid, or Oxfam, not to mention all the Jewish charitable and relief organizations, such as the Oxford Campaign for Soviet Jewry. But what is it that tells them that they are not just wasting their time? If one arrives at Oxford in order to obtain an academic degree, what impels one, what serves as the motivation to divert vast amounts of time and energy from study and the pursuit of academic excellence, to a goal that seems at the best of times to be elusive and fantastic?

The victorious allied nations who emerged from the Second World War formed the United Nations. What led them to believe that they could indeed found an international regulating body that could intervene in territorial conflicts and avert destructive war? What served as the inspiration behind the idea of a community of nations? This question is especially pertinent in light of the fact that the nations who came together to form the United Nations had just borne witness to, and participated in, the largest, most cataclysmic conflagration that had ever engulfed the earth. Twenty million people lay dead at the conclusion of the war. So what form of insanity, what denial of the evidence could have led the nations of the world to come together in an effort to seek and promote peace? Is it indeed mere coincidence that on the Wall of Peace standing in the Plaza of Nations at the UN headquarters in New York City, there is a single line from Isaiah etched in stone, which reads: "Swords shall be beaten into plowshares. . . . Nation shall not lift up sword against nation, neither shall they learn war any more" (Isaiah 2:4)?

Although we are impelled to strive for higher states of perfection that even allow us to dream of a global outbreak of peace, this occurs while we inhabit a tiny bubble of hope surrounded by wholesale slaughter. It has become increasingly illogical for anyone to still believe in the redemptive power of the human race. Amid global outrage, what motivates humankind to dare to wish for better, with the immense weight of history posed against it?

No greater evils have ever stalked the earth or killed more people than in this century. If it were possible to calculate the number of innocent victims killed in the twentieth century in war, state terror, hunger, pestilence, and starvation, the numbers could go into the hundreds of millions. Communism in the Soviet Union, China, and Cambodia was responsible for the murder, both active and passive, of at least seventy million people, while Nazism claimed at least twelve million innocent lives. The two world wars claimed a further fourteen million in lives of combatants and civilian deaths, and there were many smaller, but very bloody skirmishes. To be sure, in generations gone by there have been many wars, and the case can be made that people did not possess modern-day methods of mass slaughter or weapons of mass destruction; hence, the number of casualties was smaller. Even so, it is the programs of genocide and mass murder initiated in this century that have no parallel or precedent in the annals of history, especially since they did not even serve to the advantage of the instigators. The Nazis, for example, severely hindered their war effort against the Allies by dedicating enormous amounts of manpower and resources to the destruction of European Jewry. Yet even against this backdrop of the terrifying crimes that have been perpetrated in our lifetime, we still hope for an era of peace and brotherhood between all persons.

To take this idea further and project it on to a more universal plane, what gives the people of the world the hope that we can eventually conquer AIDS, cancer, and other debilitating and lethal diseases? Is there any reader of this book that will contend that the billions of dollars that have been poured into cancer and AIDS research are nothing but a waste of precious and limited resources? Will anyone stand outside the headquarters of the World Health Organization in Geneva and insist that we give up the search for the cure, and pour our tax money into far more tangible and realistic projects whose goals are not so elusive? After all, who says there is a cure? Maybe there will always be disease, and maybe people just have to die. Yet none of us feels this way. It is as if deep within our heart of hearts we are optimists in spite of history and in spite of the awful misery that we witness daily. But from what does this positive view of the future derive? What makes us think that we can somehow rid our streets of drugs and crime? Certainly, no one has succeeded before. Yet we still speak in political, social, and academic circles alike as though it is not just a remote possibility but something within our grasp, always inducing us to make more of an effort to finally reach our goal. But what is the source for this glimmer of hope that refuses to fade?

It springs from *Moshiah*, the Messiah, which has been the fountain of human hope, our life-source, for over three millennia. There is an awareness in the hearts of the Jews that Israel is a promised land. The promise, a destiny to be fulfilled, is the cause of our present exertions; it is not the result of a conglomeration of past events. The drive on the part of the Jewish people to perfect the world, whether consciously or subconsciously, is fueled by anticipation, by something beautiful and miraculous that defies precise formulation, that calls out to us and beckons from a not-so-distant horizon.

Even secular Zionists, who formally decried all religious terminology and motivations, often spoke with messianic overtones. They believed that although Jews were scattered throughout the world, and although Jews were largely lacking political rights and entirely lacking in nationalist claims, they could somehow refocus the Jewish agenda on reestablishing a Jewish commonwealth. They were secular, and yet they lived by messianic expectation: they believed that the Jews could be revived. No student of history would expect that we could be a strong, independent, and revitalized people after the decimation visited upon us this century. It was rather the ancient prophecies of old, white-bearded men like Isaiah, standing on stools and banging their fists in public squares, foretelling a time when "the knowledge of the Lord would cover the earth," that made the Jews once again believe that they could change the world. It was these promises of the future, forever ringing in the ears of the Jews, that taught them they could still hope for the society they would bequeath to their children, that against all empirical evidence tomorrow would be better than today.

With all of history posed against us, and with the knowledge that all those who embarked on similar quests for perfection before us have failed, we dare to keep up the struggle. Why? Because the Jews are the bearers of a dream that we must translate into reality through the Messiah.

The title *The Wolf Shall Lie with the Lamb* is taken from a verse in Isaiah that foretells the wonders that will be seen in the age of the Messiah: "The wolf shall lie with the lamb, the leopard shall lie down with the kid, the calf and the young lion and the fatling together, and a little child shall lead them." Essentially, this is meant to convey the central theme behind Jewish messianism and the messianic epoch: peace, harmony, and wholesomeness, as is stated by Rabbi Yossi HaGellili in the Talmud, "The Messiah's first message will be Peace!" (*Avodah Zarah* 3b).

Sometimes people ask whether the Messiah might already have come without the Jews being fully aware of it. There is only one answer to this, and it is provided by the great sage, Saadia Gaon, who states simply, "The Messiah can not yet have come, since we see the nations actually warring and fighting as violently as possible" (*Emunot VeDeot* 933, 8.8.).

A joke puts it in this way: A man visits a zoo and is taken to the lion's cage. He witnesses there the literal fulfillment of Isaiah's prophecy—a lion and a calf in a cage together. Amazed, he calls over an attendant. "How long have you had a lion and a calf living together?" he asks. The zookeeper tells him that it has already been well over a year. The man is amazed. "Why, it is a miracle!" "Not really," the zookeeper replies, "we have to put in a new calf every day."

The real perfection and end to suffering spoken of in the messianic idea is twofold, and could be summed up as follows. First, there is the concept of all people striving to do their best, based on the principles of justice laid forth in the Torah, to bring about a better world. Then, when the Almighty sees how much the earth's inhabitants desire a perfection of the world, He will provide the finishing touches in the form of a glorious messianic redeemer who will harness the world's resources and ideals, weave them all together, and usher in a complete utopia, an age in which godliness, goodness, and peace will pervade the earth and no one will know hunger, disease, or death.

At the root of this concept is the idea that humanity is a junior partner in creation. Since everything is created by a perfect God, it must necessarily be perfect. The world we inhabit is deeply flawed, but it affords us an opportunity to join God as a partner in the perfection of Creation. We have a choice: to improve the world and the lot of our fellows, or tear the world asunder. God wants us to better the world. Through the steady perfection of society and civilization, through the performance of more and more acts of kindness and *mitzvot*, the world achieves perfection. The actualization of that process in its entirety will be the messianic era, which will finally bring an end to all suffering and pain. The result will be a better world, people who treat each other better, and a manifestation of the underlying godliness of creation. A world in which all people can maximize their potential without intimidation and without contention. A world in which no tears of sorrow or tragedy will ever again be shed. A world in which the dreaded diseases of the past will be nothing more than a memory. A world in which no parent will ever be bereaved of a child, or a wife of her husband.

The greatest obstacle to Jewish messianism was and is that, despite centuries of promises, nothing has yet materialized. One Jewish fable speaks of a small Russian *shtetl*, where the community council decided to pay a poor Jew a ruble a week to sit at the town's entrance and be the first to greet the Messiah when he arrives. The poor man's brother came to see him from his own village, and was puzzled why his brother had been willing to take such a low-paying job. "It's true," the poor man responded, "the pay is low. But, it's a steady job."

Despite this obstacle, messianism has been immensely appealing to people in many different societies and civilizations precisely because it points to a better world than we have today. Ironically, I have even found the rational skeptics of Oxford more fascinated by messianism than any other single ideal in the Jewish faith. It is the students of Oxford themselves who so often invite me to lecture on my book and explore the themes of a messianic awakening. There are few people who are so enamored of the world as it presently stands that they are not attracted by the promise of an ideal society.

In the last few centuries, messianism has had an increasingly wide appeal for liberal, secular thinkers, especially Jewish thinkers, because it speaks of the perfection of our world, and particularly humanity itself, as a distinct possibility. Everyone wishes for an end to suffering, and as demonstrated above everyone harbors an innate, even irrational, belief in the possibility of its attainment. It is truly remarkable that even among secular Jewish intellectuals who dismiss Judaism virtually in its entirety, it is still Jewish messianism that captures their imaginations. They see these promises of a perfected world as ample reason never to despair of hope in humanity, even amid palpable darkness.

It was for this reason that Israel Deutsch proclaimed, "It is the comforting and uplifting faith in the Messiah which has sustained the Jews through the fateful times of oppression" (address, July 2, 1839). Joseph Klausner added that "the Messianic idea is the most glistening jewel in the glorious crown of Judaism!" (*The Messianic Idea in Israel*, p. 25). He even attributed the very advance of civilization almost single-handedly to messianism, exclaiming that "the Jewish Messianic Faith is the seed of progress that has been planted by Judaism throughout the whole world" (p. 531).

Another leading member of the Enlightenment echoed

Deutsch's thoughts: "From this belief in the Messiah who is to come, from the certainty which they have of conquering with him, from the power of esteeming all present things of small importance in view of such a future, springs the indestructible nature of the Jews" (Johann Rosenkranz, *Philosophy of Education*, 1886, p. 249). "The existence of Judaism depends upon clinging to the Messianic hope" (Lazar Skreinka, *Entwickelungsgeschichte der Judischen Dogmen*, 1861, p. 75).

In the *World of Yesterday*, Stefan Zweig gave eloquent voice to the understanding that it was specifically the call to messianism that had always caused the Jews to listen: "Whenever anyone—prophet or deceiver—throughout the two thousand years of exile plucked this string, the entire soul of the people was brought into vibration" (p. 104).

On the other hand, there was also a profound sense of unease felt within the heart of the intelligentsia about the very concept of a coming Messiah. This unease was largely a result of messianism's heavy reliance on godly intervention. The very raison d'être of the secular intellectual is the idea that man, by using his own innate intellect and pushing the expanses of reason beyond their limit, can solve all of his own ills. The very bedrock of Western secular academia is its presupposition that humans are the masters of their own destiny. Every moment spent supplicating even a benevolent Creator is a moment wasted from advancing the cause of the human race through humanity's own efforts.

The Jewish enlightenment especially sought to release the Jews from the strict shackles of dependency on a concept of the Divine, and many of the Jewish intellectuals of the era became prophets of the power and worth of man. Interestingly, these intellectuals used the tragic story of Jewish history to their advantage, just as the messianists did, but with a completely different emphasis. Instead of a story of triumph over persecution, Jewish history was portrayed as a disaster alleviated only by human triumphs: "The omnipotent Creator that we so often speak of was nowhere to be found in the Jews' greatest hour of need." Samuel Holdheim announced that "Israel required no Messiah in the generally accepted sense of the word because it itself suffered and agonized for its faith . . . died for its faith and was resurrected time and again" (quoted in David Philipson, *Centenary Papers*, p. 94).

The greatest Jewish "death and resurrection" is still a recent event, and is still hotly debated in both academic and social circles. An event that came long after disillusionment with the promises of the messianic age had set in: the slaughter of the Second World War. In the twelfth and most famous of his Thirteen Principles of Faith, Maimonides wrote: "I believe in the coming of the Messiah, and though he tarry, I will wait for him on any day on which he comes." During the Holocaust, countless Jews sang these words on their way to the gas chambers.

Given the preceding two centuries of "enlightenment," it was to be expected that secular Jews would react scornfully to such literal messianism: many contended that these same Jews whose last breaths of life invoked the age-old promise of messianic redemption received anything but that redemption. They say that God, if He exists at all, cannot be relied on to save the world and the human race.

Born from this apparent dichotomy—on the one hand the great appeal of the messianic idea in general, and on the other hand the distrust of any reliance on a Creator—was the largely inevitable movement of secular messianism. The overall plan to better the lot of society and all people was preserved, but the mechanisms were modified. In some cases, the adjustments were slight, but in others the alterations to the original concept of messianism were so profound that, as in the case of Christian messianism which preceded these newer secular alternatives, the original bore little resemblance to the newly organized product.

Furthermore, the Jewish enlightenment noted that it was precisely the Christian nations of the earth that had undergone a spiritual reformation from strict Catholic observance that were contributing the most to the fields of literature, the arts, and sciences. It was assumed that the Jews should consider pursuing the same course of action. Having contributed the concept of a Messiah to Western thinking, because it lies at the heart of Christianity, the Jews had finally seen it transformed from a religious to a secular ideal. Then, a proportion of Jews were willing to take the altered concept back again and assimilate it into their own understanding of the world, even though it was precisely because the messianic prophecies of world peace and redemption were not fulfilled in Jesus' time that Jews reject Christianity's messianic claims.

The Jewish intellectuals were willing to take on a new kind of messianism because the age-old promises of redemption had failed to materialize: they could not believe there was any divine hand in the salvation of mankind and were massively disillusioned. The Jewish novelist Franz Kafka bitterly summed this up: "The Messiah will come only when he is no longer necessary; he will come only on the day after his arrival" (*Parables*, trans. Greenberg, p. 65).

In many cases, humanity as a whole was substituted for the messianic figure. The German Jewish intellectual Jakob Guttmann stated that, "Judaism does not hold that the Messiah redeems mankind from sin, but declares that when mankind shall have set itself free from the sway of sin through its own powers of amendment, and shall have matured to true moral perfection, then, for it, the Messiah will have come" (*Idee der Versohnung*, 1909, p. 15).

Similarly, Samuel Schulman wrote in 1924 that "Israel must always await the Messiah. It must never acknowledge any person or event as the complete fruition of its hopes. Indeed, the essence of Jewish Messianism is the hope in an infinite ideal" (*Menorah Journal*, 1924, x. 318). Even Abraham Joshua Heschel, who was himself a Jew of profoundly held belief, could not help but partially succumb to the great temptation of substituting the efforts of mortal humans for the Messiah: "An architect of hidden worlds, every pious Jew is partly the Messiah" (*The Earth Is the Lord's*, 1950, p. 71).

In a deeply secular age, these predictions seemed to make sense. God and religion had largely been consigned, if not to the dust heap of history, then at the very least to the backwater of life. Judaism became important only as means of preserving an ancient tradition, but not as an affirmation of a way of life or a path to the salvation of the human race. It was now the collective belief in the ability of man that transplanted a need for God. The achievements and accomplishments of science bolstered this view. It appeared as though we had pushed back the frontiers of our world and there was no stopping us. Atheism was in fashion and scientific evidence appeared to back it. In fact, it was religion that now looked indefensible.

It was also the age of the superstate and the great leaders in whom everyone had supreme confidence, a fact that automatically lent itself to radical secular messianism. Why await the Messiah when the world's great leaders are already here? Immediately prior to the Second World War leaders of the caliber of Churchill, Roosevelt, Stalin, and Hitler were prominent, and although the latter two exemplified the epitome of cruelty and wickedness, they were nevertheless powerful leaders who engendered uncritical trust on the part of their respective citizens. In the eyes and minds of their followers, nothing lay outside their ability to conquer and master.

Then the war came, and suddenly the concept of the secular utopia was in tatters. Whereas many survivors of the World War II atrocities contend that the Holocaust ended our belief in God, the real story is that it ended our belief in man. How could anyone continue to believe in humanity or human institutions when one of the most culturally advanced nations of all time slaughtered twelve million people in the most gruesome and barbaric way imaginable? In fact, many scholars contend that it was precisely *because* Germany was so advanced that it spawned the atrocities of that war.

Fortunately, people finally recognized that the utopian overtones of Nazi Germany and Communist Russia were false. Both foretold of the perfection of man, Hitler through establishing the Aryan race, Stalin through the effective rule of the proletariat, but both equally were ideologies that advocated the advent of a secular utopia. What they delivered of course was not a utopia but Auschwitz and the Gulag Archipelago.

As a result, we who live in the present age have developed a deep fear of utopian ideas in general, and messianic claims in particular. This fear is compounded by the fact that a great many kooks throughout history, as well as in the present day, have claimed that they were the Messiah. Instead of bringing redemption to their flocks, their leadership has almost always resulted in unbridled cruelty and suffering to the masses who followed them.

The Jews have had their hopes dashed by false messianic expectations as well. The most famous of all the imposters was Shabbatei Zvi, but there are many others. One was a great Jewish sage, Moses of Crete. He claimed that he was the Messiah and told the Jews of the island that he was there to deliver them from the hands of their tyrannical oppressors. As they marched behind him in their proposed exodus, they came to a great sea cliff that left them nowhere to go. Moses of Crete then instructed them to hurl themselves over the cliff into the water, and he would cause a great miracle to happen in the form of the splitting of the sea, as his namesake had done for the Jewish people upon their exodus from Egypt. Needless to say, no miracle transpired and many hundreds drowned.

The Talmud has always warned that "the redeemer will come when men despair of the redemption" (*Sanhedrin* 97a). We find ourselves in an age that has despaired of the coming redemption. So impossible in our minds is the concept of a righteous redeemer coming along to remove every trace of suffering that today, in the wake of the worldwide Lubavitch campaign to raise awareness of Jewish messianism and the *Moshiah*, most Jews the world over have responded with a cynical curiosity at best, and outright scorn and derision at worst.

Allowing ourselves to fall into a pit of despair or disillusionment because of past events is something one must be very cautious of when dealing with Jewish history. Here we may return to the question of how, amid all the human suffering and disillusionment that the human race has witnessed for thousands of years, we can still hope for the future and even dream of a glorious age when peace will spread throughout the earth?

The great contemporary Jewish thinker Rabbi Joseph Soloveitchik explained: "The Patriarchic Covenant introduced a new concept into history. While universal (non-Jewish) history is governed by causality, by what preceded, covenantal (Jewish) history is shaped by destiny, by a goal set in the future" (*Man of Faith in the Modern World*, p. 70). He argued that in universal history every event is brought about by a preceding cause. Such history develops almost mechanically; origins determine events; the present is precipitated by the past.

Most historians are guided by this principle, namely that causality dictates unfolding events.

Jewish history is different, however, and proceeds in accordance with the assurances of the future. Therefore when secular scholars try to interpret Jewish history in this manner, they inevitably arrive at bizarre conclusions and distortions. Covenantal Jewish history is propelled by purpose and divine covenants pertaining to the role of the Jewish people. The destiny of the Jewish people emanates from a divine promise foretold about the future, rather than by events from the past impelling them to act in a given way. Jewish history is pulled, as if by a magnet, toward a glorious destiny; it is not pushed by antecedent causes.

The word *destiny* is etymologically related to the word *destination*. What determines Jewish historical experience is not one's point of departure but one's destination. The destination of the Jewish people, as foretold by our prophets, is a state of perfection and redemption, not just of the Jew, and not even of all humans, but of the entire universe. Rabbi Yehuda Lowe of Prague, famed as the Maharal who built the Golem, wrote: "The essential function of the Messiah will consist of uniting and perfecting all, so that this will be truly one world." The words of the prophet Zechariah still ring in our ears: "The Lord shall be king over all the earth; in that day shall the Lord be One and His Name One" (Zechariah 14:9). This is the messianic dream of Judaism and the spiritual goal of Jewish history. And this, once again, is the only response to suffering because it finally poses an *end* to suffering.

It is this covenantal understanding, and only this, that can account for the Jewish obsession with perfecting the world accompanied by the certainty that it can be achieved. If Jews took any notice of the history that has gone before, we would have given up the ghost long ago. The destiny that is foretold is an obsession that has nagged us throughout history as well as being the source of our infectious hope and enthusiasm for the future. How else can we explain why it is specifically the people who have suffered the most who are also the most hopeful and dedicate so much of their imagination and creative talents toward making a better world, or at the very least dreaming a vision of its possibility?

There is a passionate, almost irrational determination to lift up the Jewish people by every means possible, be it by creating our own homeland in this century after nearly two millennia of exile, or by rescuing Soviet, Syrian, and Ethiopian Jews from their oppression, or even by something as commonplace as building Jewish day schools throughout the world and promoting Jewish education amid mass assimilation.

These actions bear witness to an innate belief in a glorious destiny and a suprarational determination to force the arrival of the Messiah. There is no political, sociological, or nationalistic explanation that can otherwise account for the intensity and solidarity of the Jewish people in relation to these goals, despite their having been raised in distant lands and immersed in disparate cultures. Other nations have suffered lesser catastrophes and have succumbed to the imperatives of historical decline. Where are the ancient Egyptians and the ancient Greeks, the Holy Roman Empire and even the extensive British Empire today? They are the dust of history.

Judaism, with its vision of a perfect society, has influenced, indeed, brought into being, many movements and "isms" that can be referred to as secular messianic utopias. Judaism has influenced and had its impact even on those Jewish visionaries who have not even led Jewish lives. It is more than sheer coincidence that so many of the world's political ideologies have come about through Jews. On the contrary, the desire of secular Jews to perfect the world through every means is a direct outgrowth of their exposure to the teachings of the Jewish prophets, and the promises those prophets gave of a glorious culmination to the march of civilization. Even those Jews who have abandoned Judaism are still driven by its vision, but they reject a divinely ordained messianic epoch for the concept of a secular utopia. The early fathers of communism spoke almost straight out of the Bible, of a time when all of the earth's inhabitants would have according to their needs, when no one would go hungry, when there would be peace and harmony between all nations. The only real difference between what communism promised and the facts of the Jewish messianic ideal was that the former hailed a Bolshevik messiah who was to save the people, a Marx or a Lenin; what was promised was still a utopia. Even secular Jews such as Karl Marx have had this overbearing drive to improve mankind's lot, which is a direct outgrowth of their exposure to Jewish messianism.

Three thousand years of promises of hope hardened the Jew, who emerged from the Holocaust not depressed and distraught from the blows of the past, but energized with superhuman zealousness by a dream about the future that the flames of the crematoria could not extinguish. A Jew feels deep in his or her bones that destiny, not causality, is the mechanism behind the Jewish people and constitutes the dynamics of covenantal history. The future is responsible for the past. Therefore the Jew never despairs.

This is how we should address the most important of all questions related to messianism, touched upon above: its modern-day relevance. If this Messiah is the one who will bring about a positive transformation of the world, why should we work for the betterment of our world today? Conversely, why wait for something spiritual and elusive that we can carry out today via sociological, academic, or political means? The belief in the Messiah seems at odds with the belief that man is capable of making a better world.

The answer is that to believe solely in human history, in causality alone, will leave us nothing but despair and gloom. Man is a grand creature. But he must reach out and touch the hand of the Divine if he is to rise above the causal agents of history. It has always been the divinely communicated promise of a better future, a perfect epoch, that has led us to cry out against the senselessness and uselessness of pain and suffering, indeed to believe that we deserve and will receive better. Suffering has no place in creation and should not be granted any latitude in our lives, because the Creator of all life has told us so. He has communicated to us in the very first chapter of Genesis that the world was once perfect, and that the original man set in its midst to "guard it and protect it" never knew any pain. God also promised through His prophets that through a collective effort on the part of humanity, in unison with the Creator, to perfect the world, it would return to its primordial state of goodness. Any other approach to suffering and any peace made with death betrays an attitude of laziness and surrender that we dare not embrace.

We await a time described by Maimonides, the leading medieval Jewish thinker: "When the Messiah comes, war will end, God's blessing will be on all men, and none will risk his life for money" (*Commentary to Mishnah: Sanhedrin*, 1168, 10.1). We hope and pray for the imminent arrival of the Messiah and an end to all anguish and distress. May it happen now!

SELECTED BIBLIOGRAPHY

Abohav, Yitzchak. *Menora's Hamoar: The Light of Contentment*, trans. Rabbi Y. Y. Reinman. NJ: The Transcript Library, 1982.

Ausubel, Nathan. *A Treasury of Jewish Folklore*. New York: Crown Publishers, 1975.

Berkovits, Eliezer. *Crisis in Faith*. Jerusalem: Sanhedrin Publishers, 1975.

Besdin, Abraham R. *Man of Faith in the Modern World: Reflections of the Rav*, vol. 2. Hoboken, NJ: KTAV, 1989.

Birnbaum, David. *God and Evil: A Jewish Perspective*. Hoboken, NJ: KTAV, 1989.

Brandwein, Yehuda. *Tikunet Zohar Introduction*. 3 vols. New Haven: Yale University Press, 1973.

Eliach, Yaffa. *Hasidic Tales of the Holocaust*. New York: Vintage, 1991.

Fackenheim, Emil. *To Mend the World: Foundations of Post Holocaust Jewish Thought*. Bloomington, IN: Indiana University Press, 1993.

Hausner, Gideon. *Justice in Jerusalem*. New York: Herzl Press, 1966.

Herning, Basil F. *Jewish Ethics and Halakhah for our Time*. New York: KTAV, 1984.

Heschel, Abraham J. *God in Search of Man: A Philosophy of Judaism*. New York: Farrar, Straus & Giroux, 1951.

Heschel, Abraham J. *Man Is Not Alone: A Philosophy of Religion*. New York: Farrar, Straus & Giroux, 1951.

Heschel, Abraham J. *The Earth Is the Lord's: The Inner World of the Jew in Eastern Europe.* New York: Farrar, Straus & Giroux, 1950.

Hong, H. V., and Hong, E., ed. and trans. *Soren Kierkegaard's Journals and Prayers.* 7 vols. Bloomington, IN: Indiana University Press, 1967–1978.

Kushner, Harold. *When Bad Things Happen to Good People.* New York: Schocken Books, 1989.

Lamm, Norman. *Faith and Doubt: Studies in Traditional Jewish Thought.* New York: KTAV, 1986.

Loewenthal, Tali. *Communicating the Infinite.* Chicago: University of Chicago Press, 1990.

Lubavitch House. *Likutei Amarin-Tanya.* London: Kehot Publication Society, 1981.

Nachahoni, Y. *Studies in the Weekly Parashah,* vols. 1–5. New York: Mesorah Publications, 1988.

Netzach, Abraham. *Suvbota: My Twenty Years in Soviet Prisons.* New York: Empire Press, 1984.

Prager, Dennis, and Telushkin, Joseph. *Why the Jews?: The Reason for Anti-Semitism.* New York: Simon & Schuster, 1985.

Rosner, Fred, trans. *Maimonides Commentary on the Mishna: Sanhedrin.* New York: Hermon Press, 1981.

Sacks, Jonathan. *Tradition in an Untraditional Age: Essays on Modern Jewish Thought.* London: Vallentine, 1990.

Schneerson, Joseph Isaac. *Sefar Hamaamorim Kuntreistm,* vols. 1–3. New York: Kehot Publication Society, 1963.

Schneerson, Menachem Mendel. *Likuttei Sichos,* vols. 1–25. New York: Kehot Publication Society, 1971–1994.

Touger, Eliyalm, trans. *Mishneh Torah, Hilchos Teshuvah.* New York: Maznaim Publishers, 1987.

Wiesel, Elie. *Dawn.* London: Collins, 1973.

——. *Night.* London: Collins, 1972.

——. *The Town Beyond the Wall.* London: Robson, 1975.

Wiesenthal, Simon. *The Sunflower.* New York: Schocken Books, 1976.

Zohar, Danah. *The Quantum Society.* London: Bloomsbury, 1993.

INDEX

About the Author

Rabbi Shmuel Boteach is rabbi to the students of Oxford University and the director of the Oxford University L'Chaim Society. Under his directorship the L'Chaim Society has become the second largest organization at Oxford, with over 2,000 Jewish and non-Jewish members. He has brought Mikhail Gorbachev, Elie Wiesel, Bob Hawke, Javier Perez de Cuellar, Yitzhak Rabin, Yitzhak Shamir, Christiaan Barnard, and Simon Wiesenthal, to name a few, to speak at Oxford, as well as sending his weekly essays on Jewish life and moral issues to thousands of people in twenty-eight different countries through electronic mail. He is also the author of several books, including *Dreams* (1991), *The Wolf Shall Lie with the Lamb* (1993), and *Moses of Oxford* (1994). Rabbi Boteach, an American, lives in Oxford, England, with his Australian wife, Debbie, and their four young children.